FRANCE UNDER RECESSION
1981–1986

France under Recession 1981–1986

John Tuppen

State University of New York Press

First published
in USA by
State University of New York Press
Albany

For information, address State University of New York
Press, State University Plaza, Albany, N.Y., 12246

Printed in Hong Kong

Library of Congress Cataloging-in-Publication Data
Tuppen, John N.
France under recession, 1981–1986.
Bibliography: p.
1. France—Economic conditions—1981–
2. France—Economic policy—1981– . 3. France—
Social conditions—1945— . 4. France—Politics
and government—1981– . 5. Socialism—France.
6. Privatization—France. 7. Local government—France.
I. Title.
HC276.3.T86   1988   338.944   87–1980
ISBN 0–88706–580–5
ISBN 0–88706–581–3 (pbk.)

To my parents

To my parents

Contents

List of Tables

List of Figures

List of Cartoons

I would like to thank Jean Plantu, who kindly gave permission to use his cartoons.

Preface

As France moved into the 1980s the outlook for the country appeared unpromising. Economic expansion had given way to stagnation, a once-flourishing industrial sector now seemed unable to respond effectively to rapidly changing markets and new technologies, and the growing protest over rising unemployment represented but one manifestation of an increasingly divided and dissatisfied society. Over the early part of the present decade such negative trends were intensified, as France slipped deeper into recession. Yet by the mid-1980s there were indications of an upturn in the economy, despite the persistence of certain weaknesses, notably a continuing problem of unemployment and the country's high level of indebtedness.

An important change in the direction of the country's affairs accompanied this period of transition, for between 981 and the early part of 1986 France was governed by the Soc·lists. This transfer of power held a special interest, for it represented the first occasion during the life of the Vth Republic that a left-wing president and government had controlled the nation's destiny. Moreover, in their quest for a solution to the country's mounting difficulties, the Socialists adopted, at least initially, a very different range of policies from their predecessors.

It is this period of substantial change that provides the framework for the present account. Within this context the aim is to appraise the recent pattern of social and economic development in France, with particular reference to the impact of recession and the socialist prescription for revival. Rather than attempt a comprehensive review of such a broad topic, a selective approach is adopted. Thus in each chapter analysis is focused on a limited number of significant changes and key issues which became the subject of extensive debate in the 1980s; and to help illustrate these themes extensive use is made of case studies. Finally, where appropriate, analysis is carried out at a regional as well as national level, giving a spatial dimension to the study.

The text is divided into five main sections. Of these the first is designed to paint a backcloth to recent change in France, indicating its various economic, social, political and geographical dimensions. In the second chapter a more detailed appraisal is undertaken of a series of contemporary and often contentious social problems; particular emphasis is given to the subjects of law and order, unemployment and immigration. Then in Chapter 3 attention switches to the country's economic difficulties and to the opportunties for stimulating new growth. The need to restructure and revitalise the economy has been a matter of major concern, not least because of the implications for national prosperity and personal well-being: hence the considerable emphasis placed on this topic. In the following chapter the focus shifts to France's main urban areas. With a majority of the country's population now living in its towns and cities, many of the adverse effects of the recession have inevitably had most impact on these areas, contributing to the notion of an urban crisis. Increased demands for policies of rehabilitation and regeneration have resulted, themes which are examined in detail in this section. Finally in Chapter 5 the question of decentralisation is considered. This has been a vital policy issue throughout the postwar period, first in the economic domain and then more recently in relation to the growing demand for the devolution of government decision-making power; carrying through reform in this latter field became a prime objective for the Socialists, designed to underpin their wider economic and social policies.

In writing this account I have been extremely fortunate to benefit from the help and support of many people. To them all I extend my most sincere thanks, but there are a number to whom I would like to say a special 'thank-you'. Part of my research was undertaken while on sabbatical leave at Lyon and I am most grateful for the assistance given by colleagues in the Department of Geography at the University of Lyon III where I was based during my stay. In particular I wish to thank Paul Mingret, not only for his advice and ability to provide a seemingly endless supply of contacts, but also for his extreme kindness to all my family. Other university colleagues to whom I am particularly grateful, at Lyon and elsewhere, are Bernard Barbier, Jean Billet, Jacques Bonnet, Marc Bonneville, Pierre Bruyelle, Etienne Dalmasso, Charles Gachelin and Michèle Joannon.

Numerous other people in many different spheres of French life were most generous in offering their assistance, providing information, explaining policies or generally helping to guide my enquiries. In this respect I am especially grateful to Françoise Gaspard and Claude Belot for their willingness to discuss with me a wide range of issues, and to Jacqueline Letellier and Jocelyne Lerouge for supplying numerous statistics. I would also like to express my appreciation for the help given by Aline Adam, Jean-Pierre Aldeguer, Brigitte Belloc,

Philippe Brom, Tilly Bussman, François Chevalier, Gisèle Clare, Marie-François Crozat, Dominique Fache, Yves Jenn, Marie Masson, Jean-Pierre Portefait, Michel Senelet, Christophe Tampon-Lajarriette and Bruno Voisin. As I travelled around France the kindness and hospitality of many friends was greatly appreciated; in particular my thanks are due to Agnès, Françoise, Germain, José, Mario, Marguerite, Monique and Vincent.

On the technical side I am very grateful to Gustav Dobrzynski for his skilful execution of the maps and diagrams, and to Diane Wilson for her expert typing of the text, a task she undertook with much patience and good humour. Very special thanks are merited by my family, not least my wife Valerie who coped admirably with her own job, a move of house and to France, typing the original draft and looking after the rest of us. Finally, 'thank-you' to Emma and Helen for reminding me that there are in fact more important things in life than France!

JOHN TUPPEN

1 France in the 1980s

As the further substantial increase in oil prices in the late 1970s plunged the western world into deeper recession, the formerly buoyant French economy appeared decidedly less dynamic. Lower growth rates and rising unemployment represented but two of a series of disturbing negative trends, contributing to the emergence of new strains and divisions in the country's society. The changed performance of the economy was clearly illustrated by the difficulties encountered by industry: once viewed as the powerhouse behind France's remarkable and sustained postwar economic expansion, this sector now appeared to have lost much of its former vigour. In a climate of growing disenchantment over the management of the economy and of increasingly widespread expression of the desire for change, the election of a socialist president and socialist government in 1981 appeared to many people to offer new hope in the quest for solutions to the country's mounting economic and social problems.

Yet the euphoria which surrounded the Socialists' victory became short-lived. Despite commitments to a substantially higher rate of economic growth and to a sharp decline in unemployment, the reality of their first years in government proved very different. Stimulating demand failed to revive a sluggish economy and unemployment continued its inexorable rise. As a consequence, a radically revised economic strategy was adopted, owing far more to monetarist principles than to Keynesian philosophy which underpinned the government's original policy. In retrospect, with the economy appearing to founder under socialist rule, the strict economic management under the previous Barre administration became viewed far more favourably; yet during the late 1970s the then government's policies were much criticised despite being accompanied by a relatively high rate of growth. Instead of a continuing improvement in living standards, people were now faced with a progressive erosion of purchasing power. The Socialists also appeared unable to reverse a number of other unwelcome trends, not least a continuing breakdown in law and order, leading to a more violent and fragile society. Young people in particular seemed increasingly vulnerable, as a heightened sense of disillusionment pervaded this section of the community; entry into the labour market had become progressively more difficult and the chances of a satisfying career greatly diminished.

It is therefore ironic that, as many of these problems appeared to be easing and, in particular, as the French economy seemed to have been placed on a firmer base and sounder course, the Socialists should have been ousted from power in the general election of March 1986. By this time high inflation had been eradicated, the level of unemployment had stabilised (at least temporarily) and France's international trading position had become more competitive. The re-emergence of such positive trends might be seen to imply an inherently healthy economic base, devoid of some of the fundamental weaknesses which appear to have characterised other European economies, not least Britain's.

Contemporary patterns of development have also been moulded by a series of longer-term structural changes affecting the country's society and economy. These include the considerable rise in the number of retired people, the continuing increase of women in the labour-force, deindustrialisation and the drift of population away from the country's nineteenth-century industrial centres in favour of the more dynamic southern areas and newly industrialised regions. Many of these features were apparent prior to the last decade, but the onset and deepening of the recession has made their impact more pronounced.

French society in the 1980s has been characterised by a phase of substantial transformation. Change has been a composite process, embracing various social, economic, political and geographical dimensions, and as it has occurred, has become linked with a series of key policy-issues relating to the way in which the country's economy and society should be organised and managed. Initially the Socialists sought to guide development by a planned approach. Thus the country's progress was charted first by an 'interim plan' covering the years 1981–83, and then by the IX Plan for the period 1984–8, built around the joint priorities of modernising France and devolving power from the capital. In this introductory section the aim is to paint the backcloth to these different features of contemporary change under the impact of recession.

THE ECONOMY UNDER RECESSION

Despite the weaknesses which became apparent in the French economy in the wake of the oil crises, France still enjoys the reputation of a dynamic and innovative manufacturing nation, playing a leading role in the development of Western Europe's advanced-technology industries. Yet at the onset of the present decade, debate on the economy centred on France's deteriorating economic position and the unlikelihood of a continuing high rate of expansion. Growth rates had begun to slip noticeably compared with the late 1970s: between 1976 and 1979 the French economy grew by an average of over 3 per cent each year (Figure 1.1). Certainly this already represented a substantial fall compared with the beginning of that decade (when annual growth rates averaged twice this figure), but when viewed in relation to the subsequent further decline in rates the economy still appeared relatively dynamic. In 1980, following the 'deuxième choc pétrolier', the country's GDP increased by only 1.4 per cent, since when the level of growth has remained at a constantly low level, averaging only 1.1 per cent per annum between 1980 and 1985.

France has not been alone in experiencing a depressed economy as similar trends have been reflected elsewhere amongst other advanced western countries. At the beginning of the present decade the prevailing economic climate was unconducive to strong growth. A substantial downturn in economic activity had occurred, international trading had tended to stagnate, and inflationary pressures remained strong: it was not only the price of crude oil that had risen sharply but also that of other energy products and a wide range of raw materials for manufacturing industry. A further boost to inflation was then provided by the considerable strengthening of the dollar as the first Reagan administration came to power in the USA. Rising unemployment represented an additional widespread problem: already by the end of 1980 there were just under 8 million people registered as unemployed in the EEC alone, representing 7.2 per cent of the total work-force. Governments in member countries were also coming under increasing pressure to cut public expenditure and were faced with the dilemma of how to assure adequate funding of generous social welfare schemes adapted to a period of strong growth and rising incomes rather than recession and growing expenditure.

The difficulties of the French economy in the early 1980s were not limited just to low growth rates (Figure 1.1). In 1980 and 1981 the inflation rate exceeded 13 per cent, a level above the EEC average and more than double the rate in West Germany. The country's foreign trading balance, already in debt, deteriorated further with the deficit rising to over 100 billion francs in 1982; a similar worsening of the balance of payments was occurring. At this time consumption appeared to be holding up relatively well, but home production was

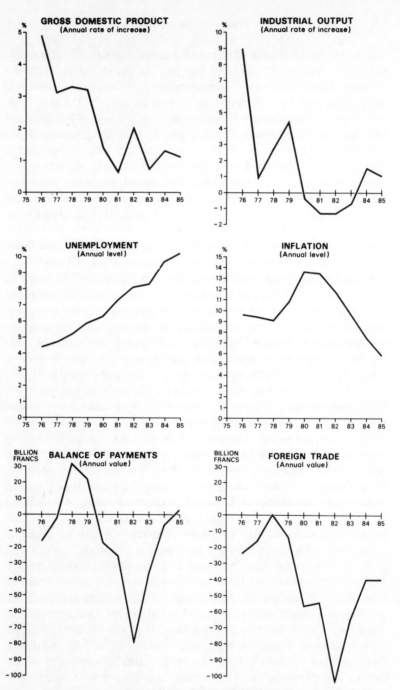

Figure 1.1   Performance indicators of the French economy

satisfying a lower proportion of demand, reflecting the reduced competitiveness of certain sections of French manufacturing. The problem of unemployment had also become far more significant. In 1974 those people out of work accounted for only 2.3 per cent of the working population, slightly below the average for West Germany which stood at 2.6 per cent. However, by 1981 the French rate had jumped to 7.8 per cent, standing by then at over two percentage points higher than the comparable West German figure. There were other indications of the deterioration in the country's economic situation. Industrial production had stagnated and the prospects for a future rise in output seemed increasingly endangered by the falling rate of investment in manufacturing: high interest rates (base rate stood at 15.9 per cent in mid-1981 compared with 10.85 per cent four years later) offered little incentive for investment in factories and machinery. Finally growing budget deficits and high government spending had combined to increase substantially the country's external debt.

Compared with the bleak picture presented by the French economy in the early 1980s, the position by the middle of the decade appeared to indicate a substantial improvement (Figure 1.1). Overall growth was still sluggish (averaging 1.3 per cent in 1985), but certain key negative features were in the process of being eradicated. The foreign trading deficit had been greatly reduced with the result that in 1985 the balance of payments account returned to the black for the first time in six years. Other favourable signs included a higher rate of industrial investment, which rose sharply in 1984 and 1985, and an increase in manufacturing output: having fallen consistently each year between 1980 and 1983, production expanded again in the following two years. Furthermore, by 1985 the jobless total had stabilised, at least temporarily. But, above all, the level of inflation had fallen dramatically to an average rate of 5.8 per cent for 1985 (although this was still slightly higher than the average for the EEC), with the expectation that this downward trend would continue.

Just as in the early 1980s France's worsening economy could be seen as representative of a more general pattern of depressed western economies, so too by the middle of the decade the revival of the French economy might be considered reflective of a wider improved economic situation in these countries. There has been a common trend to much lower levels of inflation, international trading has become more buoyant as demand has increased, and raw material and energy prices have fallen. The sharp drop in the price of oil, initiated in late 1985, and the fall of the value of the dollar against leading West

European currencies suggested even further improvements were likely in western economies.

Some caution, however, seems advisable in assessing the revised position of the French economy and the prospects for future expansion. Despite encouraging signs of recovery, the economy could hardly be described as particularly dynamic: growth is still occurring at a relatively low rate, industrial output is only expanding slowly and investment in productive activities has been below the levels achieved by major competitors. Weaknesses persist in the foreign exchange balance, not least in terms of the deficit in trade with EEC partners; moreover, the amelioration in the balance of payments account has been partly attributable to the high level of earnings from tourism, but this source of income has been artificially inflated by the past strength of the dollar. Unemployment may have stabilised in 1985, but is generally judged to remain unacceptably high. By early 1986 there were still over 2.4 million people out of work; over the five years of socialist government more than 600 000 jobs were lost in the economy.

Under the Socialists a new approach to the management of the economy was launched. Initially their strategy was largely determined by a major commitment to reduce unemployment. It was argued that such a goal could be achieved by increasing demand and promoting a high rate of economic growth; and in the attainment of this objective an important role was to be played by the investment and employment strategies of a much enlarged public sector and by increased government expenditure. In the latter field the new administration was considered to possess considerable room for manoeuvre following the sound management of the country's finances by Raymond Barre; however, subsequently the Socialists' ability to spend, and their predilection for such action, became viewed as a contributory factor to the country's growing economic difficulties. But at this stage reducing inflation was not seen as a major priority.

In a generally depressed international economic climate the Socialists' reflationary approach proved unworkable and, as the government's financial problems became more serious, was replaced in 1982 by a policy of restraint which was further reinforced in the following year. Stricter controls were placed on spending and policy became determined to a far greater degree by economic rather than social considerations. The government showed a progressive move away from its original idealist and interventionist stance to a more pragmatic and liberal approach to the management of the economy (particularly under the leadership of Laurent Fabius), based partly on a sounder understanding of the needs of the business community. Furthermore it seems not unreasonable to suggest that on many key issues, such as the need to rationalise major sectors of industry, the Socialists hesitated too long, their early industrial and general economic policies lacking direction and incisiveness. By the time these shortcomings had been remedied, in electoral terms at least, for the Socialists it was too late. With the change to a right wing government in 1986, a further shift towards liberalism occurred, as market forces became accepted as an essential determinant of economic policy.

Despite such changes in approach to the running of the economy, and the Socialists' claim that France's improved economic standing by the mid-1980s was largely the result of their careful management, (a view which conveniently set aside the misguided strategy of their first year in office), the extent to which any individual government's policies are capable of affecting wider underlying economic trends remains questionable. External factors frequently play an important if not dominant part in determining the performance of any particular country's economy, as economic activity has become increasingly international in scale. Thus, in the case of the pronounced fall in the rate of inflation in France, this has not occurred in isolation: the downward trend is reflective of a general deflationary tendency throughout western economies, aided by falls in raw material and energy costs and moderated wage demands (Figure 1.2). Nevertheless this should not diminish the significance of the cut in inflation which represents a major economic change in the 1980s during the Socialists' reign at Matignon. Conversely, the inability to achieve a reduction in unemployment, an essential election pledge, might be seen as the principal 'failure' of socialist rule, although again jobless totals remain consistently high throughout·the EEC (with over 16 million people registered as unemployed at the beginning of 1986), suggesting that the scope for any one government to achieve a substantial reduction is limited (Figure 1.2). It is even questionable whether unemployment could be brought down significantly by a strongly reflationary policy. Faced with the adverse impact of fundamental technological changes on the pattern and level of employment, high unemployment is seen increasingly as a basic structural problem of the economic system, largely insensitive to short-term variations in demand.

Short-run change in the economy has been accompanied by the continuing transformation of the underlying productive system, a

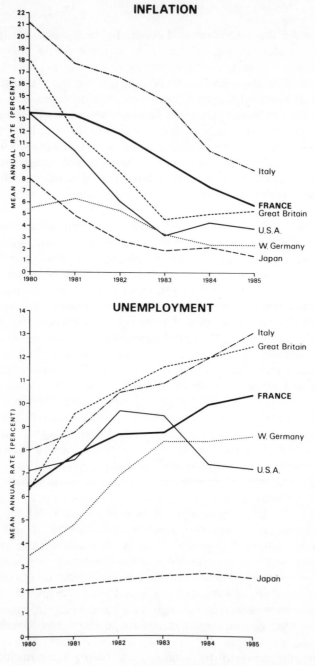

Figure 1.2   *Changing trends in inflation and unemployment*

theme which may be illustrated by modifications to the nature of company size and ownership, and by the changing sectoral and spatial distribution of activity. Over the last twenty-five years the business community in France has been characterised by an increasing concentration of ownership, so that the country's economy is now dominated by a series of large multinational groups. Within the industrial sector alone nearly 60 per cent of the work-force is controlled by firms employing over 500 workers, while in the economy as a whole France now possesses nine major groups with a labour-force exceeding 100 000 and a similar number of companies with an annual turnover in excess of 50 billion francs (Table 1.1).

Table 1.1   The major French companies, 1984

a.	*Turnover*	*(Billion francs)*
	Elf-Aquitaine	177
	Française des Pétroles	159
	Electricité de France	118
	Renault	118
	PSA (Peugeot)	91
	CGE (Compagnie Générale d'Electricité)	74
	St Gobain	61
	Thomson	57
	Rhône-Poulenc	51
	Gaz-de-France	48
b.	*Employment*	*('000)*
	SNCF	248
	Renault	213
	PSA	187
	CGE	162
	Michelin	130
	St Gobain	125
	Electricité de France	125
	Thomson	112
	Rhône-Poulenc	79
	Elf-Aquitaine	76

Source: L'Expansion, no. 269, October/November 1985.

Despite the high degree of influence now exerted by large corporations, by international standards the concentration of control in France is less developed than amongst competitors; no French company squeezes into the ranking (by turnover) of the world's 'top twenty', and even in Western Europe France only manages three groups amongst the leading twenty companies compared with six in the case of West Germany.[1] However, as most of these major companies have been engaged over recent years in drastic surgery (involving the closure of plants and the reduction of their workforces) to enhance their competitive position, it might be argued that France's comparative weakness in this field is an advantage rather than a handicap! Indeed while there has been an underlying tendency since 1974 for large companies to shed labour, the country's small and medium-sized firms have proved far more dynamic, showing an overall increase in employment.

The expansion of the economy and the related increase in the role played by large groups have been accompanied by a vastly increased international dimension to business activity. Encouraged first by the creation and development of the Common Market and by the general freeing of world trade, the movement has been greatly amplified by multinationals anxious to extend their market areas and control, and to diversify their activities. There are numerous examples of this process, ranging from the substantial rise in external trade to the growing level of investment by French-based companies in foreign markets, compensating a parallel movement by outside investors into France; in industry alone, firms in which foreign-based companies have a majority holding control nearly 700 000 employees. West German, Swiss, British and other European firms are all represented in France, although the majority of investment has originated from the United States, with Japanese capital becoming increasingly important over recent years. Many companies are long established (e.g. Shell, Esso, Philips), but there has been a growing trend towards investment by groups concerned with electronics and data-processing, following the lead given many years ago by IBM. Much of the capital is again from the United States (e.g. Digital Equipment, Hewlett-Packard, Wang), and now Japan (e.g. Sony, Pioneer, Canon), reflecting both the strength of such manufacturers in high technology fields and the corresponding weakness of French and West European companies.

Since the last world war a major shift has occurred in the respective contributions made by the three broad sectors of the economy to national wealth and employment; the land and the factory have been increasingly abandoned for the office. Technological advance and changing patterns of consumption have switched jobs away from manufacturing to control, administrative, research and educational functions. Now employment is concentrated overwhelmingly in the service sector, accounting for over 61 per cent of the total. Well over one in every three people in employment works in an office as the number of office workers has more than doubled since the early 1960s. The expansion of the state's health, educational and welfare services has made a substantial impact on this increase, as too has the growth of the activities of local government, recently boosted by the effects of decentralisation. More significantly firms and households have become major consumers of a growing range of services. Specialists and consultants in finance, insurance, property, advertising and many other fields have become in increasing demand; private medical and educational facilities have grown in importance; services associated with leisure, sports and recreational activities have similarly expanded and, in an increasingly 'consumer orientated' society, the number of people employed in retailing has also risen.

Industrial employment now takes a lowly second place, accounting for only 31 per cent of the total work-force. The secondary sector, however, still produces 42 per cent of the country's added-value suggesting that cuts in manpower have been translated into increased efficiency in the use of capital. Agriculture's role as an employer is now much diminished, giving full-time jobs to less than 1.6 million people, representing just under 8 per cent of the labour-force. But such figures undoubtedly undervalue many people's perception of the role played by agriculture in the economy, for in a country where the major shift of population from the countryside to the town has occurred in the last forty years many people still have strong rural ties. Furthermore, ever since Valéry Giscard d'Estaing 'discovered' France's 'pétrole vert' in the mid-1970s as a valuable natural, and national, resource capable of further development, agriculture has been promoted as one of the country's growth activities for the future (although it is uncertain that many of the still numerous small, upland dairy farmers, overburdened by their debts, would concur with this assessment!).

Sectoral changes in the pattern of employment have been accompanied by similar modifications in the regional distribution of jobs. Since the onset of the recession the trend towards the loss of jobs in the country's older industrial regions has been reinforced, affecting areas in a broad arc stretching from the Seine valley through northern and north-eastern France (with the notable exception of Alsace) and southwards towards traditional manufacturing centres such as St Etienne (Figure 1.3). In contrast much of the south and west of the country has experienced an increase in jobs, although in many cases

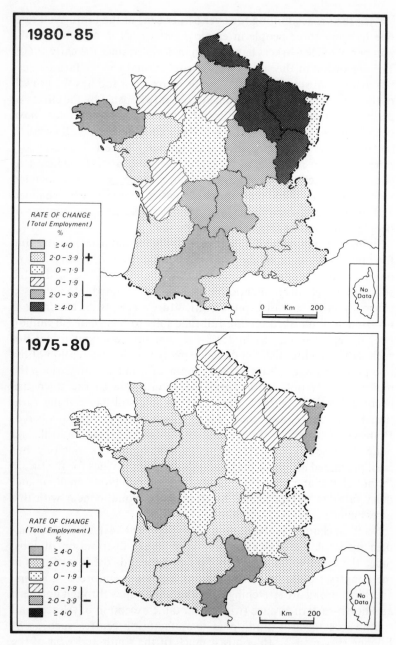

Figure 1.3   Regional patterns of employment change

this has involved only a modest rise. Regions in which there is a strong component of tertiary employment (such as Provence-Alpes-Côte d'Azur and Languedoc-Roussillon) tend to have held up relatively well; the same is also true for those areas which have benefited from decentralisation; thus parts of the Paris basin, particularly to the south and west of the capital (regions such as Basse-Normandie, Centre and Pays de la Loire) have had the advantage of a rapid growth of employment over an extended period which, due to the creation of new factories and offices, has helped rejuvenate the structure of regional employment and attenuate the depressant effects of the recession. Such generalisation may be misleading. Take the case of the Paris region (Ile-de-France). Within this area there is now an overall decline in employment, but the considerable loss of jobs in central and inner areas contrasts sharply with the continued growth on the periphery. Nevertheless even such intra-regional variation, and the implication of a relatively complex pattern of spatial changes in employment when viewed in detail, makes it hard to avoid the conclusion that the country is now faced with a growing geographical divide in the dynamic qualities of its productive activities.

SOCIETY IN TRANSITION

In the same way that the French economy has been subject to a series of structural changes, altering its basic form and character, similar processes have operated to modify the country's society. One illustration of such continuing transformation is offered by changes to the pattern of growth and structure of the country's population. By 1986 there were over 55 million people living in France, but the rate at which this population has been increasing has slowed considerably since reaching a peak in the 1960s; the present rate of growth averages only 0.4 per cent per annum compared with a figure over twice that level little more than a decade ago. The large increase previously accounted for by immigration has now greatly diminished, while birth rates have exhibited a continued decline, currently standing at around 13.5 births per 1000 population. A falling number of births is also reflected in a declining average size of families and changing attitudes towards the family are also seen in relation to marriage. There is now a pronounced downward trend in the number of marriages (in marked contrast to the position in the 1960s and early 1970s), while the number of divorce cases has risen sharply: there are currently around

280 000 marriages and 100 000 divorces each year compared with figures of 400 000 and 45 000 respectively in the early 1970s. One final example of the population's changing composition is provided by modifications to the age structure. France is now faced with a progressively ageing population, particularly as the birth rate has fallen, implying in the longer term a problem for those in work of supporting a much larger non-active section of the community.

Change has been equally apparent in the composition of the country's labour-force, with a key feature being the continuing growth in the number of women in or seeking employment. Nearly 40 per cent of those people in work are now women and 64 per cent of women aged between 25 and 54 have either a full- or part-time job.[2] The trend, which has led to a minor revolution in French lifestyles, has been brought about by a combination of social, economic and psychological influences. These include a modified perception of women's role in society, fewer constraints on mothers due to smaller families and increased child-care facilities, and more job opportunities with the expansion of the service sector where female employees account for over half of the labour-force: over 4.5 million women now have some form of office job. With this growth there has also been a substantial increase in the number of women working part-time, reflecting the personal convenience and practicality of such an arrangement; but part-time work generally has become widespread, now providing over 2.3 million jobs, and over recent years has often represented a means by which employers have been able to avoid redundancies. A further case of underlying change is seen in the continuing shift taking place in the size and relative importance of different socio-economic groups in society. Most apparent has been the declining importance of blue-collar workers following the rapid growth of this group during the late 1950s and 1960s. Now, as their number declines, they have come to represent a lower proportion of the country's labour-force, accounting for approximately a third of the total, a share similar to the position thirty years ago. In part this reflects the basic long-term switch of employment away from the primary and secondary sectors in favour of tertiary and quaternary activities, covering such fields as education, research, government administration and services, retailing and a varied range of private-sector services provided for businesses and households. Since the onset of the recession the accelerating deindustrialisation of the economy has only served to accentuate this trend and emphasise the growing importance of white-collar occupations in society.

The recession has highlighted and often accentuated other modifications to the character of the country's active population. There are now, for example, fewer young people joining the labour-force each year, as the number choosing to remain in the educational system has increased, often reflective of the difficulties encountered in entering the labour market. Activity rates have been similarly falling amongst the older workers, as early retirement has become far more widespread. Both trends, however, have not prevented a substantial rise in unemployment. While this latter feature undoubtedly reflects a contracting labour market, the situation has also been aggravated over recent years by the need to absorb the much larger cohorts of young people resulting from the baby-boom of the 1960s.

For many people the gradual and sometimes imperceptible character of underlying structural changes within society results in a general lack of awareness of their occurrence. Yet there are many other forms of change in contemporary French society which have a greater sense of immediacy and relevance. Modifications to living standards are one example. Much of the period since the end of the Second World War has been associated with a remarkable increase in personal affluence, producing a substantial rise in the level of household consumption over the last thirty years. However, the country's more recent economic difficulties, particularly as they intensified in the 1980s, have shown the previously-assumed inevitability and automatic character of such improved material well-being to be unrealistic. The depressed character of incomes and subsequently of consumption

Table 1.2   Annual change in spending power

	Rate of change (%)
1976	2.8
1977	3.3
1978	5.2
1979	1.6
1980	−0.1
1981	2.8
1982	2.8
1983	−0.7
1984	−0.7
1985	0.5

Source: Ministère de l'Economie.

has become one of the most obvious manifestations of the recession on French society. The average purchasing power of families continued to rise by over 4 per cent each year between 1976 and 1980, yet for the period 1980–85 the yearly mean fell to just under 1 per cent, with a decrease in spending power occurring in 1982 and 1983 (Table 1.2).

Patterns of consumption have not followed an exactly comparable path, as families have used savings to compensate for shortfalls in earned income. Nevertheless, sales of certain types of product have appeared highly sensitive to constraints on income, notably clothes and durable goods such as cars and household appliances. A more sober attitude has also become evident in French people's attitudes to holidaymaking. In 1984 the previously upward trend each year in the number of families taking a holiday was broken, accompanied by a lower average length of stay, despite the introduction of a statutory fifth week of paid holiday in 1982. Such generalisation, however, needs to be treated with some caution, for contrasts in personal circumstances and behaviour patterns frequently vary considerably between different social groups. Under the Socialists, for example, the lower-paid manual worker achieved a more substantial proportional increase in income than many white-collar counterparts, particularly in comparison with certain managerial staff who experienced a cut in real earnings.

There are grounds, therefore, for suggesting that despite the recession, in the 1980s the standard of living of the more modestly paid worker has been relatively well protected. While this may be true in narrow monetary terms, it has not prevented the spread of a growing sense of malaise amongst many people in the working and lower-middle classes who have seen many of their aspirations remain unfulfilled. The years of sustained postwar economic expansion had offered such people the prospect of a continuing rise in material well-being and of upward social mobility, hopes which could be satisfied most obviously in terms of owning a better home and achieving a higher-status job. As incomes increased regularly in real terms and in a situation of a highly fluid and expanding labour market these expectations did not appear unrealistic. But, in the face of recession, such hopes have been thwarted. Social promotion no longer represents a natural process: careers have been blocked and personal affluence has increased far more slowly, and with these trends the possibilities for upward movement in the housing market and particularly for home ownership have been reduced for many people. Not unnaturally this change has engendered a sense of frustration amidst a substantial sub-section of society in a country where there has long been a sharper division between rich and poor than in Britain, contributing to a latent source of discontent within the latter group.

A sense of dissatisfaction, however, is not restricted just to this segment of society. Increasingly over recent years a general feeling of disenchantment, associated with a growing expression of unrest, has become a far more widespread and visible feature. Society appears more violent, not least through the rise in international terrorism, lacking in tolerance, generally less caring and more divided. Within this framework two key issues have aroused particular public concern: the need for more efficient action to combat the continuing rise in criminal activity and the similar requirement for an effective means by which to control immigration and assimilate France's already large foreign population. But there are other manifestations of discontent. Poor housing conditions have become a particular source of complaint. Specific problems have been linked with many of the disproportionately large and ill-conceived high-rise estates in the suburbs of major towns and cities where living has become increasingly intolerable through a combination of neglect, inappropriate allocation policies and bad management. But generally France faces a growing housing crisis as the older stock of accommodation in the large rented sector (and particularly in the quasi-public section of the market) is in increasing need of repair and rehabilitation.

An essential requirement for this latter process to be effective is the availability of more resources, a principle which applies also to the ability to maintain at their past level the country's extensive range of social services. The recession has brought into question the capacity of the social security system to fund the benefits it is now required to pay, especially as the expectation of and demand for improved medical care have continued to grow, and the level of both unemployment and pension payments has risen substantially. Recent experience in France has shown the difficulties of continuing to provide the standards of care set by the social progress of past decades.

The Socialists might justifiably claim that, despite such problems, their record of achievement in social policy while in office was considerable. Indeed, while widespread apprehension was initially aroused by the prospect of left wing parties managing the economy, greater confidence was inspired by their intended programme of social reform. It has since resulted in lowering the age of retirement, a shorter working week, raising the minimum wage, longer paid holidays, a new framework for management-worker relations and the abolition of the death penalty. However, certain of these measures have still provoked controversy not least over the considerable financial burden that their introduction imposed both for individual firms and for the economy as a whole. Attempted change in other fields, notably education and control of the press also aroused resentment and dissent, while the Socialists' image as the party of social progress was not enhanced by their inability to resolve success-fully certain new problems generated by the recession, illustrated by the increasingly difficult plight of the least well-off members of the community.

A NEW POLITICAL FRAMEWORK

Social and economic change in the first half of the present decade has been set largely against the backcloth of a socialist administration, as left wing parties were swept to power in 1981 for the first time during the life of the Vth Republic. In May of that year François Mitterrand achieved a narrow victory over Valéry Giscard d'Estaing to become President; the Socialists then won a popular victory in the ensuing general election, obtaining 285 of the 491 parliamentary seats. With the Communists the Left had an overall majority of 167 seats in the National Assembly, offering it an exceptionally strong base from which to pursue its intended programme of reform (Table 1.3).

The Socialists saw their rise to power as reflective of a widespread movement for change, involving a much modified attitude to the management of the economy and to tackling the country's mounting social problems. Their new approach was designed to lead to a more equitable and considerate society, involving a stronger role for government in the outline and execution of policies. But increased state intervention was not intended as a means of perpetuating the conservation and centralisation frequently associated with govern-ment control. Instead it was designed to promote the modernisation of the French economy and was to be accompanied by major reform to devolve power away from Paris; indeed the two processes were seen as interrelated. Restructuring the country's industrial sector was considered a vital element of this transformation, necessary to restore France's position as a competitive trading nation and thus to generate increased wealth to help finance an ambitious programme of social reform. Modernisation was not envisaged as a process requiring

Table 1.3   Composition of the French National Assembly

	Number of seats
1981	
Socialist Party	285
Communist Party	44
RPR	88
UDF	63
Non-aligned	11
	491
1986	
Socialist Party (and other Left)	215
Communist Party	35
RPR	148
UDF	129
National Front	35
Other Right	14
	577

Source: Le Monde, Les Elections Législatives du 16 Mars 1986 (1986).

brutal surgery, the cost and effectiveness of which would be measured in terms of lost jobs. Instead it was conceived as a means to relaunch output (in response to increased internal demand), creating more employment; where jobs had to go every effort was to be made to cushion the impact of this loss.

Responsibility for the realisation of the government's legislative programme was first entrusted to Pierre Mauroy, the new Prime Minister. However, despite his government's initial popularity, support for its policies was to decline significantly following a relatively short 'état de grâce'. In certain fields achievements were substantial, notably in relation to social reform and decentralisation. Similarly significant progress was made in freeing broadcasting from its previous restrictions. Legislation passed in 1982 enabled the creation of private radio and television stations, ending the previous state monopoly. The result (an explosion of local radio networks, now exceeding 1700 in number, and the provision of three additional television channels by 1986) was widely acclaimed, although the controversy which was later to occur over the allocation of the new television franchises, notably for the fifth channel, could not be foreseen. But the downfall of the Mauroy administration was caused primarily by the government's inability to pursue its original economic strategy.

Having embarked on a programme of revitalisation and expansion in 1981, three years on, many of the government's policies appeared unrecognisable and their consequences unimaginable. The main priority was now restraint, with far greater emphasis upon efficiency and profitability, policies which Pierre Mauroy found increasingly difficult to sell to his traditional trade union and working-class supporters. 'La vie en rose' could hardly have been expected to lead to large-scale redundancies in key strategic industries (coal, steel, ship-building and cars), adversely affecting some of the main bastions of socialist support in areas such as the Nord; nor could it have been envisaged that unemployment would have risen to a total of over 2.3 million people.

A growing sense of disillusionment, amongst at least part of the electorate, at the government's change of course, was suggested by the poor showing of the left wing parties in the European elections of 1984; and by the increasing lack of popularity of both the President and Prime Minister. Various factors appeared to have conspired to weaken the government's position – its own inexperience, an unfavourable international economic climate, a major reversal of policy over management of the economy and continuing disagreements between the Socialists and their erstwhile communist allies. Crisis point was reached in July, triggered by the deepening controversy over reform in 'private' schools. Pierre Mauroy resigned his office, followed shortly by the decision of the Communists not to participate in the new government on the grounds that the Socialists refused to modify their revised economic strategy to accord greater priority to reducing the level of unemployment. This marked the break-up of the much vaunted 'union de la gauche', with the irrevocable character of this split confirmed in the following December when the Communists voted with the opposition against the government's budget for 1985.

To help revive confidence in his administration François Mitterrand nominated Laurent Fabius to succeed Pierre Mauroy as Prime Minister. His youthfulness (he was 37 when appointed) was intended to provide socialism with a rejuvenated image, although his age was also considered by some as a disadvantage, particularly in view of a lack of ministerial experience. Yet here was an astute, articulate, apparently self-assured and competent politician, very different in style and outlook from his older and more convivial predecessor, with his strong attachment to the working-class movement. The new Prime Minister's wealthy, upper middle-class background contrasted sharply with the humbler origins of Pierre Mauroy, and represented a seemingly unlikely pedigree and potential disadvantage for a socialist leader. However, judged by the initially favourable response to Fabius in opinion polls, this was not the view of the electorate.

Under the leadership of Laurent Fabius a further reorientation of government policy became evident, especially in the economic field where a shift occurred away from the highly interventionist strategy of the 1980s; consideration was even given to the partial denationalisation of firms brought under state control in 1982. Certain objections were raised within the ranks of the Left at this injection of liberalism and at the apparent adoption of policies broadly similar to those advocated by the Right, such as the reduction in the rate of income tax. However, from an electoral point of view, socialist leaders, and particularly François Mitterrand appreciated the need to capture more of the middle ground in politics if the party's base was to be widened and strengthened. Hence the search for 'une troisième voie' embracing a 'société d'économie mixte',[3] which lay mid-way between the extremes of a completely free-market economy and a collectivist system. None the less, acceptance that the private sector has a significant role to play in the country's economic revival represented a difficult process of conversion for many Socialists.

Despite a change of Prime Minister the Socialists' decline in popularity persisted, culminating in their defeat in the general election of March 1986. Fabius had not achieved the anticipated revival, with his own image now appearing flawed, following a series of mishandled affairs. These included an unseemly struggle in the summer of 1985 with Lionel Jospin, the First Secretary of the Socialist Party, over management of the strategy for the forthcoming elections, and open disagreement with François Mitterrand concerning the latter's invitation to the Polish leader General Jaruzelski to visit France in December 1985. Furthermore the government of Laurent Fabius had shown far less reforming zeal than its predecessor, despite a number of important innovations such as the introduction of community service work to help ease unemployment.

Yet by the early part of 1986 it appeared that the government's revised economic strategy was achieving some success. By then the Socialists also appeared far more competent administrators than when they first embarked on government, although they had apparently not lost their art of mishandling potentially 'explosive' issues as demonstrated by the notorious Greenpeace incident (Watergate à la française) in the autumn of 1985. However, this particular event appeared to arouse greater concern and indignation outside rather than within France, and to provoke little long-term electoral damage to the Socialists. Instead their ultimate downfall was related to a deeper sense of disappointment over the failure to fulfil certain of their original promises, particularly concerning the creation of jobs and the corresponding reduction in unemployment, and to respond successfully to the desires of many French people for an improved quality of living in a more cohesive and harmonious society.

Given these unfulfilled aspirations, it is perhaps surprising that the Socialists' defeat in March 1986 was not of greater proportions. They obtained only 216 seats (32 per cent of the vote) in the new parliament, compared with 285 seats in 1981, but still represented the largest single party with the right wing coalition (RPR and UDF) gaining only a slender majority over the Left (Table 1.3). Various hypotheses have been put forward to explain this comparatively strong and unexpected standing of the Socialists, (including the vigorous campaign fought by François Mitterrand and tangible evidence of an improving economy); but it has been generally accepted that the decision taken in 1985 to adopt a system of proportional representation for the then forthcoming general election exerted a significant influence on maintaining a strong socialist presence in the National Assembly. This modification of the electoral system was officially justified on the grounds that it produced a more equitable and representative voting procedure, but the suddenness of the change might imply that it was also seen as an ingenious move by the President to limit electoral damage to his party. If this were the aim, François Mitterrand's strategy could be regarded as highly successful, an assessment which seems quite reasonable in view of the new government's decision to revert to the pre-existing system; it would also confirm his reputation as a machiavellian character, unpredictable and at times impenetrable, but clearly an extremely astute politician.

One other effect of the introduction of proportional representation was to provide Jean-Marie Le Pen's Extreme Right party with its first parliamentary seats; thirty-five members of the National Front were elected, as the party captured just under 10 per cent of the vote. In part this result would seem to reflect the increased concern over issues of immigration and law and order, although extreme politics hardly appears to represent the most effective means through which to tackle such sensitive matters. As for the Socialists' former allies, the Communists, their interventionist policies and tactics of confrontation no longer appeared appropriate to the country's current problems or capable of generating large-scale popular support. They held only a similar number of parliamentary seats to the National Front, the party suffering its worst electoral result since the end of the Second World War, reflecting a progressive decline in its popularity; forty years ago the Communists represented the largest (and natural) party of the Left.

In March 1986 France reverted to a right-wing government, headed by Jacques Chirac, a situation which produced extensive debate over the ability of a President and Prime Minister of opposing political parties to 'co-habit' successfully; such an arrangement is unprecedented under the Vth Republic. Although François Mitterrand remained in office, the change of government brought a new approach to the design of social and economic policies. In their election campaign both the main parties (RPR and UDF) forming the right wing coalition had emphasised their commitment to the creation of a more liberal society, and when first outlining the new government's proposed policies before the National Assembly Jacques Chirac stressed the importance attached to personal liberty, free enterprise and the need to reduce the excessive 'dirigisme' of the state.[4] Undoubtedly this gave a distinctive image to the new administration, although if these principles were of such fundamental importance it is tempting to enquire why greater progress towards their implementation was not achieved under previous right wing governments!

In the economic sphere less state intervention was seen as critical in establishing a more efficient productive sector, capable of generating a higher rate of economic growth, which in turn should provide the necessary pre-conditions for an increase in employment and the additional resources to enable social as well as economic progress to be achieved. The objectives, therefore, were not dissimilar from those set by the Socialists in 1981, although the means by which they were to be attained differed. In this context it is also somewhat ironic that the reduction of unemployment should have become a major priority of the Chirac government, for this was exactly the position adopted earlier by the Mauroy administration as the Socialists sought to demonstrate the appropriateness of their policies to a problem whose solution had constantly eluded their predecessors.

Evidence that the new administration was wedded to a liberal philosophy was clearly seen in its economic strategy, where central goals included the removal of price controls and restrictive legislation on competition, denationalisation (now known as privatisation, supposedly to avoid unnecessarily antagonising President Mitterrand)

and the rather ill-defined concept of creating an environment conducive to higher investment. In the area of social policy the principle of greater freedom was again evident in matters such as the provision of more parental choice in the type of schooling available to children, and the lessening of state intervention in the media, both subjects which led to considerable disagreement under the Socialists. A further important commitment of the Right was to improve people's sense of security and above all to seek to combat more effectively international terrorism, again a major source of polemic under the previous socialist administration; for the RPR and UDF 'la sécurité est la première des libertés'.[5] In highlighting these priorities Jacques Chirac succeeded in creating a new sense of urgency over the need for action; some might interpret this as a positive response to the seriousness of related problems but a more cynical view might conclude that such an attitude and the need for immediate results were not unconnected with the approaching presidential elections set for 1988!

Over the last decade French society has experienced another significant shift in the balance of power, as the strength and influence of the country's main trade unions now appear substantially diminished. Management has found itself in a stronger position than for many years and prepared to take a much firmer line in pushing through plans of rationalisation and resisting excessive wage claims. Such new 'toughness' was forcibly demonstrated by Peugeot in its insistence on reducing the work-force at its troubled Talbot plant at Poissy. Ten years ago managements in general were much readier to accede to workers' demands. But unions, under a left wing administration, found themselves in an ambiguous and frustrating position. Although broadly sympathetic to the policies and aspirations of such a government, the sharp rise in unemployment and stagnation of workers' purchasing power forced them to a more critical stance; yet the very increase in the jobless, which they sought to combat and had such difficulty in accepting, greatly compromised their bargaining power.

The labour-force in France has never been highly unionised, certainly by the standards of countries such as Belgium, Italy, West Germany and Britain where upwards of 40 per cent of the working population are union members. It is now estimated that less than 20 per cent of French workers belong to a union. Nevertheless, in the 1960s and early 1970s the trade unions represented a considerable political force, led by the largest and most militant group, the CGT. Yet faced with the recession and its adverse consequences for many traditional union supporters in terms of lost jobs, the movement has been thrown into increasing disaccord and disarray. The dissipation of union power has been accompanied by declining membership, by growing differences of opinion and of strategy between the main union bodies and by greater difficulties in mobilising members to support strike action. Over recent years the number of working days lost through strikes has decreased substantially, falling from 3.6 million days in 1979 to a total of 0.9 million in 1985. Workers have also displayed a growing tendency to reject strike calls, as was forcibly demonstrated in October 1985 when the CGT failed in a major bid to paralyse Renault's plants (once one of its key strongholds) and to gain widespread support for a one-day general strike. The politics of confrontation, still inspired by the desire to pursue the historic class struggle, appear increasingly outmoded as a means of resolving the problems currently facing the country's labour-force, particularly in a depressed economic climate. Through the continued pursuit of such a strategy, the unions have fostered the impression that their principal aim is to stubbornly maintain the status quo even if this is counter-productive, rather than to contribute positively to the creation of more efficiently-run enterprises. Such an attitude was highlighted by the CGT's unwillingness to co-operate with the Socialists' proposals for more flexible working practices, yet this is widely viewed as an essential requirement if more jobs are ultimately to be generated in the economy.

Part of the explanation for the weakening of union power lies in the substantial rise in unemployment and the greater insecurity of employment, conditions which have created, not unnaturally, an increased reluctance amongst workers to participate in disruptive action which might jeopardise their jobs; similar trends have been apparent elsewhere in Europe. However, the modified role of unions has also been conditioned by basic changes in the organisation of society and in working practices. Automation and computerisation may lead not only to fewer jobs in specific activities but also to very different requirements from the labour-force, particularly in terms of a new range of skills. These tendencies have eroded support for traditional blue-collar unions, not least in those industries such as steel, shipbuilding and cars, long-characterised by a militant work-force; moreover it is these activities which have frequently been most adversely affected by reduced demand and lower labour requirements. The expansion of the teriary sector and therefore white-collar employment, traditionally weakly unionised, has further diminished the influence of the organised labour movement; and a similar effect has resulted from the rapid growth of small businesses in the private sector. Indeed if an increase in the membership of trade unions is to occur, it will be through adapting their appeal to cater for the needs of these groups and recruiting within their ranks.

Unions ought to perform a significant function in sustaining and promoting the country's continued economic development and in ensuring that the work-force benefits from this process. The challenge to French trade unions is to become fully involved in this movement rather than tending to remain, as at present, on the fringe. Unions need to adopt a more progressive attitude and demonstrate that they are able to work in harmony with management rather than in constant opposition. Some progress towards increased dialogue has already been achieved by the Auroux labour laws, which were passed in 1982; a key objective was the desire to improve relations between management and the work-force by ensuring that regular contact occurred between the two sides. In addition, greater involvement of unions in company decision-making should elicit from them a more positive contribution to economic growth; certainly this is indicated by the experience of countries such as West Germany and Japan.

A SPATIAL DIMENSION TO CHANGE

Imbalance between the regions has long characterised the processes of social and economic development in France. Marked spatial contrasts have been evident, for example, in rates of population growth, the structure of employment, income levels and living standards. This underlying pattern of regional disparity has been further modified over the last decade, not least because the impact of the recession has had a significant geographical dimension. The latter feature might appear most obvious in relation to the heavy losses of jobs in many of the country's traditional staple industries such as steel, textiles, heavy engineering and coal which frequently exhibit a marked spatial concentration in their distribution, so that regions housing a high proportion of these activities would be expected to have been particularly badly affected by the downturn in the economy.

Evidence to support this contention is provided by regional trends in employment which reveal a pronounced decline in jobs, especially in the secondary sector, in the older industrial regions such as Nord – Pas-de-Calais and Lorraine. However, in reality the situation is more complex, as the scale of job losses in these areas appears less than might be anticipated given their unfavourable employment structures which feature a large number of declining activities. This suggests that other factors (notably government decentralisation and regional policies) have been effective in stimulating the expansion of replacement activities. Conversely jobs have held up much better in many of the country's southern and western regions where there is no legacy of contracting outworn heavy industrial areas to depress the level of employment. On the contrary, industrialisation is frequently of more recent origin, notably in regions such as Brittany, much of it again related to decentralisation in the 1960s and 1970s. However, even in these areas industrial employment is now falling, although at a much slower rate than in the traditional northern industrial centres: it is only the continued growth of jobs in tertiary activities that has ensured an overall increase in employment.

One factor contributing to the continued expansion of the service sector in the above regions has been the still relatively strong growth of population and the creation of related employment as the need for services has increased. In fact, spatial variations in the pattern of demographic change represent a further significant dimension of regional contrasts in France. One of the major changes to have occurred since the 1960s has been the progressive decline in the attractive role played by Paris. It is in the country's south-eastern, traditionally under-industrialised regions, essentially Languedoc-Roussillon and Provence-Alpes-Côte d'Azur, where the highest growth rates are currently recorded. In contrast northern regions, with a long history of manufacturing activity and related urban development, such as Nord – Pas-de-Calais, Champagne-Ardenne and Lorraine, feature a stable or progressively declining total population. This opposition is even clearer when only migrational trends are considered, for there is now a growing dichotomy between many areas in the northern part of France, including the Paris region, featuring a pronounced net loss of population through migration, and a similar group of regions in the south where there is a strongly positive balance.

Different models have been proposed to provide a simple conceptual framework in which to analyse these various forms of inter-regional contrast. In the late 1940s attention was first drawn to the severe imbalance which existed in many spheres of life between the capital and the rest of France. But this idea of a basic opposition between Paris and the provinces was then superseded by the notion of an essentially east-west division between the more industrialised and urbanised regions of eastern France, epitomised and dominated by Paris, and their less developed western counterparts. Elements of both models are still observable but changes, such as those brought by decentralisation policy and the recession, have rendered their continued use less appropriate, particularly as the capital has lost both jobs and population. Instead a new spatial division has begun to emerge as many southern areas (and certain parts of western France) have displayed far greater dynamism, even in a generally depressed economic environment, than regions in the north of the country. Not only have these two broad areas performed differently in terms of economic and demographic change, but there is also evidence of a drift of both jobs and people towards France's southern 'sun-belt', suggesting a fundamental reordering in the relative importance of the forces influencing the location of economic activity.

Such generalisation conceals many intra-regional contrasts in development patterns, not least the clear shift of population and certain forms of economic activity away from major cities, particularly their inner areas. Just as the early postwar years were characterised by a strong movement of urbanisation, more recently suburbanisation and exurbanisation have become equally prominent counteractive trends. Most of France's large urban centres are now losing population as people demonstrate a preference for living in outer suburbia or surrounding semi-rural districts compared with inner suburbs; the former areas are often perceived to offer a superior quality of environment and a higher standard of accommodation. Jobs have displayed a similar migrational tendency as first industry and increasingly tertiary activities have shifted towards the periphery in search of more space, lower costs, and greater proximity to both their workers and their clientele. Similar factors have also persuaded considerable numbers of firms and individuals to reject the large city and its various diseconomies in favour of smaller urban centres, with these towns as a group now displaying the highest rates of urban growth in France.

These various trends outlined above testify not only to the diversity of social and economic conditions in France, but also to their dynamic quality, reflecting a high level of mobility amongst the population and businesses. But change is apparent even here. In the period of expansion prior to the recession inter-regional migrational flows of population had increased substantially; the labour market displayed a similar and related fluidity, with the considerable movement of people between jobs frequently associated with a change of residence and region. A decade later, however, in a very different economic climate, a modified picture of mobility had emerged.[6] Inter-regional shifts of population, although still substantial, had diminished and fewer people were changing employment, reflecting a growing reluctance to relinquish the relative security of an existing job. Not only did this serve to constrain spatial mobility, it also had the effect of increasing the difficulty of entry to the labour market, especially for young people and women. As such this represents but one of the problematic features of contemporary French society.

2 Society in Disarray

A NEW SOCIETY?

Modern French society remains divided. The country is still characterised by substantial inequalities in wealth, opportunities for employment and living standards, contrasts which are evident between people of different occupational groups and between the various regions. Against this background the cohesiveness of society has been further weakened by the divisive effects of recession. In such circumstances, therefore, the election of a Socialist president and government might have been seen as an appropriate opportunity to embark on a new era of social reform. Certainly this was the view of the Socialists themselves, particularly François Mitterrand who, to enhance his image during the presidential election campaign, had sought to portray himself as 'l'homme du changement'.

The commitment to this goal was forcibly demonstrated in 1981 and 1982 with the introduction of a wide range of new legislation, but by 1983 the country's worsening economic problems meant that further progress in this field had to take second place to measures aimed at counteracting the increasingly serious social consequences of industrial modernisation and restructuring. Key issues now became the sharp rise in unemployment, the growing sense of insecurity and increased racial tension and conflict, issues which form the basis of subsequent and more detailed analysis in this chapter. These problems were not new, but their seriousness had been accentuated by the recession, and many people saw them as being increasingly interrelated; thus high unemployment and a rising crime rate were linked to the continued growth of the immigrant population. For some, socialist policies themselves had contributed to this situation, notably through a less punitive attitude to the maintenance of law and order, a less restrictive policy on immigration and a misguided economic strategy which had only served to increase unemployment.

Despite some reorientation of priorities in their social policies, one consistent goal retained by the Socialists was a commitment to improving the conditions of the working class, recognising such people's vulnerable position in a period of economic crisis and a longer-standing failure of previous administrations to introduce adequate improvements. The government's action focused on three key areas of change. First it aimed to make workers better off materially through a higher minimum wage (the SMIC was raised by 25 per cent in the first twelve months alone of the socialist reign) and enhanced family allowances; second, it reduced the statutory working week to 39 hours, with the hope that this would be further reduced to 35 hours by 1985 (an aim which was subsequently abandoned); and third, workers were to be given a greater say in how their firms should be managed. Many of the changes embodied in these reforms were designed to contribute to the resolution of wider social issues. Thus, by enabling people to work shorter hours it was originally hoped that this would help reduce unemployment through increased work sharing.

However, not all of these measures appear to have produced the desired effect. A shorter working week has not resulted in the anticipated increase in new jobs, and some ambiguity surrounds the extent to which legislation designed to improve workers' rights (lois Auroux) has achieved this goal. Indeed considerable controversy came to surround much of the Socialists' programme of reform.

In part this might be seen to reflect the excessive haste with which certain measures were formulated and, therefore, their ill-conceived character, but it also resulted from a misjudgement of public opinion and from the inherently contentious nature of certain policies. Changes in the field of education were to provide a prime illustration of this aspect of socialist policies, a somewhat surprising outcome given the general consensus that reform was necessary.

Reforming education

When the Socialists took power, the country's educational system was already under increasing challenge from a variety of forces. High birth rates in France which persisted until the mid-1970s ensured the continuing need to provide a growing number of places in schools and higher educational establishments. More significantly demand had grown for fundamental revisions to the curriculum and to teaching methods, and particularly to adapt these to the changing requirements of the labour market. The Socialists had other basic philosophical motives for intervening in education, notably to eradicate inherent inequalities which still existed. Change to the system was also implied within the government's wider strategies of modernisation and decentralisation.

Thus from the first months of socialist rule, reorganisation of the educational system became an integral and key component of government policy. Three goals were to underpin subsequent action. First it was considered essential to widen the range of educational opportunity, particularly for children of parents with modest financial means. Second, there was a need to reduce the apparently excessive number of 'failures' produced by the system, reflected in the high level of teenagers abandoning full-time education, poorly qualified, at the age of 16 and of students leaving university with no qualifications; both trends were seen as contributing to high youth unemployment and the rising incidence of juvenile delinquency, increasing the urgency and desirability of tackling this problem. Third, in a rapidly changing technological environment, the need for a greater technical orientation to many teaching programmes was considered vital. Thus, both economic factors and the desire for a greater element of social justice lay behind the Socialists' plans to reform education.

Yet in 1981, as the government initiated this programme, it would have been difficult to predict the controversy and animosity engendered by certain elements of its policy. Polemic centred on the proposals to transform the system of public and private education in schools, producing an acrimonious debate which lasted more than three years. What started out from the government's point of view as an attempt to create a fairer system of educational provision, resulted in claims that its reforms would cause discrimination and a loss of personal liberty. After widespread expressions of protest, culminating in the marching of an estimated 1 million people through Paris on 24 June 1984 (ending symbolically at the Bastille), the government withdrew its proposals in a spectacular volte-face, representing a remarkable victory for public opinion. Whatever the benefits originally envisaged, the ultimate costs were high – Alain Savary the Minister of Education resigned, followed shortly by the Prime Minister, the government's credibility was strained and time and effort had been diverted from arguably far more important issues such as the need to revitalise the economy.

There has long been debate over the relative merits and roles of state or public schools and their equivalents in the private sector, although over time opinion has tended to be polarised and attitudes hardened. The term 'enseignement privé' (private education) has become synonymous with the 'free sector' of the educational system where freedom is equated with the notion of liberty to teach in an unrestricted manner without constraints applied by, for example, the state. Although this term theoretically covers a wide range of schools, in practice it relates almost entirely to Catholic institutions, these representing approximately 98 per cent of the private or free sector. ('Free' is something of a misnomer because in many cases parents are expected to contribute to the cost of education, even if the amount paid is small.) Thus two parallel and competing systems of education have developed in France. In 1959 the position of private institutions was considerably strengthened through the adoption of the 'loi Debré'. To help overcome some of the financial difficulties experienced by a number of these schools, one of the main provisions of this Act was to provide a revised and increased level of state funding. One further outcome was to demarcate more clearly and rigidly the position of the main political parties on this issue: the public sector became strongly identified with the Socialists, while its Catholic counterpart drew particular support from centre and right wing parties.

Increasingly the private sector became viewed as a privileged partner in the educational system, associated not only with the Church but also with more affluent members of society; in terms of occupational class the influence of private education compared with the public sector is particularly prevalent even now amongst those children whose parents fall within the categories of upper management, the liberal professions and heads of industry, as well as those who are farmers.[1] Not only were the Socialists opposed to this situation but also to state funds being used to subsidise the private sector, reflected in the slogan 'à école publique, fonds publics; à école privée, fonds privés' (public money for state schools: private resources for private schools), adopted by many of the unionised staff in the public sector who were active in seeking change. There was also resentment that the private sector had acquired a generally high reputation for the quality and innovative character of its education contrasting with the image of a less progressive and less efficient public sector. Against this view was the attitude that parents should be free to choose the system under which their children were educated, this representing a fundamental right; defending the 'école libre' became a symbol for the maintenance of personal liberty and choice within society, a philosophy strongly supported by the 'conservative' parties.

Already, while in opposition, François Mitterrand had announced his preference for a single, unified state system of education and it was, therefore, of little surprise that such a reform should be proposed once he was invested as President. The basic proposition of the government was the eventual integration of private schools and their personnel into the state system, where the freedom of parents to select a particular school (for religious reasons, for example) would be respected. But the liberty of action in teaching and the appointment of staff, and the financial independence previously enjoyed by 'l'école libre' would disappear. Initially it appeared that such change would be accepted, for even the Church recognised that some modification of its privileged status had become almost inevitable. However, as negotiations failed to progress and became increasingly politicised, and opposition to the reform sharpened, this likelihood began to recede. The government's first formal proposals set out in the latter part of 1982 by Alain Savary were rejected by Church leaders; subsequent modifications put forward a year later proved acceptable to neither the Catholic sector nor advocates of the state school (for some elements of private education were retained). By the end of 1983, as the prospects for a negotiated settlement appeared increasingly remote, the government indicated that legislation might have, therefore, to be imposed.

By this time, however, substantial support had been mobilised in defence of 'l'enseignement privé', despite its relatively minor role: currently there are an estimated 10 000 Catholic schools responsible for the education of just over 2 million children, but this represents only 15 per cent of the school population in France.[2] But size was largely immaterial. Above all the defence of the 'école libre' stood for the maintenance of individual freedom of choice. It might be seen as of little surprise, therefore, that opinion polls showed 70 per cent of the French population in favour of retaining this sector.[3] Support was further manifest at a number of large regional demonstrations in the early part of 1984 at Lyon, Bordeaux, Rennes, Lille and Versailles. But it was the massive gathering in the capital in June of the same year which finally persuaded the government of the deep resentment to its proposed measures, leading to their hasty withdrawal and the associated political upheaval. The battle was therefore lost, with the Socialists forced into retreat. Negotiations over the role of private education had been resumed by the autumn in a very different climate and under the more pragmatic direction of Jean-Pierre Chevènement, the new Education Minister. Rather ironically they resulted in legislation which resembled many aspects of the original Savary proposals, giving the state greater control in the running of non-public schools although retaining the principle of a separate and state-funded private sector as laid down by the loi Debré. By now, however, interest in the issue had waned.

Thus the outcome might be seen as a victory for the protection of parents' rights to choose freely the manner in which their children are educated, yet even the Socialists had never envisaged the disappearance of sectarian education, arguing instead for the maintenance of a plurality of institutions but embraced within a single, unified state system. However, ultimately it was perhaps the somewhat arrogant approach of the government and the intention to impose the reform, as much as its implied attack on individual liberty, which thwarted this initiative.

Crisis on the campus
A further incidence of controversy over educational policy arose with proposals to modify the university sector. Despite the upheavals of 1968, more than a decade later French universities still appeared in need of reform. Such institutions, through their bureaucracy and immense diversity of activity, allied to the independent spirit of the teaching and research staff, had proved remarkably resilient to change. In general many seemed increasingly outmoded and more isolated from the society they were designed to serve, resulting in their inefficient operation and a decline in status and image. Too many university courses appeared too remote from the realities of the labour market in a period of recession, particularly in arts and social science disciplines where the principal traditional market for graduates (the teaching profession) had experienced a substantial cut in recruitment; too few of their research units appeared to be engaged in fruitful links with the industrial and commercial worlds; too many students were leaving the system without completing their programme of study or obtaining a degree; and the majority of students still originate from relatively affluent families, especially in 'élite' disciplines such as medicine, while overall only one out of every five young people of university-entry age actually takes up a place in such an establishment. Universities have become viewed as increasingly less attractive centres of education, particularly in the training of specific skills linked to subsequent professional life (although, as in Britain, the extent to which this represents the intended function of universities is much debated). By comparison many of the country's 'grandes écoles' and IUTs (Institut Universitaire de Technologie) have acquired a much higher reputation, appearing far more innovative and adaptive, and their courses displaying considerably greater relevance to the

needs of business and industry. Yet universities (including the IUTs) represent a substantial force and major educational and research resource embracing 46 000 teaching staff, and nearly 1 million students spread amongst over 140 centres.

The Socialists, therefore, pledged themselves to modernising the university system, aiming to make it more democratic, more efficient and more responsive to society's needs. Underlying these intentions were the notions that universities should welcome an increased number of students, and provide them with a wider range of opportunities and improved quality of training which would have a greater professional orientation. However, these proposals provoked anger from both students and lecturing staff, seen in a series of protest marches and demonstrations in the early part of 1983. A key feature of government changes was the revision of the first two years of university study (the 'premier cycle') with the aim of greatly increasing their interdisciplinary character: by widening the initial choice of subjects the intention was to facilitate the subsequent orientation of students. Certain staff, already with numerous commitments, showed little enthusiasm for the idea of a substantial reorganisation of this first cycle, although it was designed to provide students with more choice and more vocationally orientated courses, and as such to increase the attractiveness of university entry; moreover, through more careful guidance and advice by university staff, it was hoped that a greater number of these students would successfully complete this initial course of study.

From the student point of view resentment was aroused by what they saw as a greater degree of selectivity which would result from these new courses and the associated process of orientation. Selection has long been opposed, not least by the Socialists themselves when the same changes towards a more cost-effective and selective system of higher education, with courses orientated much more to professional outlets were proposed by Alice Saunier-Séïté, Education Minister under Valéry Giscard d'Estaing. Indeed, at a much wider level the issue of selection remains a major unresolved issue in the French university system. In theory once the 'Bac' has been obtained entry to university is automatic for those who wish to follow a course of higher study. But many students subsequently drop out and, for those who continue, an increasing number encounter difficulties in finding employment with their degrees, especially in Arts disciplines. In contrast it is in those universities where selection on entry is applied, such as the IUTs and medicine faculties, where the results are more encouraging.

Yet the idea of the more widespread practice of such selectivity has always been resisted, for it is seen as an attack on a fundamental right.

Despite opposition, the reforms outlined above and other changes (including a new form of doctoral research degree, and changes to university teachers' contractural obligations increasing their hours!) were introduced in the early part of 1984. But it is far from clear that they will revolutionise or rejuvenate the system. Yet if the university sector is to project a new image and produce a radically restyled form of education, fundamental change is essential. Certainly some advances towards these goals are evident. On the teaching side a series of new 'first cycle' courses is now in operation in many universities, while to develop and widen the community role of these institutions, there are now many instances of a much stronger emphasis on courses for adult education (la formation continue); and in the research field increasing efforts are being made to bridge the gap between the frequently abstract context of much of the work traditionally undertaken in academia, and the strongly applied demands of the industrial and commercial worlds.

Nonetheless, there is also evidence that many features of the system remain highly resistant to change. Despite attempts to advise students more fully on possible degree courses, French universities still appear far less caring than their British counterparts. Student facilities for sports or social activities frequently remain inadequate or non-existent, extra-curricular activities are limited and staff are frequently extremely inaccessible. The 'turbo-prof', commuting to or from the capital, is still very much alive and will no doubt continue to flourish with advances such as the TGV and its spread to an even greater number of regions. Academics who act in this way would no doubt argue that until Paris ceases to represent overwhelmingly the prime focus of research activity, the situation is likely to persist – vive la décentralisation! There are also internal cleavages which need removing, not least the division between the professorial corps (frequently seen as 'mandarins') and their 'lecturer' colleagues, for this is detrimental both to students and good working relationships within the profession. Yet the solution to these problems and to the need to create an enhanced image for universities remains elusive, not least as the change of government in 1986, and the new administration's commitment to repeal the reforms of Alain Savary and provide universities with greater autonomy, seemed likely to herald a further period of instability and uncertainty.

The theme of modernising education and adapting teaching programmes to the changing demands of society is evident at other levels within the system. It is not just university graduates who need to be better prepared for their subsequent professional lives, but also school leavers. Hence the Socialists' search for new approaches in secondary schools: in particular the aims were to introduce far greater emphasis on technological subjects and computer-based studies, and to provide the opportunities for teenagers to undertake some specific professional training (if they wished) while still at school. Even primary education has not escaped this desire to adapt education to the rapid technological changes affecting society, with a major programme launched in 1985 to equip schools with microcomputers and to train staff in their use. However, traditional values have not been neglected and indeed Jean-Pierre Chevènement, while Minister of Education, placed considerable emphasis on the need not to neglect the three Rs and to raise standards, to the surprise of certain of his colleagues although to the apparent general approval of a majority of French people. But the change of government has again led to a rethinking of these initiatives, helping to foster the view that the French educational system remains in a state of crisis requiring stable direction: long-term improvement is unlikely as long as education is such a volatile political football.

Although curriculum development is important, schools at both primary and secondary level have been faced with a number of other challenging and problematic issues. As in Britain, morale within the teaching profession has tended to decline, reflecting factors such as dissatisfaction over the level of salaries and a deterioration of working conditions, particularly in certain inner-city suburbs and the 'grands ensembles'. Here teachers' difficulties are compounded by the growth in anti-social behaviour, the rise in the use of drugs and the high proportion of immigrant children in many classes. The latter trend has frequently provoked strong reaction and resentment amongst the parents of French children who view this feature as a cause of lowering educational standards. Some attempt has been made to provide schools with additional resources to combat these problems (through for example the creation of priority education areas), but teachers still have to work in a difficult and delicate social environment. Moreover, their ability to influence the above conditions is limited, for in many cases the destabilising forces within schools merely reflect many of the fundamental ills of society as a whole.

CRIME ON THE INCREASE

In the early hours of Sunday, 29 September 1985 a young North African was stabbed to death in the centre of Lyon by three 'bouncers' from one of the city's night clubs; the young man's 'crime', apparently, had been to object to the manner in which his friend had been evicted from the club – he was kicked into the Saône. In the same month the extreme left wing organisation 'Action Directe' claimed responsibility for a number of bomb attacks in the Paris suburbs on firms supposedly having links with South Africa: despite considerable material damage and several injured people, in this instance no one was killed. Earlier in the year, however, three guards employed by a security firm transporting wages through the northern suburbs of Marseille were less fortunate; they were killed instantly when, from a pursuing vehicle, a rocket launcher was used to fire explosives into their van, completely destroying it. Only the previous day two policemen and a security guard were killed in the 18th arrondissement at Paris when another security van was attacked.

Such events represent one of the least attractive aspects of French society in the 1980s, yet robbery, violence and terrorist attacks appear to have become common features of contemporary France, still provoking outrage but no longer astonishment. Already the first half of the present decade has produced an extensive and varied catalogue of major crimes and acts of terrorism. Violence has flared in Corsica as part of the continuing campaign of the separatist movement; Middle Eastern terrorists have placed bombs in the French capital with two people killed, for example, on the Champs-Elysées in March 1986; the North African community in France has been the subject of violent attack, but so too have other racial minorities – in August 1982 six people were killed and a considerably greater number wounded when Palestinian extremists raided a Jewish restaurant in the rue des Rosiers in Paris; express trains, including the TGV, have become a further terrorist target – in 1982 a bomb exploded in the Paris-Toulouse express (le Capitole), killing five people; and over seven months in the latter part of 1984 and early 1985 twenty-one people were murdered in Marseille, as a series of accounts were settled amongst the city's gangland fraternity. In such circumstances it is not surprising that headlines have suggested that 'les français ont peur'.

There is now a popularly held view that during the 1980s society generally has become less safe in the face of an increasing breakdown in law and order. Opinion polls comparing attitudes in the late 1970s and mid-1980s have shown a strong rise in the proportion of people (now representing a substantial majority) who consider that they live in a more violent and increasingly insecure environment.[4] Politicians, particularly of the right wing parties, have not been slow to seek to capitalise upon this issue, with the result that during the Socialists' years in power the question of 'l'insécurité' became a major topic of debate.

None the less, some disagreement has arisen over the extent to which crime has actually increased significantly. Official statistics certainly confirm a substantial rise in criminality during the early part of the 1980s (Table 2.1). Whereas the number of recorded criminal acts rose by approximately 27 per cent between 1974 and 1979, the rate of increase over the period 1979–84 more than doubled to 58 per cent. All the major categories of crime have been affected by this trend, with some such as armed robbery and drug trafficking displaying particularly high rates of increase. Similarly the incidence of relatively minor offences such as car theft and personal robbery has risen sharply, notably in major cities and especially Paris. An illustration of this latter trend is given by the growing number of criminal offences (notably robbery) committed on the capital's metro system. In 1981 there were 1110 reported attacks on people, but by 1984 this number had risen to 4101: in the same year it was estimated that at least 10 000 people were robbed while using the underground.[5]

There is now some suggestion, however, that the general upward trend in criminality has slowed, at least temporarily. In 1983 and 1984 a decelerating rate of increase was recorded, while for the first six

Table 2.1   The increase in criminal offences, 1974–84

Type of offence	Number of offences ('000)					
	1974	*1980*	*1981*	*1982*	*1983*	*1984*
Offences against the person	87.8	111.1	119.2	131.2	139.9	142.3
Public order offences	112.3	227.8	252.2	305.4	317.0	333.6
Robbery and theft	1455.1	2150.3	2384.5	2939.2	2966.5	3073.1
Other	172.2	138.3	134.1	137.9	140.6	132.5
Total	1827.4	2627.5	2890.0	3413.7	3564.0	3681.5

Source: INSEE, *Annuaire Statistique de la France* (1985).

months of 1985 government figures showed a drop of almost 5 per cent in the number of crimes compared with the similar period in the previous year. There may not be any widespread appreciation of this change, but at least it implies that socialist policies have not been completely to blame (as the Right has frequently indicated) for France's recent crime wave.

Rising crime levels might imply that society in France is more violent and less safe than in other neighbouring European countries. However, there would appear to be little firm evidence to support this view. Acts of terrorism have remained constant features of life in countries such as Great Britain, West Germany, Italy and Belgium, although their origins may vary from one country to another. Paris may appear a relatively unsafe city compared with a number of other major urban centres in Europe, but the contrast is not great and levels of violence are substantially below those recorded in certain American cities such as Chicago, New York and Los Angeles. Finally, the demands in France for a stronger fight against crime, partly through more effective policing, have been echoed equally forcibly in many other European countries.

Debating the issues

Given the concern over the increased incidence of criminal activity, it is of little surprise that the issue should have become highly politicised. For the parties of the Right one of the principal factors encouraging a rise in crime has been the laxness of the socialist government's approach to the question and its reforming attitude. Traditionally the Socialists have adopted a less repressive attitude than their centre and right wing opponents in the policies they have advocated to combat higher crime rates. As early as 1981 the socialist members of parliament led the move to abolish the death penalty and to remove certain controls over terrorists; by 1983 parliament had also voted to offer 'community work' as an alternative to mandatory imprisonment for various forms of relatively minor offence. Such measures were interpreted as representing a more lenient attitude towards criminals, an approach which was widely condemned by other political parties. The Socialists were also faced with dissention from within the ranks of those responsible for enforcing the law, not so much in opposition to their general policies in this field, but to the decline of working conditions and morale in the related services. Thus in June 1983 the Paris police took the unprecedented action of demonstrating in front of the Ministries of Justice and of the Interior, to be followed shortly afterwards by a strike of prison officers, angered in particular by the high level of overcrowding and the difficulties of working in frequently outdated penal institutions. Inevitably such events helped to strengthen the view that the Socialists were unwilling or incapable of mounting an effective campaign against criminal activity.

Jacques Chirac and his party (RPR) have become strong advocates of a tougher policy towards fighting crime, although it would appear that the differences between the Right and Left are as much related to the degree of repressive action that is required as to fundamental differences in approach. It is rather the Extreme Right, and in particular its leader Jean-Marie Le Pen, who have proposed more radical alternatives. The National Front favours the restoration of the death penalty and is firmly committed to a policy of much stiffer sentencing. While it also proposes an increase in the size of the police force, notably in certain sensitive areas of the major cities, the party does not see a lack of resources as a major obstacle to the more effective control of crime. For the National Front the most important factor is the need for a fundamental change of attitude and of those in power being prepared to adopt a much harder line. Initially the RPR sought to disassociate itself strongly with such a viewpoint, but given the considerable support that the views of Monsieur Le Pen appear to have generated, it has been forced itself to adopt a more radical tone to its declarations. Certainly this became apparent when the Right was returned to power in 1986.

To imply that rising crime rates and deteriorating standards of protection against criminals have been due predominantly to the policies pursued by a particular political party would seem to show a lack of understanding of the complex social, psychological and economic character of many criminal acts. Indeed even politicians themselves have sought to dispel this simplistic notion, although one of the most frequently implied alternative 'explanations' seems equally doubtful. Certain political figures, notably on the extreme right, have been unable to resist the temptation of suggesting that a breakdown in law and order is linked to the country's still growing immigrant population. As a result a new popular stereotype of the criminal has emerged; such a person is young, of foreign birth or descent, preferably North African, probably unemployed and lives in an insalubrious inner-city district or one of the interminable 'grands ensembles' on the urban periphery. Such views might be seen as particularly disturbing, not least because of their apparent ready acceptance by certain members of society. Frequent press reports are to be found of attacks on North African immigrants, which in certain cases have resulted in death, where the implied attitude of those responsible has been to diminish the importance of the crime due to the victim's immigrant status. One of many similar instances was recorded at Menton in the early part of 1985 when a young Moroccan was shot dead by an unemployed Frenchman with no other apparent explanation than he and his companion 'n'aimaient pas les Arabes'.

Seeking to link the presence of a large immigrant population to an elevated level of criminality would seem at best highly mischievous and at worst highly dangerous, serving only to inflame racial prejudice and encourage the actions and attitudes described above. Yet those who choose to advocate these views justify their attitude by reference to certain correlations which can be observed associating the presence of a large immigrant population with high crime rates. Thus criminality tends to be most prevalent in the country's major cities (especially Paris) and certain industrial regions such as the Nord, as well as throughout the 'Midi'; and it is in these same areas that are found the highest concentrations of immigrants. However, it could also be argued that many other sub-groups within society are found predominantly in the larger towns and cities, an almost inevitable consequence in a country where three-quarters of the population are officially classified as urban residents. Moreover there has long been a strong link between high crime rates and urban areas.

Statistics relating to the number of people in prison have also been used to support the view that immigrants represent a significant source of criminal behaviour. In 1985, over 27 per cent of the total number of inmates were non-French, representing a rate, which in relation to the size of the foreign population in France, is over five times higher than the equivalent proportion amongst French nationals;[6] moreover this rate has increased considerably over time, for in the mid-1970s it stood at around 18 per cent. However, this position needs to be qualified. It might be argued, for example, that as the country's immigrant community tends to be subject to a greater degree of surveillance by the police than is accorded to native French people, it is not surprising that a proportionally higher number are brought to justice; moreover, given the comparatively marginal and uncertain nature of residential areas from which many foreigners appear to originate in France (at least as far as the police and magistrates are concerned), there is a greater tendency to hold suspects awaiting trial rather than to release them on bail, as might be the case with a French person.

One of the reasons officially advanced to explain the more rigorous control of foreigners is that this is essential to deal effectively with problems such as illegal entry to, or residence within, the country. While this may be so, as such offences relate only to the immigrant population, their inclusion in figures relating to levels of crime or to prison inmates tends to result in bias against these people. It is also suggested that as a large number of crimes appear to be associated with a relatively youthful, poorly educated and male population, often unemployed, and that as immigrants (and particularly many of those originating from areas such as Algeria, Morocco and Tunisia) tend to be over-represented within these groups, then it is only natural that this situation should be reproduced in crime statistics.

While this latter argument again serves to explain why crime appears to be more prevalent amongst immigrants, it also raises certain issues concerning the conventional view of crime and the criminal, for it ignores one significant and arguably rapidly growing field of criminal activity – white collar criminality; and, due to the arguably greater 'intellectual' character of such crime, its incidence might be supposed to be less widespread amongst the immigrant population. In 1985 a report produced by the Centre de Recherches Sociologiques sur le Droit et les Institutions Pénales indicated that on the basis of crimes committed over the period 1980–82 offences such as tax evasion and financial fraud cost the country a substantially greater amount than more conventional forms of robbery from individuals and from property.[7] Yet there is a frequent reluctance on the part of those institutions affected by such theft to declare its existence or to prosecute those involved, rendering this form of crime extremely difficult to detect. Furthermore, in view of the essentially 'concealed' nature of such activity, its impact upon the general climate of insecurity could be considered relatively insignificant.

The quest for a solution

Devising appropriate and effective strategies to produce a safer society represents an intricate and challenging task, not least due to the issue's many and frequently interrelated features, and the need to alter strongly-held opinions and to convince people that improvements are taking place. Not only has the question of insecurity taken on an increasingly political aspect, but in the fight against crime, the growing manner in which individuals have sought to protect themselves has caused disquiet, implying the need for a revised and stronger official lead. Potentially lethal booby-traps placed to deter intruders from homes or work premises, and direct action in shooting would-be assailants or burglars have become increasingly common responses in a more violent society.

Not surprisingly, therefore, one response has been to reinforce the traditional means of law enforcement, principally by seeking to transform the image and efficiency of the police, where morale amongst officers had been considerably eroded. In 1985 Laurent Fabius claimed that the modernisation of the police force represented a major priority for the government, with legislation passed in the latter part of the same year designed to achieve this goal. Although 10 000 additional jobs in the service were created during the first two years of socialist rule, the basis of more recent changes has been to enhance the effectiveness of the police by increasing the range and quality of support services. New equipment is to be provided, more modern and efficient premises built and, above all, strong emphasis is to be placed on computerising records and generally using the computer to expedite enquiries, this latter policy coinciding with much wider attempts being made within society to encourage the greater use and awareness of new technology.

Other initiatives include a revised approach to policing, including the introduction of the system, familiar in Britain, of the 'neighbourhood bobby'. By this means it is hoped to forge an improved relationship between the public and the police, and to provide a more effective counter-measure against the rising trend in locally-based vandalism and minor criminal offences, particularly evident in many large postwar housing estates. As part of the new image for the police, uniforms are also changing, involving the disappearance of the symbolic 'kepi'. However, it is unlikely that such cosmetic alterations alone will lead to greater respect for or co-operation with the police in a country where mutual mistrust and dislike have long been features of the relationship between the French citizen and the forces of the law. Nor are the measures designed to produce a much more technically efficient force likely to result in a rapid improvement for their introduction represents a fundamental and much longer-term change. But whatever the shortcomings attached to these various forms of transformation, for a government to be seen to take such action to reinforce law and order is politically advantageous, particularly as most of the changes are uncontroversial.

Certain other reforms undertaken by the Socialists have proved more contentious, as with the adoption of a new approach to sentencing for various relatively minor offences. Thus, since 1983, instead of imprisonment courts now have the option of replacing this traditional form of punishment with an order for the guilty party to provide a set number of hours of work for the community; for example, a hundred hours for attempted robbery. The work might involve activities such as street cleaning, gardening in public parks or building repair. Support for this approach is provided by the arguments that it will help reduce the problem of overcrowding in prisons by removing a number of minor criminals and that in many cases placing such offenders in a prison environment is inappropriate due to the high rate of recidivism which it encourages. However, right wing opposition to this type of innovation sees such measures as offering an inadequate deterrent. The contrasting reaction to this change, therefore, serves to highlight the difference between the Socialists' more reformist approach to tackling the problem of insecurity and the more repressive measures advocated by the conservative element of the political spectrum.

There is, however, general agreement that the level of criminality is unlikely to be significantly reduced by more effective policing and legal reform alone. Change is also required in many of the basic conditions which influence criminal behaviour. Improvements need to occur, therefore, in living and housing conditions, in the availability of employment, in educational and training opportunities for teenagers, and in generally reinforcing those systems providing assistance to less fortunate members of the community. Appreciation of this wider dimension to criminal behaviour led to the decision in 1982 to set up a special enquiry team into the broad question of insecurity, headed by M. Gilbert Bonnemaison, Deputy at the National Assembly for the department of Seine-Saint Denis in the Paris region. The commission's final report,[8] when completed later in the same year, recognised the importance of interrelated action in the above fields and of local initiatives in combating crime; and the application of these principles is now to be seen in the methods adopted to tackle the varied social, economic and environmental problems of an increasing number of large, working-class housing estates (see Chapter 4).

It might still be questioned whether even these measures will have a substantial impact on reducing crime, for the rise in violence, the increase in criminal activity and the general mounting sense of insecurity could be attributed, at least in part, to a more fundamental breakdown of conventional values in society, by no means confined to France. Nonetheless amidst this rather bleak picture there are indications of at least a temporary halt in the rise of recorded crimes; and there is one industry which has profited considerably from the growth of a more criminal society – the manufacturers and installers of security equipment!

THE BATTLE AGAINST UNEMPLOYMENT

Over the last decade, in common with most other West European countries, France has experienced a substantial rise in unemployment. Already, therefore, in 1981 the newly elected socialist government was confronted with the unwelcome problem of a sizeable and still mounting total of people out of work; and it was of little surprise that the need to reverse these trends should be seen as an urgent priority, and a major political imperative for a socialist party. This was clearly indicated by Pierre Mauroy when he declared in July (of the same year), while setting out the government's future programme, that a prime objective would be to put France 'back to work', and that economic policy would remain centred around maintaining and, wherever possible, creating jobs. These might be seen as ambitious goals, however, for as the then Prime Minister subsequently explained, in tackling unemployment the government had to face the underlying problem of a labour market which faced each year the arrival of 750 000 school leavers, while only 500 000 people were simultaneously withdrawing from employment through retirement.[9]

None the less, in a climate of some optimism as the economy was reflated, a dual-fronted attack was mounted on unemployment. One arm of the government's strategy was directed at reducing the number of new entrants to the labour-force each year by offering a range of alternative pursuits for school leavers, hopefully aiming to give them some practical experience or specific training before applying for a job; the other arm aimed to encourage a greater number of workers to retire, particularly at an earlier age. More generally the Socialists' philosophy towards combating unemployment was founded on the notion of the need to share out work more equitably amongst the population; as such this could be seen as a prime illustration of the new mood of national solidarity. Thus, the essence of the government's approach had become the 'social management' of unemployment, where forced redundancies should be contemplated only as a last resort; and, as the jobless total appeared to stabilise throughout 1982, this strategy gained credibility.

By the following year, however, a much changed picture of unemployment had emerged, against the background of growing economic problems and a very different approach to running the economy: reflation had given way to deflation and it had become quite clear that many branches of industry required drastic surgery if they were to compete effectively with foreign manufacturers. Overmanning was a major and widespread problem, and as many firms were faced with a declining demand for their products, redundancies often became an integral part of restructuring plans. The protective barrage that the government had sought to maintain against rising unemployment through its 'traitement social' approach finally gave way as the weight of economic casualties increased under the recession. Faced with this situation, a more pragmatic and less idealistic strategy was required by the government; consequently new measures were prepared in an attempt to limit the adverse effects of job cuts. Nevertheless throughout 1983 and 1984 the level of unemployment climbed inexorably, creating its own problems as the average length of time people were out of work increased, as the number of long-term unemployed rose and as young people in particular encountered increasing difficulty in obtaining work, especially on a permanent basis and in an occupation offering a defined career structure. Nevertheless, by the latter part of 1985 there were indications that the overall level of unemployment had again stabilised, lending some support to the government's claim of the efficacy of its revised economic policy.

A left wing government representing parties committed to policies of enhanced social welfare might be seen as having a special responsibility for seeking to reduce unemployment; indeed the Socialists themselves might well argue that they had been given a clear mandate by the electorate to tackle this issue. Certainly opinion polls in the early 1980s showed unemployment to be the primary concern of a majority of French people, outdistancing by a considerable margin disquiet felt over the apparently increasingly insecure nature of society.[10] But any government, not just a socialist administration, could be seen to have strong reasons for wishing to eradicate the 'cancer' of unemployment and its numerous undesirable side-effects. Anguish, frustration and a profound sense of demoralisation are common forms of human suffering induced by unemployment, and the state could be considered to have an important moral responsibility to help counteract these problems. A correlation can also be made between areas in which a high level of unemployment exists and an elevated incidence of other social ills is apparent, implying, therefore, that reducing the number of people out of work should represent an integral part of policies designed to rehabilitate certain residential districts or improve the quality of life of various sections of the community. Finally, not only are there considerable social costs generated by unemployment, but there is also an important economic cost, represented by the substantial payments of benefits to those out of work, which governments are naturally anxious to contain.

The scale of the problem

Compared with a situation of virtually full employment in the early 1970s, unemployment had already risen very substantially by the beginning of the present decade. In 1970 the total number of people out of work averaged 262 000: ten years later the corresponding figure stood at 1.4 million. France had not 'exploded' as President Pompidou had once predicted should the level of unemployment ever rise above 1 million, but the scale and rapidity of the deterioration in the labour market came as a severe psychological shock to a population long conditioned to high rates of economic growth and a shortage of manpower. Such background helps to explain why the subject of unemployment should have become a major preoccupation of the French and why union reaction has been particularly hostile. Since 1981 the situation has grown considerably worse, so that by the beginning of 1986 over 2.4 million people were registered as unemployed, representing 10.3 per cent of the work-force; during the Socialists' reign the number of people out of work increased by approximately 750 000. In 1984 alone, a year in which a series of major restructuring operations affecting key branches of French industry resulted in an average of 35 000 workers being made redundant each month,[11] the number of people out of work rose by nearly 300 000. More recently, however, the jobless total has stabilised (as throughout the latter half of 1982 and most of 1983) even marginally declining throughout most of 1985, implying some success for remedial measures.

Whatever the potentially encouraging signs which emerged in 1985, the continuing high level of unemployment and its sharp increase over recent years offer some indication of the adverse impact of recession on the previously buoyant French economy. Yet when France is compared with its European neighbours its record, at least as far as limiting the scale of employment losses, appears commendable (Table 2.2). Over the first half of this decade the other major industrial nations of the EEC have experienced a higher rate of increase in unemployment, notably in West Germany and the Netherlands, and the proportion of the country's labour-force without a job is below the Community average and that of trading rivals such as Britain, Italy and the Benelux; only West Germany has a significantly lower rate of unemployment. Viewed outside Europe, however, France's position is less encouraging, with the United States and Japan recording rates (in 1985) of 7.3 per cent and 2.6 per cent respectively.

Table 2.2   The increase in unemployment in EEC member countries since 1980

	Base year 1980 = 100 Index of increases 1985
EEC (10)	196.1
Belgium	151.2
Denmark	137.6
West Germany	256.3
Greece	229.4
France	165.1
Ireland	227.2
Italy	187.4
Luxembourg	236.6
Netherlands	233.9
UK	205.6

Source: Eurostatistics 1 (1986).

The unemployed

Certain groups within society are at a greater risk from unemployment than others (Table 2.3). Overall more women are registered as unemployed than men, while blue-collar workers, shop assistants and clerical and secretarial staff represent the occupational categories most affected by job losses. Young people within the age-band 16–25

Table 2.3   Selected characteristics of the unemployed population, 1985

a. *Unemployment by age and sex*

Age range	Men	Women	Overall
		Unemployment rate (%)	
15–24	24.5	30.5	27.4
25–49	6.2	9.7	7.7
50 and over	5.9	7.1	6.4
Total	8.5	12.6	10.2

b. *Unemployment by socio-economic category*

Socio-economic group	Unemployment rate (%)
Managerial and executive staff	2.8
Technicians and junior executives and administrators	4.5
Office and shop workers	10.8
Manual workers	13.7
Overall	10.2

Source: INSEE, *Enquête sur l'Emploi Mars 1985* (1985).

have also been particularly vulnerable to the adverse effects of the recession, and over 40 per cent of total unemployment in France is accounted for by this group, one of the highest proportions in the EEC. Not only do such people face considerable difficulties in obtaining a job, but once in employment their position may remain insecure, for they have often been obliged to take only temporary or part-time work with the associated risk of a fairly rapid return to being unemployed. Many of these characteristics are not new, but were accentuated in the 1980s by the worsening of France's economic problems. An apt illustration is provided by the considerable rise in male unemployment, notably affecting manual workers aged between 25 and 49, a group which has been particularly sensitive to cutbacks in manufacturing industry and the building trade. As the number of people out of work has grown, so too has the proportion of long-term unemployed and the average length of unemployment, which at the beginning of 1986 stood at over 15 months compared with only 10 months five years previously.

Spatial contrasts are also evident in the pattern of unemployment and in the manner in which jobless totals have progressed over recent years. Traditionally rates have been highest in many of the country's less industrialised regions of western and southern France where employment opportunities have been inadequate to cope with the combined effects of a rapid increase in population and an occupational shift from farming and rural-based activities to manufacturing and services located primarily in urban centres. Since the onset of the recession, however, France's older industrial areas have become the prime focus of rising unemployment, with the result that some of the highest rates of increase have been recorded in the country's northern and eastern regions in areas such as the lower Seine valley, the northern coalfield and steel making towns and the heavy industrial 'basins' of Lorraine. Yet the pattern of spatial contrasts in unemployment rates has altered little since the onset of the recession (Figure 2.1), suggesting that the underlying causes for these variations pre-date this period.

Assessing unemployment on a regional basis may be deceptive, for the problem is often far more localised in character. Thus despite a particularly low rate of unemployment for the region of Alsace as a whole, this conceals severe difficulties in many of the former textile towns of the Vosges foothills such as Thann and Guebwiller where rates are much higher. Even in the Paris region, inner industrial suburbs such as those found in the department of Seine-St Denis (to the north of the centre) feature unemployment rates considerably in excess of the regional average. Similar intra-regional contrasts are also apparent in the heavy industrial regions. In northern France one of the worst affected zones has been the Sambre 'basin' in the eastern part of the region, close to the Belgian frontier and centred on the town of Maubeuge. This area, housing around 40 000 people, has a long association with metal working and over 80 per cent of the industrial labour-force is still employed in this branch. But factory closures amongst the once major and prestigious employers of the valley (Cockerill, Vallourec, Jeumont-Schneider) have sapped its industrial strength, leaving a legacy of rising unemployment now affecting 20 per cent of the work-force; few hopes exist for a reversal of this situation, despite the region's designation as a special development area (pôle de conversion) in the early part of 1984. It might be concluded, therefore, that one important implication of such spatial variability is that remedial measures should be equally flexible in their design and application.

The high level of unemployment is often primarily explained in terms of the general down-turn in economic activity, originally triggered by factors such as the rise in oil prices and the disruption of world money markets which first occurred in the early 1970s. Simi-

53

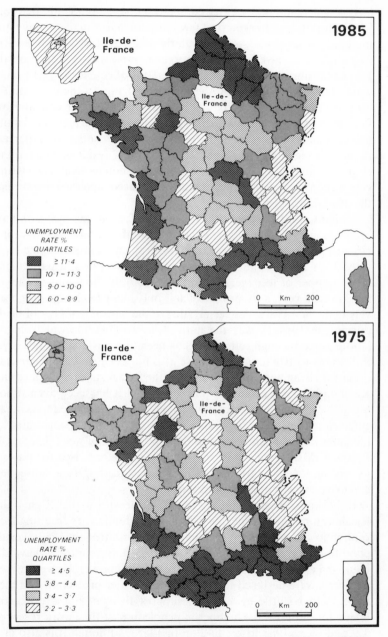

Figure 2.1   The regional pattern of unemployment, 1975 and 1985

larly less demand and greater competition have been translated into lower output, lost markets and few jobs. Advances in technology and increases in labour costs, particularly as a result of a high level of wage inflation, have further encouraged employers to dispense with jobs or to substitute capital for labour. (It is of course not just France which has been affected by these changes.) But to these essentially economic influences may be added a number of other contributory factors of an essentially sociological character. Thus the labour market has been faced with the need to absorb a substantial increase in women seeking work, whether this be as a result of necessity or choice. Arguably, therefore, as this phenomenon has coincided with a general contraction in employment it has placed increased pressure on the availability of jobs.

It might also be argued that the worst effects of the recession have been accompanied by a particular set of unfavourable demographic circumstances, further aggravating the problem of unemployment. As a result of the continuing 'baby boom' in the 1960s, a particularly large number of teenagers (around 200 000) are now joining the job market each year, a situation which is only likely to change progressively in the late 1980s; conversely, due to the reduced number of births during the 1914–18 war the natural level of withdrawal from the labour-force through retirement has been at a particularly low level. Politicians of Right and Left have also not been slow to blame each other for rising unemployment. Thus the Socialists have claimed that Raymond Barre's economic policies, which it has been argued hastened the collapse of certain industrial branches and failed to generate sufficient investment in French industry, directly contributed to increases in redundancies and to those people out of work. In contrast President Mitterrand's governments have been criticised for the lack of realism in their early economic policies, leading to a subsequent explosive growth in unemployment.

It has also been popularly held (at least by the Right) that legislation requiring official sanction for redundancies resulting from economic causes, and the tightening up of controls in 1982 over the conditions governing temporary and fixed-term contracts have discouraged employers from taking on extra manpower. However, these measures were designed to give workers greater protection and there appears to be little evidence to support their supposedly negative effect; for example, the number of people in part-time work rose from 1.9 million in 1982 to 2.3 million in 1985,[12] although it is also clear that many employers, as an economy measure, replaced full-time posts by part-time jobs. In the case of requests for redundancies, research shows the majority have been granted, although the need for administrative control has slowed the process.[13] Yet despite the apparently marginal impact of this measure, one of the first actions of Jacques Chirac's new government in 1986 was to seek its reform. There is a certain irony in this situation, however, for it was not a case of dispensing with ill-conceived, socialist legislation, but with a system of control introduced in 1975 by none other than Monsieur Chirac while Prime Minister under Valéry Giscard d'Estaing!

Protecting the unemployed

At the time of the onset of the recession in France a comprehensive and generous system of unemployment benefit existed. It was not impossible for a worker who had lost his job, claiming redundancy payments and other benefits such as a retraining allowance, to end up with a higher net income than when he was employed. During the latter part of the 1970s the relatively generous character of such assistance provoked little controversy; indeed in more general terms the existence by then of an elaborate and protective system of social security could be interpreted as one of the significant achievements of the extended period of postwar economic expansion. However, as the number of people out of work continued to rise rapidly, with a corresponding increase in the payments of unemployment benefit, the system's financial equilibrium came under increasing strain. In such circumstances benefits were seen to be too generous and to be paid in certain cases for an excessive period; the thesis was also advanced that if unemployment pay was set too high this would discourage people from seeking work (always assuming that jobs were available for them) and restrict labour mobility. It was, therefore, left to the Socialists to proceed with the unenviable task of reforming the system with the aim of effecting substantial economies, a process in many ways anathema to a government elected on a platform of social reform.

The administration of the greater part of unemployment insurance in France, covering essentially the private sector, is undertaken under the umbrella of an organisation known as UNEDIC (Union Nationale Interprofessionnelle pour l'Emploi dans l'Industrie et le Commerce). This body is managed jointly, and on an equal basis, by representatives of the employers' organisations and unions. Its functions are primarily those of policy formulation and co-ordination, for the system of unemployment benefits is actually run through a series of regional offices (referred to as ASSEDIC – Association pour l'Emploi dans l'Industrie et le Commerce), federated to the UNEDIC. There are now 43 ASSEDIC in France (as well as a further five in the country's overseas territories). They are non-profit making organisations and were established (along with the UNEDIC) in 1958 as part of a national convention signed by the employers and unions. Benefits became payable in accordance with an official charter which set out conditions of entitlement related to the previous length of employment, level of remuneration, and amount of unemployment contributions which had been made.

By the early 1980s this system had encountered increasing financial difficulties. In 1976 benefits paid out by the ASSEDIC amounted to only 10.9 billion francs (although this already represented a five-fold increase since the early 1970s), yet by 1982 this total had risen to 72.2 billions.[14] At the same time income was failing to cover expenditure producing a rapidly mounting deficit, calculated at 8.8 billion francs in 1983.[15] By now the ASSEDIC were having to cater not only for a large increase in unemployment payments but also a substantial outlay related to early retirement pensions. To resolve these problems the UNEDIC was faced with the choice of raising its income through higher contributions, or cutting the length and duration of benefits. Both were unpopular courses of action, and it was partly for this reason that the UNEDIC proved unable to agree on the most appropriate action, with the result that the government intervened (as it was legally empowered) to propose its own solution.

Extensive and difficult negotiations followed which in 1984 eventually produced a revised system of unemployment benefits within a new 'régime d'assurance-chômage', and a new convention between management and unions. Various economies were effected through reductions in the amounts payable to redundant workers and the length of time such benefits could be claimed, increases in the levels of contribution, notably by employees, and a redefinition of the regulations governing the eligibility for benefit. But the main innovation was to introduce an additional form of assistance, the solidarity scheme ('régime de solidarité'), funded directly by the state. Its resources were designed to assist two specific categories of unemployed person – first, unemployed school-leavers who had made insufficient contributions to be eligible for unemployment benefit, and second, the long-term unemployed who were no longer entitled to further assistance under the normal system of benefit. Assisting people in this latter situation was seen as a particular priority due to the general absence of any other form of help open to them, for however undesirable it might be that school-leavers should be unemployed, a wide range of measures had been introduced to offer them at least a temporary alternative to this condition. But despite this change it might seem regrettable, although inevitable, that as the problem of unemployment has become worse and the length of time a person might be without work has increased, the level of financial assistance generally available for any individual has fallen.

Under the system established in 1984 the normal maximum duration of ASSEDIC benefits has become two years (although in many cases considerably less for this limit applies only to those aged 55 and over), while the level of payment cannot exceed 75 per cent of the previous salary; in certain circumstances payments may continue for up to a further 18 months (again for those aged 55 and over). Once this period has expired an unemployed person is paid a small basic daily allowance, known as the end of entitlement allowance – 'allocation de fin de droits' (set originally in 1984 at 40 francs) for a limited period, and once this entitlement is exhausted a similar amount may be claimed under the state's 'régime de solidarité'. Those people unemployed aged between 50 and 55 might be seen as particularly vulnerable under the present system; they frequently face the difficulty of being considered too old to be employed in a new job, yet they are too young to qualify for early retirement benefit. However, if they remain unemployed, benefits normally last for only 18 months, with the possibility of an extension for a further 12 months; then if still unemployed and with access to no other resources, as someone 'en fin de droits', their daily entitlement becomes a meagre 40 francs (1984). Thus, in contrast to Britain, there is no comprehensive social security net in France to assist such people.

By mid-1985 nearly 400 000 unemployed workers were being paid this minimum allowance, a total which has regularly increased over recent years. The existence of so many people in this position has helped focus concern and political debate on those who have become the 'new poor': not just individuals receiving a minimum unemployment allowance but many more, such as those who are unable to meet their financial commitments through being out of work or who receive no benefit at all. Around 40 per cent of those people actively looking for a job are not in receipt of unemployment payments, although not all of this group might necessarily be considered poor: one element is represented, for example, by wives whose husbands are already employed, seeking to enter the labour market.

Particular attention was drawn to the plight of these people during the excessively cold spell in the early weeks in 1985. The problem manifest itself most openly in the major cities, where the entrance halls of the main railway stations became increasingly inhabited by the homeless and the destitute seeking some warmth and shelter. In Paris the situation was especially acute, with an estimated 15 000 wandering the streets.[16] Here metro stations were left open at night to offer some protection for such people – at Luxembourg and Nation heating and camp beds were even provided – and 'soupes populaires' were organised to offer some nourishment: by mid-January 160 centres providing a temporary home for more than 8000 were in operation throughout the Paris region.[17] While the 'sans abri' represent but a minority of the unemployed, their particular predicament clearly demonstrated the need for a new initiative to assist the increasing number of less fortunate people in society. Yet with the winter past, their situation seemed again forgotten, although in recognition of the inadequacy of the minimum level of unemployment benefit which stood at 43 francs at the beginning of 1985, this was raised by nearly 50 per cent (to 63 francs) in July of that year – only to create new financial problems for the UNEDIC. Thus some additional albeit modest relief is being provided for the long-term unemployed, but this does not disguise the fact that those people who are now jobless remain one of the major casualties of the recession.

Fighting unemployment

While in terms of social justice it is important to try to ensure an adequate and just level of unemployment benefit, such action merely serves to alleviate rather than resolve the problem. The basic issue facing many western governments remains, therefore, how to reduce most effectively the currently high levels of unemployment. In the long term it might be argued that the only way in which a substantial fall will be achieved is through recreating those conditions necessary for a new period of substantial and sustained economic growth. How this should be achieved is, however, less clear, but is unlikely to depend on action taken solely by the French, unless it is assumed that protectionism is a realistic strategy to pursue. However, even the Socialists would appear to have accepted that such an approach to economic management is unrealistic, given the likely long-term effects of creating a less efficient productive system and, therefore, ultimately even higher unemployment. Instead there appears a general consensus (with the exception of the Communist party) for the need to establish a more efficient and competitive economy through the adoption of essentially monetarist policies. A prime goal has thus become the reduction of inflation, despite the undesirable short-term side-effect of higher unemployment.

This policy obviously contrasts sharply with the Socialists' original remedy for conquering the rise in the number of unemployed – reflation, accompanied by a positive lead from the government in creating jobs. But such a strategy proved untenable. Not only did it produce bizarre policies of recruitment with bodies such as the SNCF recruiting new staff (4500 in 1981 and 1982) at a time when its traffic was declining (to be followed a year later by a reduction in employment, in line with revised government thinking), but also an unacceptable rise in the level of inflation and deterioration in the balance of payments. Hence the abandonment of this approach.

Moreover, seeking to resolve the problem of high unemployment through a macro-economic approach represents an essentially long-term strategy, implying the need for a series of complementary measures which might be expected to produce a more immediate impact. Numerous initiatives have been launched since the onset of the recession, by governments of both left and right wing tendencies, with this objective. The differences between their respective programmes of action appear to have been related more to a shift in emphasis or priority rather than to a basic contrast in strategy. Amongst the measures introduced by the Socialists, three distinctive strands to their policies might be detected – first, a desire to create more employment through various forms of work sharing; second, an attempt to persuade more workers to retire early, hopefully providing increased opportunities for others to take over their jobs; and third, a varied package of schemes designed to temporarily divert young people away from the labour market by offering them the chance of an extended education, professional or technical training or some form of paid community service work.

The concept of an increased sharing of employment and a more flexible approach to work was strongly advocated by both Pierre Mauroy and Laurent Fabius during their terms of office as Prime Minister. Both saw this approach as a central feature of efforts to reduce unemployment, and indeed one of the prime motives behind the original desire to institute a working week of 35 hours was to enable this process to occur. But obtaining agreement on this issue, particularly to allow legislation to be enacted, has proved extremely difficult. Even the modest reduction to a 39 hour week (in 1982) was only achieved amidst controversy. Unions were unwilling that this should be accompanied by a reduction in pay, while management was adamant that if the measure was to increase flexibility and efficiency then this was essential. Relatively little progress has since been made beyond this stage. Employers have become increasingly wedded to the idea of fewer restrictions governing the deployment of their work-forces: a more flexible pattern of shift-working and a more flexible attitude to the number of hours worked in a particular week would offer them the opportunities of more easily adjusting output to demand and of increasing productivity. But on the union side doubts have been expressed, notably by the CGT, over the implications of such measures concerning their effects on wages and on manage-ments' ability to manipulate their work-forces.

This did not deter the socialist government from continuing to pursue this policy. When trying to secure agreement on this question in the latter part of 1985, Monsieur Fabius argued that it was only through 'l'aménagement du temps de travail' that unemployment could be reduced significantly. For the jobless total to fall in this manner he proposed that up to 400 000 jobs would have to be created each year until the end of the century, arguing that only half this total was likely to be achieved simply through maintaining a high rate of economic growth: the rest would have to come from changed attitudes to work and the sharing of employment.

The ability of a more flexible approach to working practices and of job-sharing to generate employment in large numbers, however, would appear questionable. In his account of his years as Prime Minister, Pierre Mauroy claims that the introduction of the 39 hour week and a fifth week of paid holiday created at least 40 000 jobs.[18] But a study by INSEE suggests a much lower total, with the reduction in the working week leading to between 14 000 and 28 000 new employment opportunities.[19] It would seem somewhat doubtful, therefore, whether this approach has the potential to generate jobs on a sufficiently large scale. The logic of Laurent Fabius might also be challenged, for it seems unrealistic to separate the notion of economic growth from that of changed and more efficient working practices. The two would appear highly related, with a reduced labour input and much shorter working week having played an integral and largely spontaneous part in the rapid postwar economic growth in France. Indeed, it could be argued that one of the factors prompting the socialist government to persevere throughout its years in office with attempts to legislate on this matter was the continuing and growing number of agreements on more flexible working being drawn up on an ad hoc basis between individual firms and their employees.

Encouraging workers to retire early, hopefully making way for younger people to take their place, came to represent a favoured strategy for tackling unemployment in the early 1980s. The concept of early retirement, however, has a further significance, for unions in France, supported by the Socialist party, have long campaigned for a lowering of the legal age at which workers could retire and become entitled to their full pension rights. Consequently when the official age of retirement was reduced to 60, a measure which took effect from 1 April 1983, this was hailed as a major social advance. Moreover, the legislation was passed with the understanding that those who wished to continue working beyond this age were under no obligation to retire. However, this did not prevent the rather pointed observation from government critics that the change had been particularly timely in the sense of encouraging a greater number of people to leave the labour-force during a period when the supply of workers considerably exceeded the demand. But despite a sizeable increase in those seeking to retire each year (in 1983 there was nearly a 50 per cent increase over 1982) only workers still in employment who have completed $37\frac{1}{2}$ years of retirement contributions are eligible to benefit from the lower age limit, a requirement which excludes certain potential 'takers' particularly amongst married women.

As far as easing the problem of unemployment is concerned, it has been the government's effort to persuade an increasing number of people below the official age of retirement to leave that has been crucial. The option of early retirement was strongly pushed in the early 1980s when the conditions under which this took place were particularly favourable; in certain cases, prior to the lowering of the retirement age, for those people over 60 the previous level of salary was guaranteed. Behind this policy was again the desire that firms would take on new and preferably much younger workers to replace those lost through retirement. To promote this idea a system of 'solidarity contracts' was introduced between the state and individual firms whereby the government would contribute to the payment of a generous pension (up to 70 per cent of the previous wage) to those workers aged between 55 and 60 who left and were replaced. Initially the policy appeared relatively successful, with a number of state-owned firms such as SNIAS and SNECMA leading the way in signing contracts with the government. But two factors curtailed its more widespread application; first, many companies were seeking to reduce their work-forces, not maintain them as this system prescribed, and second, where contrasts were negotiated the financial cost to the government was seen to be high.

Largely as a result of the adverse effects on manpower levels of the major industrial restructuring programmes announced in the early part of 1984, and particularly to help resolve the serious overmanning problems of Citroën, the government proposed a new formula for trimming labour-forces without redundancies. This scheme was termed 'congés de reconversion'; it was designed to allow firms to offer workers ultimately willing to accept redundancy to undergo first a retraining course of, for example, six months during which time they would again be paid up to 70 per cent of their previous salary. While this occurred, legally they remained employees of the company so that should the opportunity arise they could be reintegrated into the labour-force, assuming for example that the firm's previous difficulties had been eliminated. Alternatively the worker, following retraining, would be much better equipped to obtain an alternative job. This at least was the theory behind the scheme but in practice the measure has been interpreted in some quarters as a thinly veiled attempt to postpone redundancy and disguise the 'true' level of unemployment. In effect it represents another form of 'early retirement', for in those heavy industrial regions such as the Nord, Lorraine, Le Creusot, and St Etienne, or shipbuilding towns such as Dunkerque and La Ciotat, where this measure has been applied, the idea of the availability of alternative jobs is much more myth than reality.

While the policy of promoting early retirement to help alleviate unemployment has certain attractions, it might also be seen to have certain limitations, and as a result it has attracted criticism. First, it has proved a highly expensive strategy; by 1983 it was costing more than unemployment benefit. Second, it represents a significant waste of expertise and experience which is difficult to replace. Third, there is the unwelcome sense of demoralisation and frustration amongst many of those deprived of their job and therefore of making a 'meaningful' contribution to society. Finally, the strategy has helped create a situation of increasing inequality amongst those who have ceased working during their fifties. For the unskilled or semi-skilled worker of a small firm, forced into redundancy, his benefits and chances of new employment are minimal; yet his counterpart previously working for one of the country's major companies and having accepted an early-retirement package should be able to enjoy comfortably his new-found leisure. Despite the heavy job losses in industries such as coal and steel, there have been no enforced redundancies: instead enhanced payments through schemes negotiated with the government have 'encouraged' workers to leave the industries. Some would argue that this is hardly social justice.

'Les jeunes'

While early retirement may help to reduce some of the pressure on the job market, it would appear to have made only a relatively minor contribution to reducing the number of young people who are unemployed. For reasons that are still not fully understood France has been singularly unsuccessful compared with the majority of western countries in finding employment for this sector of the population. There are over 8 million young people in France aged between 16 and 25, representing roughly 15 per cent of the total population, but this group accounts for approximately 40 per cent of the total unemployed: over 1 million are now jobless. But this is only part of the problem for this generation, for it is estimated that up to a further 500 000 are employed only on a short-term or part-time basis, or are following some form of fixed training programme: in all these cases the long-term prospects for work are often bleak.

In such circumstances it is not surprising that 'les jeunes' have become viewed as a section of the population that is becoming increasingly excluded from many aspects of social life. The lack of employment and therefore low level of income which have become the basic characteristics of many young people, may result in their inability to participate in various recreational and leisure pursuits, in the need to delay leaving the parental home to set up home for themselves and in couples' postponing having children. For some the difficulties of obtaining work might be seen as a necessary, albeit undesirable, hurdle to be surmounted – a challenge. However, for many more, particularly those who have no or few qualifications and have therefore already experienced the sense of failure at school, the outlook must be extremely depressing, with the frustration caused by the prospect of continued unemployment leading to feelings of bitterness, disenchantment and revolt. These young people are therefore in increasing danger of becoming marginalised within society and it is tempting to point to a link between this condition and the rapid

1. Tackling youth unemployment. A high level of youth unemployment became a major cause for concern in the 1980s.

rise in problems such as drug abuse and criminality amongst certain sections of French youth.

In recognition of these dangers, and of the particular problem faced by France in the late 1970s and early 1980s with the still large cohorts of school leavers (resulting from the postwar baby boom) entering each year a highly depressed labour market, successive governments have sought to introduce special measures to cope with this situation. Thus, between 1977 and 1981 Raymond Barre instituted a series of 'pactes pour l'emploi' (employment pacts) which offered young people the opportunity to undertake various forms of training or work experience. Despite certain criticisms concerning the usefulness of some of the courses which were provided, and the high cost of the operation, over this period around 1.7 million people took part in these programmes.

A similar priority has been shown by the Socialists, but their approach has been modified. In order to guide its thinking, one of the government's first actions, in June 1981, was to invite Bernard Schwartz, then professor at the University of Paris-Dauphine, to submit his proposals on the most effective means of preparing young people aged between 16 and 21 for their subsequent working lives so as to prevent them from being condemned to the ranks of the long-term unemployed. The resulting report, which was presented later in the same year, became the basis for subsequent government action.[20] Professor Schwartz was a strong advocate of the need to offer young people as many opportunities as possible to prepare themselves for their future lives, not just in employment but in a much wider sense linked to their different roles in society. On the specific issue of work he stressed the importance of providing all school leavers with some form of work experience or professional training; but he also recognised that grouped under the 'umbrella' term of young people was an extremely varied range of individuals with their own identities and aspirations. Consequently schemes designed to help this group needed to reflect this diversity.

In the early part of 1982 the government began to translate some of the Schwartz report's recommendations into actual policy measures, notably on the issue of training. Various schemes were introduced, differing in their detail, but in many cases based on the principle of providing 'sandwich' courses, combining practical experience with continued study: these initiatives, therefore, were grouped around the idea of 'formation alternée' or 'formation en alternance'. For teenagers aged between 16 and 18, the emphasis was primarily on the initial orientation towards a future career and to provide them with some basic form of qualification, while for young people over this age, the aim was to provide an increasing level of actual work experience. These measures were not necessarily completely new, therefore, but rather a remodelling and repackaging of schemes already operating under the 'pactes pour l'emploi' but with greater choice and more flexibility, and arguably a more sensitive approach to young people's needs. They also represented a logical complement to the process of extending technical education in schools.

Obviously if the system was to be effective, it was essential to make people aware of opportunities and to select the course most appropriate to their needs. With this objective, the government undertook to reinforce the existing structure of services where people could obtain the offices of advice (the ANPE – Agence Nationale pour l'Emploi (job centres): and the PAIO – Permanences d'Accueil, d'Information et d'Orientation (induction, information and guidance services)) by promoting the creation of a series of special centres throughout the country where expert guidance could be obtained: these were termed 'mission locales' and designed to act as local task forces. By 1985 over 100 existed, spread somewhat unevenly around the country, although relatively strongly represented in the major urban and industrial regions. These centres were designed not to provide courses and training themselves, but to try to promote the existence of as many such opportunities as possible within their respective areas, being in constant dialogue with the various relevant partners (schools, colleges, potential employers, health and housing services, social security services, police), and to provide every assistance to a young person in finding and then persevering with a particular course of study or training, or work experience. Informing young people of opportunities, and in the process gaining their interest and trust, were considered vital tasks, designed to counteract the feeling amongst this group that society was uncaring and disinterested in their plight and problems; and much of the government's strategy in this field was obviously directed towards those unable to help themselves adequately – the disadvantaged members of society: the children of problem families and problem estates. Assessing the success of these initiatives is difficult. Certainly young people appear to have been interested by these possibilities: for example, in 1984 the various 'missions locales' helped 64 000 people,[21] and it is estimated that sandwich courses alone are taken up by an average of around 300 000 young people each year.[22] But the main issue for many people is whether this leads to a permanent job. Here the evidence is less encouraging, illustrated by the results of the 'mission locale' at Reims; here only 20 per cent of those assisted by the centre appear to have obtained subsequent employment.[23]

Indeed at a national level the continued rise in the number of young people out of work during 1984 led the government in September of the same year to reinforce its policies of aid. In part this resulted in an extension of the programme of sandwich and vocational training courses, but principally it led to the introduction of community work (travaux d'utilité collective – TUC). This scheme was initially designed for those aged 16–21, providing work for up to a year's duration. Young people would be employed on a part-time basis (80 hours a month) for which they would be paid 1250 francs by the state; to this an employer could add up to a further 500 francs. Convinced of the usefulness of the scheme, in 1985 the government extended it to cover those people aged 21–25 who had been jobless for at least one year. The type of work involved varies considerably – cleaning metro stations for the RATP; tending gardens or street cleaning for local councils; and answering reader enquiries at the library are just some illustrations. By the early part of 1986 190 000 people were employed in some form of TUC, although it had originally been anticipated, at least by President Mitterrand (!), that this number would have risen to 300 000 by this time.

Considerable debate has surrounded the introduction of the TUCs (again an idea proposed by Professor Schwartz). Cynics suggest that they represent jobs which have been artificially created, invented purely as a temporary palliative for high unemployment; for some the low rate of pay implies exploitation. However, a more realistic assessment might conclude that the system at least provides young people with a greater sense of purpose than remaining unemployed and hopefully provides some work experience, although in many cases this appears limited. Consequently once the period of community service is terminated, the prospects for further employment become remote. But whatever the shortcomings of the scheme, this and related measures have arrested the upward climb in youth unemployment, despite its continuing high level, and as such could be regarded as a success.

Doubtless the Socialists would wish to claim some credit for the efficacy of their policies in stabilising unemployment during 1985, although it is ironic that this should have been achieved amidst a climate of austerity and constraints on government expenditure, in direct contrast to the strategy of reflation, expansion and higher public spending originally intended to reduce the number of people out of work. However, the continuing high level of unemployment has remained widely condemned, leaving little room for complacency. Jacques Chirac echoed this view by making the fight against unemployment one of his government's first priorities, introducing a series of measures aimed particularly at helping young people. In essence they represented a strengthening of previous socialist policies, with a new initiative to encourage companies to retain trainees by a reduction in firms' social security payments for such workers. But the programme is likely to be expensive and assumes that companies will respond to the government lead. Behind such policies, however, a change of philosophy to the problem of unemployment may be detected, for the Right sees ultimately the ability to reduce the jobless total as resting with a freeing of the economic system. It is for this reason that the idea of reducing government controls on redundancy took on such a symbolic importance for the new administration.

Debate has continued over the wider social and economic ramifications of high unemployment. It is suggested, for example, that this has been a significant factor in the growth of the 'black economy' which is now estimated to 'employ' almost one million people and generate a turnover equivalent to that of the car industry. Certainly the practice would appear to have expanded, especially in branches of activity such as agriculture, ready-to-wear clothing, car repair and the building industry: in the latter case the contention that up to 10 per cent of new houses being built each year (representing around 20 000 units) were the 'product' of 'le travail noir' caused considerable surprise and controversy.[24] However, factors other than unemployment influence the working of the black economy, and it has even been suggested that with more people out of work the opportunities of 'borrowing' employers' materials and equipment to carry out this activity are similarly reduced, constraining its further expansion.

Greater controversy has been generated by attempts to explain the cause of high unemployment. For a certain body of opinion the country's large immigrant population is seen as a major factor. Irrespective of the reality of the situation, the two issues have become interwoven, representing just one of the reasons why immigration has also developed as a major social issue in the 1980s.

IMMIGRATION: CONFLICT, CONTROVERSY AND MISUNDERSTANDING

The presence of a large foreign community in France (exceeding 4 million people) has become a highly contentious issue in the 1980s, producing important social, economic and political ramifications. Slogans such as 'La France aux français' and 'immigrés = chômage

= insécurité' are typical of sentiments which have been expressed increasingly openly, even if it is only by a minority of the population; these themes have been exploited ruthlessly by Jean-Marie Le Pen and his followers.

Despite the National Front's blatantly racist stance, by obtaining 11 per cent of the vote in the European elections of 1984 and achieving only a slightly lower proportional score in the local (municipal) elections of 1985, the party gained widespread notoriety and, at least in its own eyes, enhanced credibility. Its position was then further consolidated by the strong showing in the 1986 general election. Other electoral surprises have also served to publicise the policies of the National Front, notably in the re-run local elections at Dreux in 1983. Here the Le Pen camp, in an unusual coalition with the RPR, finally succeeded in ousting the Socialists from power and with them the former mayor Françoise Gaspard, who has long campaigned on behalf of France's immigrant community. For several months the small town of Dreux (35 000 inhabitants) became the centre of an intense and at times bitter and violent campaign focused on the issue of immigration, the debate fuelled by the extreme stance of the Right. Whether Monsieur Le Pen's supporters deserve the recognition they have now achieved might be questioned, but it is certain that the emergence of the Extreme Right as a much more powerful force in politics has pushed the question of immigration to the centre of the political arena, and helped focus and polarise public opinion on this issue. But it is not just those opposed to the large immigrant presence in France that have publicised this issue. The increasingly forceful expression of racialist views has produced its own reaction, demonstrated by the growth of organisations such as 'SOS – Racisme' (which became famous through its adopted slogan 'touche pas à mon pote' – hands off my (Arab) friend) which aim to combat this trend.

Yet France has a long tradition of immigration, associated particularly with people of European origin, that in the past has rarely generated the same tensions and passions which surround the current polemic. By the early part of the present century there existed already an established and substantial inflow of Belgians into the country, subsequently to be superseded by the arrival of a growing number of Italians, Spaniards and Poles, notably in the 1930s. Then, in the more recent postwar period, these groups were joined by the Portuguese, who first began to arrive on a substantial scale in the early 1960s. However, over the last 40 years a more fundamental and significant change has affected the pattern of immigration. During this time the number of people of North African origin (principally Algerians and, to a lesser degree, Moroccans) migrating to France, and subsequently remaining in the country, has risen sharply. In the early 1950s North Africans represented little more than 10 per cent of the total immigrant population in France, but now they account for over 40 per cent. Their arrival has brought a new dimension to the issue of immigration, for unlike many other groups of foreigners the presence of these people is readily apparent not only through the difference in skin colour, but also through their frequently contrasting life-style, which in many cases is strongly conditioned by their Muslim religion. In addition, they have frequently become identified with many of the undesirable characteristics supposedly associated with immigrants such as unemployment, high crime rates and large families. The eventual integration of this North African population into French society represents, therefore, a particularly delicate and challenging task, and presents many problems which do not generally arise with other immigrant groups of European origin.

A further basic change is now also to be seen in relation to the position and standing of immigrants in France. Postwar immigration was largely motivated and sustained by the continuing demands of the rapidly expanding French economy for labour; but, as elsewhere in Western Europe, the expectation amongst many people in France was that this 'imported' labour-force would not remain a permanent feature of the country's society. However, it is now clear that such a view was misguided. In 1974, with the first signs of a downturn in economic activity, the further recruitment of foreign workers was officially stopped, a measure which has remained in force ever since. Yet relatively few immigrants have returned to their source countries and amongst those already settled in France many have sought to bring in their dependants. For the French, therefore, there has been an increasing awareness that the large foreign population is a permanent rather than temporary feature of the country's society. Furthermore, despite frequent references to 'immigrants' when describing these people, the use of this term is often inappropriate, for many of the children born of foreign parents in France have, or later take on, French nationality; for them France is their 'home' and cultural ties with this country are far stronger than those with the society of their parents.

The reality, however, for many French citizens would appear to be that immigration has gone too far. Certainly this was the reaction of nearly 60 per cent of the respondents in a national opinion poll on this subject conducted in the early part of 1984.[25] The presence of a large foreign population and the continued increase in its size, despite the existence of government controls to limit further arrivals, have contributed significantly to the popularly-held view that France is in danger of experiencing a process of 'colonisation in reverse'. Immigrants have become the scapegoats for many of the country's current social and economic ills. But French people are not alone in expressing feelings of anxiety, incomprehension and resentment. Foreign communities have to withstand the burden of rejection placed on them by certain elements of French society; they have to cope with frequent abuse and widespread discrimination. At the same time, and as their numbers have increased, they have sought to maintain their cultural identity. Yet in such circumstances the assimilation of this population and its harmonious co-existence with French people represent difficult goals to achieve.

How many foreigners?

Precise assessment of the number of foreigners in France is difficult. The results of the most recent census (1982) indicate a total of just under 3.7 million residents of non-French nationality in the country, representing nearly 7 per cent of the population. However, this is generally regarded as an underestimate, for certain doubts exist over the accuracy of census returns: under-recording may occur due to factors such as the high level of illiteracy amongst some immigrant groups, the difficulty of effecting a census in severely overcrowded residential districts and the unwillingness of those without the required authorisation to stay in France to declare their presence. An alternative estimate of the number is provided by the Ministry of the Interior. Their statistics suggest a total closer to 4.2 million foreigners in 1982, a figure which had risen to 4.5 million by 1985. But such calculations are also subject to error, for they are based on the number of valid resident permits issued to foreigners and fail to take account of those people leaving France before their permit expires and failing to inform the appropriate authorities (as is often the case): they include as well an estimate of clandestine or illegal immigrants, whose number in 1985 was considered to total approximately 300 000.

Given these discrepancies it seems reasonable to assume that there are now at least 4 million foreigners resident in France. However, there is a view that merely taking into account those people of foreign nationality is an unsatisfactory measure of the impact of immigration on society and particularly of the way in which the size of the immigrant population is perceived by others. Such an approach fails to incorporate many people who might be construed as foreigners – the children of foreign parents who automatically assume French nationality at the age of eighteen (or in the case of Algerians born in France after 1963, at birth) unless they request otherwise; children in families where at least one parent is French; immigrants who have themselves acquired the status of French nationals and people of French nationality originating from the country's overseas departments and territories.

This question is especially sensitive in relation to the population of North African origin. Such people, not unnaturally, are generally viewed as foreigners, although in many cases they may hold French nationality. Officially this population is no longer increasing but many French citizens view reality very differently, as each year approximately 100 000 children are born to parents of North African descent. For the French this represents a substantial rise in the foreign population, whereas technically many of these children are French. As racial tension and discrimination are strongly associated with the 'Maghrebins' such attitudes are disturbing, particularly as the number of people living in France of North African nationality or descent is estimated at around 2.5 million, far in excess of the 1.5 million who were officially enumerated as Algerian, Moroccan or Tunisian.

The continued increase in the overall number of foreigners has also contributed to the controversy surrounding the issue of immigration. Growth rates were highest in the late 1960s and early 1970s when they exceeded 4 per cent per annum, although since then the pace of increase has slowed considerably. Nonetheless, even the far more modest rate of expansion observed between 1975 and 1982 (averaging just under 1 per cent per annum) was still twice the level of that recorded for the country's population as a whole. Furthermore, one of the main features of this period was the continuation of a high rate of growth amongst North African migrants, whereas the inflow of population from more traditional European sources started to decline, accentuating the Arab presence in France and contributing to the problems outlined above.

Since the beginning of the present decade the slowdown in immigration has been further confirmed; in 1984 the rate of increase was slightly less than 0.4 per cent. Nevertheless this has not prevented a very substantial rise occurring since the early 1960s in the actual number of foreigners resident in France: between 1962 and 1982 the total increased by over 1.5 million, a rise of 70 per cent. In the early 1970s, before restrictions on entry were introduced, the net increase of the French population each year through migration was upward of 150 000. Now, in the mid-1980s, the total is much more modest, amounting to around 16 000 in 1984; but this overall figure still conceals a number of divergent movements. In that same year approximately 40 000 new migrant workers entered the country, together with a further 20 000 dependants of existing immigrants; but these flows were counterbalanced by what has become over recent years a growing stream of return migrants, estimated in 1984 to number 45 000. As implied above, however, the major factor ensuring the continued growth of the foreign population in France is the high birth rate prevalent amongst these people, a situation which arguably is much harder to control.

Despite the continued growth of the North African contingent and its position as the dominant group of foreigners in France, overall the immigrant population is characterised by a considerable diversity of races (Table 2.4); not only is there an important European component, but also increasingly significant Black African and Asian communities; in the latter case the rapid rise in the size of this group has been associated particularly with the arrival of refugees from countries such as Vietnam and Cambodia. In other respects, however, there is an underlying similarity in many of the structural and occupational characteristics of the foreign population.[26] Immigrants

Table 2.4   Major immigrant groups in France, 1984

Immigrant group	Total ('000)
Portuguese	860
Algerians	777
Moroccans	520
Italians	426
Spaniards	380
Tunisians	215
Black Africans	153
Other	1139
Total	4470

Source: INSEE, *Tableaux de l'Economie Française* (1985).

still remain a relatively youthful section of the community. Over 50 per cent are under the age of 30 and a third are less than 20: respective figures for the country's French population are 44 per cent and 28 per cent. Their families tend to be larger than those of their French counterparts (with an average of 3.3 members, rising to 4.0 in the Algerian case, compared with a mean of 2.7 in French families) and, in particular, the number of young children is often much greater; for example, only 6 per cent of French households have at least three children under the age of 17 and only 0.5 per cent of these families have a minimum of five such children, yet in the case of the Algerian and Moroccan communities these proportions rise to 30 per cent and 11 per cent respectively. In many instances these people are poorly housed, with over 40 per cent of foreigners living in conditions of overcrowding.

Immigrant society still remains predominantly working-class, with the majority of those in employment possessing few qualifications or skills, and performing essentially menial tasks. Slightly more than half work in manufacturing industries; nearly two-thirds are 'blue-collar' workers and as many as 40 per cent are classified as unskilled manual workers. Again some of the extreme conditions are found amongst the North African population. Certain changes, however, are occurring. The loss of jobs in industry has had a significant impact on the immigrant work-force, with a fall, for example, of over 20 per cent between 1975 and 1982 of the numbers employed in the car industry. Not only has this induced higher unemployment but, as with French workers, it has also resulted in a sectoral shift within the labour-force in favour of service activities. This latter trend has been further encouraged by the far greater presence of women amongst the foreign population, largely as a result of family regrouping, and their growing search for employment: 42 per cent of foreigners in France are now women.

The theme of diversity is again apparent in the uneven spread of foreigners between different regions of France; for although immigration is seen as a national issue, there is considerable spatial variation in the degree of concentration of this population and, therefore, of the possibility for its presence to directly influence public opinion. Two main features underpin distribution patterns. First, immigration is a phenomenon which is primarily urban-based, associated particularly with the country's larger towns and cities: two-thirds of all foreigners live in urban centres with a population exceeding 100 000. Second, its effects are more evident in three regions

– Ile-de-France, Rhône-Alpes and Provence-Alpes-Côte d'Azur – which together house nearly 60 per cent of France's foreign population (Figure 2.2). Consequently the effects of immigration might be seen to be most apparent in the more urbanised and industrialised areas of eastern France, focusing particularly on the capital. In contrast throughout much of the still essentially rural, central and western parts of the country, the incidence of immigrants is extremely low; in the region of Rhône-Alpes nearly 10 per cent of the population is made up of foreigners, yet in Brittany the proportion is under 1 per cent.

The impact of immigration on an area may not always be simply a function of the number of foreign residents. At Marseille, for example, immigrants officially account for 12 per cent of the city's population, yet it is only necessary to walk along the celebrated Canebière (without even venturing into the slum dwellings lying immediately to the north) to be convinced that this vastly under estimates the immigrant (essentially North African) presence in the city; for the above figure fails to take account of those foreigners who are visiting Marseille or who are temporarily there 'in transit'; with its sea and air links, the city plays a vital role in movements to and from countries such as Algeria and Morocco. Estimates suggest that around 1.3 million North Africans pass through the city in this manner each year.[27]

It is, however, Paris and its suburbs which act as the prime destinations for immigrants. The 1.3 million foreigners resident in and around the capital represent over 36 per cent of all such people living in France, and more than 13 per cent of the total population of Ile-de-France. Furthermore, over time there has been an increasing polarisation of immigrants on Paris, accentuating their presence within the region's population. This appeal of the capital appears related partly to the great diversity of its labour market, offering at least the hope of some form of employment. Equally the strong existing base of foreign communities acts as a valuable system of support for newcomers, providing a potential source of assistance in finding accommodation and work, and generally assisting in the often difficult process of adapting to a very different lifestyle. However, the continued expansion of the capital's foreign population has not only occurred through the arrival of successive waves of new migrants; increasingly it has also come to reflect the high birth rate prevalent amongst these people (a factor which has increased in significance as a growing number of families have become reunited in France), although it is difficult to

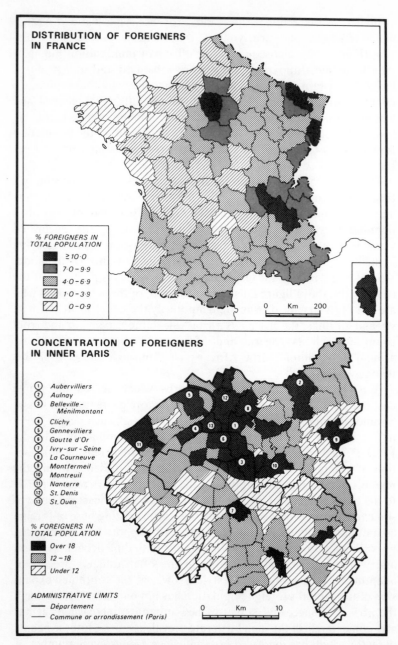

Figure 2.2   The foreign population in France, 1982

know how many parents declare their children as of French nationality rather than their own.

The foreign population is not spread evenly throughout the Paris region: instead a number of distinctive 'immigrant' quarters have developed in which the bulk of these people are housed, situated either in run-down, inner-city areas or in more peripheral locations amongst the anonymous tower blocks of the vast estates built to 'solve' the country's postwar housing shortage, but increasingly rejected by those French people who were once delighted to be offered the possibility of such a residence. This pattern is repeated elsewhere in other large urban centres where there is a substantial immigrant population. In the capital itself immigrants are concentrated primarily in many of the city's northern, industrial suburbs, ranging from inner areas such as Belleville and St Denis, to the 'grands ensembles' of La Courneuve and La Rose des Vents at Aulnay (Figure 2.2). But the pattern has been changing, particularly through redevelopment of slum properties. Belleville offers a prime illustration of this transformation. Its immigrant population has been increasingly squeezed out as the number of cheap and often squalid furnished rooms, essential to the existence of such people in inner areas, has diminished under the destructive force of the bulldozer. Immigrants therefore have been forced towards the subsidised, 'social' housing estates of the periphery, the only other low-cost option open to them.

Contentious issues

The now sizeable total of foreigners living in France, the realisation that many of these people regard themselves as permanent residents, and the existence of a very different economic climate from that pertaining twenty years ago when the first major waves of immigrants arrived, are among the influences which have combined to make immigration a highly controversial, emotive and potentially explosive issue in the 1980s. Immigrants have become a source of reproach for various reasons. It is argued by many people that the presence of a large contingent of foreign workers has provoked unemployment amongst their French counterparts; that immigrant families represent a major drain on the resources of the social security system; that foreigners have been the cause of a substantial rise in crime and insecurity; and that it is not uncommon for these people to make little attempt to integrate themselves into French society. Not unnaturally, though, amongst the foreign community there is often a very different perception of the situation. From the immigrants' point of view it was, after all, the French who originally encouraged their presence due to the absence of an adequate supply of indigenous labour. Yet now such workers and their families are the source of considerable animosity, which they regard in many cases as unjustified. These people also suffer from the fact that they often work in difficult conditions, are relatively poorly paid and live in accommodation of only marginal standard. Immigration is, therefore, a diverse and complex issue, with attempts to assess or clarify the situation frequently rendered difficult by the lack of reliable information or detailed research. Not only does this lead to misconceptions, but often prejudice and misinformation appear to dominate appraisals of this subject.

The widespread view that foreigners have been responsible for the recent increase in crime, especially juvenile delinquency, illustrates this latter feature. Certainly, as discussed previously, there is evidence to support this general contention, but when the situation is analysed more closely a number of misconceptions seem to prevail. It is by no means clear, for example, that crime rates are significantly higher amongst young, unemployed immigrants living in large peripheral housing estates (a popular target for those who condemn foreigners) than amongst similarly aged French people living in such areas. There are also marked variations in the degree of criminality between different immigrant groups: Alain Griotteray indicates that rates tend to be substantially higher amongst people from North Africa compared with those originating from countries such as Spain and Portugal.[28] However, as Françoise Gaspard explains in a rather different view of immigration in France,[29] such raw statistics ignore the far greater likelihood of someone originating from Algeria or Morocco being stopped, searched and questioned by the police; in other words the suggestion is that this section of the population is kept under surveillance to a far greater extent than many other immigrant groups and particularly the French, and it is therefore of little surprise that arrests amongst this section of the immigrant population should be higher.

There are certain French people who would claim that the presence of an ever-growing immigrant population has heightened the feeling of insecurity, particularly amongst those residents in areas of the city where there is a high concentration of foreigners. Such a view is difficult to confirm or deny, but even if immigrants do increase anxiety amidst the French population, it is also clear that this effect is not one-way. Immigrants too may find their personal security threatened as they live with the stress and fear induced by the abuse and violence to which they are at times subjected. Crimes, particularly involving bodily harm and with racial overtones, directed primarily against the Arab population, now appear more widespread. One of the worst illustrations of such aggression occurred in November 1983 when a young Algerian, travelling on the Bordeaux-Ventimiglia express was beaten to death and then thrown from the train by three Frenchmen, for no other apparent reason than they found Arabs objectionable. Their action brought strong condemnation, even inspiring the film *Train d'enfer* produced by Roger Hanin, himself a 'pied-noir', which carried a strong anti-racist message. This crime was particularly horrific, and revealed a disturbing feature that has been shown to accompany other acts of violence: none of the 92 passengers on the same coach as the victim sought to intervene and restrain his aggressors.[30] It is of some concern that such events do not appear particularly exceptional: between 1980 and 1984 over 40 Arabs were murdered in France, underlying a very real sense of 'insécurité' prevalent amongst a significant section of the immigrant population.[31]

The idea that foreigners make excessive and even unwarranted demands on the country's social services has been fostered by certain well-publicised accounts implying abuse of the system – illegal immigrants receiving child allowances and other benefits is one example. It is also not uncommon for such payments to represent a substantial amount for foreign workers employed and entitled to be in France; a manual worker with a large family of more than 6 children could reasonably expect to double his monthly income through child allowances alone. But this applies equally to French households. It is just that large families are a more frequent occurrence amongst the immigrant population, leading to the impression that this sector of the community is receiving preferential treatment. Similarly, foreigners cost the country's health service less per head than French people, partly because of their lower average age. Indeed, in a number of cases foreigners might be seen to be at a disadvantage; those who have left their wives and children in their countries of origin receive a lower rate of benefit (based on the cost-of-living in their home country) than if their families were with them in France. Certainly the social security system is abused (with, for example, benefits claimed for fictitious illnesses to extend holidays spent in the home country), but the French themselves are far from innocent in the use of such practices. There is considerable disagreement over whether the immigrant represents a greater cost to the community than the average French person, but what should not be in dispute is a foreigner's entitlement, having made the required social security payments, to the same range of services and benefits.

Greater controversy is generated by the role which should now befall those many immigrant workers for whom apparently there is no further need. By 1985 approximately 18.5 per cent of the foreign labour-force was unemployed compared with only 9.6 per cent of the French working population; certain nationalities were particularly badly affected, notably the Algerians with an unemployment rate of nearly 26.5 per cent. This meant that there were over 270 000 foreigners out of work leading to the suggestion that now there is no work for these people they should be returned to their countries of origin, to avoid an unneccessary and expensive burden on the French economy. This sentiment was expressed even more forcibly by the National Front during its campaign for the municipal elections in 1983 when it adopted the slogan 'deux millions de chômeurs, deux millions d'immigrés'. The implication was quite plainly that if foreign workers were sent 'home', then unemployment would be substantially reduced. Whatever the racial overtones in this simplistic assertion, it is not difficult to understand its attraction amongst certain sections of the French working-class community, especially those in the industrial suburbs of the major urban areas faced with redundancy and few prospects of alternative employment. Yet such an assessment has two basic flaws. First, 'home' may well be France rather than countries such as Morocco or Portugal, especially for young people; and second, given the unattractive and even dangerous character of many of the jobs undertaken by foreigners, it is far from clear that they would be replaced by French people if they vacated their employment.

This view also ignores much of the history surrounding the mass inflow of immigrants to France. The shortage of manpower for industry was perceived as so acute in the 1960s that even leading political figures such as Georges Pompidou were advocating the importance of immigrant workers as a means to ease pressure on the labour market. Companies actively sought to recruit foreign labour, not just in France but often in the countries of origin. Similarly factories were located to benefit from this supply of relatively cheap and, at the time, pliable immigrant workers; such was the case with the large Citroën factory opened at Aulnay in the northern Parisian suburbs in 1973, where subsequently over 75 per cent of the 'blue collar' labour was represented by immigrants.[32] It has even been argued that had certain firms invested in new plant rather than inexpensive foreign labour in the 1970s they would not have experienced the loss of competitiveness which became a prominent feature a decade later. More recently, as firms have been forced to cut their work-forces, a reduction in the number of foreign workers has been seen as an option least likely to provoke opposition, although this has not always been the case. In 1982 violence erupted at Citroën's Aulnay plant as the immigrant work-force went on strike protesting at their unjust treatment and harsh working conditions, where they had few of the same rights as French workers and had little chance of promotion, condemned to life on the assembly line; but this did not prevent the subsequent reduction in foreign workers employed at the factory. Nor has this been avoided in other car factories where similar protests have occurred. In such instances, however, it is not the status of being 'foreign' which in itself causes redundancy, but rather the fact that immigrants are generally equated with unskilled workers and it is this group which has been most severely hit by the combined force of the recession and the introduction of new technology. Few foreign workers have the aptitude, inclination (and often the opportunity) to train for new skills.

The immigrant worker might be seen, therefore, as largely powerless to resist these forces of change. Yet this only serves to reinforce the feeling of exploitation amongst such people; strongly encouraged to come to France, expected to work under arduous conditions when they arrive and rejected once they are no longer required. Certainly there is no obligation for a foreigner who has been made redundant to return home, although various firms (including Citroën) and the government have set in motion programmes with this aim. A worker may remain in France and draw unemployment benefit; but as in many cases social security contributions have only been paid for a relatively short period, the length of entitlement to benefit is equally limited. After that assistance is restricted to a meagre minimum payment; unemployment for the immigrant may become, therefore, a particularly painful burden.

With few skills, and a highly depressed demand for labour, the chances of re-employment might also appear remote. Foreigners would also claim, whether they are young entrants to the labour market or older workers in search of a new job, that discrimination frequently restricts their chances. It is, however, extremely difficult to assess the existence or significance of such a factor, although numerous anecdotes confirm that it is perceived by many foreigners as a major influence. Two stories from Les Minguettes, a 'problem' estate on the outskirts of Lyon (see Chapter 4) highlight this feeling. Aïcha is in her mid-twenties, and one of a family in which there are nine children.[33] In giving her account of the anguish associated with job-hunting, she explained to a reporter of *Le Monde*: 'I would go to the local job centre and to various employment agencies offering temporary work. As soon as I said that I was Algerian or they saw my blue visitors' permit there was a subtle change of attitude. I understood.' A similar report recounts a common and highly pessimistic attitude among young 'second generation' North Africans about the chances of obtaining work:[34] 'Even French people can't get a job. What hope have you got when you're called Mohammed and you say you live at Les Minguettes?' Whatever the degree of truth these statements contain about the problems of obtaining employment, they also indicate the sense of rejection by French society felt by many foreigners, especially amongst those originating from or having family ties with North Africa.

Yet French people might well retort that it is not so much their refusal to accept immigrants that causes the isolation of this group, but more the unwillingness of foreigners themselves to become integrated into local communities. This raises the question, therefore, of whether assimilation is an achievable goal. Few would argue that integration is an easy task, particularly when dealing with certain categories of immigrant in which there is a high level of illiteracy, a lack of familiarity with urban living, and where people are used to very different routines and lifestyles. But there is also a feeling that certain foreigners wish to retain their separate identity, a sentiment associated most with the Muslim (and, therefore, North African) population. In reality, however, the issue is not so straightforward. Many Algerians and Moroccans do not see their religion as a bar to integration, yet at the same time they are anxious to retain their own cultural roots and identity; hence their demands, now granted, for Arabic to be taught in those French schools where there is a strong North African presence. Yet this has often only served to inflame further local French opinion against such families and their separate culture, in situations where there is already protest at the high proportion of immigrant children in classes.

The sense of isolation and rejection is perhaps most evident amongst certain second-generation immigrants born in France of North African parents. They have been brought up amidst a French cultural background, although in many cases do not feel part of this society and are subjected to racially inspired attacks. Their demands are for an equality of treatment, free of the discrimination and prejudice which they now perceive to exist. For them there is also a special dilemma: the option of 'returning home' is not available, for links with North Africa are tenuous and their status there is one of an outsider and foreigner.

In recognition of the many problems faced by immigrants in France and of the obstacles to integration, a number of tentative steps were taken by the Socialists to improve the situation. Since 1981 foreigners have been allowed to form together freely in various types of association – to assist and protect workers; to organise sporting activities; to combat illiteracy and to promote their own cultural identity. More significantly in 1984 it was agreed to provide all foreigners legally entitled to be in France with a ten-year work and residence permit, replacing the previous system which required the annual renewal of these authorisations. The measure was supported by both the government and opposition, and had been seen by immigrants as an important step in assuring their security in France; it also represented tacit recognition by the government that the majority of immigrants were not, as first envisaged, temporary 'guest' workers but permanent residents. However, the Socialists ducked one major issue – the right for immigrants to vote; yet this was promised by President Mitterrand. Without full citizenship immigrants are always likely to experience a feeling of alienation, although some would not wish the extra responsibility and accountability which forms an integral part of such change. It is not surprising, perhaps, that the Socialists should have baulked at introducing this measure (even for local elections), for it is politically explosive. Furthermore, much of the Socialists' traditional support comes from the working class suburbs, yet it is here in the 'banlieue rouge' that anti-immigrant feeling has often been strongest, fuelled in certain cases by the Communists who have long sought to draw attention to the threat that foreign labour represents to the jobs of the French worker.

Which way forward?

Faced with a potentially explosive issue, politicians have proposed a series of solutions to tackle the problem of a large immigrant presence in France. But finding appropriate policy responses represents a challenging task, for not only is it necessary to take account of the discontent and resentment evident amongst French people, but also to recognise the fears and frustrations felt by the immigrant community itself. Over the last decade the two principal right of centre parties (now represented by the UDF and RPR) have generally adopted a more repressive attitude to immigration than the Socialists. Under Valéry Giscard d'Estaing the main thrust of government policy eventually became the reduction of the immigrant presence in France, encouraging the widespread return of foreign workers to their countries of origin: in practice this proved unsuccessful. More recently the Right has campaigned against the automatic nature of the process of acquiring French nationality, arguing that one of the essential conditions for this to occur should be the demonstration of a willingness on the part of the immigrant to integrate into French society (although how this should be judged is less clear!).

The Socialists sought a more enlightened approach although they reaffirmed the previous government's commitment to preventing any new phase of immigration. Their policy became centred around three key principles – first the need to prevent the illegal entry of immigrants; second to facilitate the return of those people who wished to leave France; and third to promote the integration into French society of those foreigners who effectively had become permanent residents and to prevent discrimination against these people or their unfair treatment. Arguably it is this latter policy which is most significant for not only does it apply to the majority of immigrants, but it is also crucial to the quest for racial harmony. While there has been some disagreement over the most effective means to attain these goals, general support for such an approach has also been forthcoming from the Right.

The problem of illegal immigrants is not new, but previously during a period of strong economic growth when the demand for labour was high, the issue raised little concern. Since the onset of the recession, however, it has been viewed more seriously, but despite successive efforts to control the problem, the number of immigrants illegally resident in France was estimated to have increased rather than to have diminished during the late 1970s. Thus, prior to the introduction of stricter controls on entry by the Mitterrand government, it was decided to declare an amnesty for existing illegal immigrants: during a period of six months covering the latter part of 1981 and the early part of 1982 those people without papers who reported their presence would be given the necessary documents to enable them to remain legally in France. Over 130 000 cases were dealt with in this manner, although amidst considerable disquiet from certain quarters of the opposition parties. While not opposed to the principle (they themselves had employed it), they protested at the apparent laxity with which it was implemented; they argued that the government had provided an unprecedented opportunity for numerous clandestine immigrants in neighbouring countries to come to France and readily obtain legal status, with the result that during this period immigration into France increased considerably. There is no proof that this was the case, but the publicity attracted by the expression of such opinions helped discredit the Socialists and undermine their immigration strategy. It also tended to confirm the emerging popular view that while certain of its ideas might be sound, the government had little notion of how they should be implemented, with the difficulties then being encountered in introducing legislation on nationalisation and decentralisation adding weight to such an interpretation.

Since the completion of the above 'regularisation' process, through the tightening of controls, illegal entry has become far more difficult, at least theoretically. However, in practice this appears less certain, with current estimates suggesting there may now be a considerably greater number of clandestine immigrants than in the early 1980s. Effective control can be difficult to achieve. There is little, for example, to prevent any foreigner ostensibly arriving to holiday in France remaining permanently, although tougher sanctions have been introduced against irresponsible employers of illegal immigrants and it is now more difficult for wives and children to join husbands already working in France. Previously families tended to arrive and then sort out the necessary administrative requirements; now the entry of families has to be sanctioned before arrival, and before this authorisation is given checks are also made to ensure that the husband has the means to support and house his dependants. Thus, although estimates indicate that the number of illegal immigrants is still high, even the socialist government moved towards a more restrictive approach on this issue.

When Lionel Stoléru (a former Secretary of State for Immigration) introduced a system of grants (l'aide au retour) in 1977 to encourage immigrants to leave France, his policy was condemned by the then socialist opposition as being an inadequate and reprehensible attempt to 'buy off' an unwanted work-force; and once in power the Left abolished this measure. However, by 1984, as large-scale redundancies amongst manual workers in various major branches of industry had become inevitable, a similar policy was reintroduced. The scheme was first applied in the troubled car industry to assist Peugeot and Citroën in the reduction of their manpower. In essence, as previously, it constituted a financial inducement for foreign workers to return to their home countries; but in detail a number of changes had been made. Grants were to be much more generous, and were to include the repayment of pension and other social security contributions, an allowance to assist the worker to re-establish himself in his own country and the cost of the return fares. Arrangements could also be made by an immigrant's French employer, prior to his departure, to provide some form of training to assist in the task of finding a job once he returned. Policy, therefore, had shifted away from providing a simple inducement to leave, to offering a more comprehensive approach to return migration, where the emphasis was placed on assisting the reintegration of the worker into his home country.

Payments under this revised scheme have been relatively generous, amounting to between 70 000 and 100 000 francs in the case of certain former employees at Peugeot with a long record of service. Generally some success has been claimed for the measure, with over 9000 applicants seeking grants in the first three months of 1985 alone. But this does not necessarily represent widespread approval. Immigrant leaders, now far more educated in their rights, see the payments as still too low and feel workers should receive greater compensation if they agree to give up their job and with it the right to return to France. Even if a worker himself is tempted by this offer, it is often rejected by his family, particularly the children, who have been brought up in France. Furthermore, it is far from certain that foreign governments would welcome the large-scale return of migrants. This is especially true in North African countries where the payments sent by workers to their families represent a substantial inflow of income (currently estimated at 2 billion francs a year in the case of Morocco alone), and where difficulties would be created in absorbing a large number of workers into already fragile economies. Although not admitted publicly, it is also doubtful if the French government would appreciate the large-scale return of immigrants under the above terms due to the high cost this would entail.

Ultimately, however, measures designed to facilitate the departure of redundant immigrant workers and their families, or to prevent the illegal entry of foreigners are unlikely to reduce significantly the non-French population now permanently resident in the country. Consequently there remains the difficult task of effecting the satisfactory integration of these people into French society, so that racial conflict ceases to be a significant issue. Any strategy employed to achieve this goal is likely to represent a delicate compromise, for it has to balance the need to ensure that there is no discrimination on racial grounds against immigrants in fields such as housing and employment, with that of persuading French citizens that foreign residents are not being shown undue favour. Moreover, achieving racial harmony is not a matter on which it is easy or realistic to legislate, although certain governmental measures such as the ten-year residence and work permit might be seen as an important backcloth to creating a climate of security and stability in which the immigrant can seek to establish his roots in France.

If relationships between communities are to be improved, it seems essential that increased dialogue should occur, so that mutual understanding is improved and misconceptions dispelled. This might imply a far greater number of local initiatives, centred on those areas with a high immigrant population and where there is a history of unrest or conflict. Increasingly a number of government-led schemes have adopted this approach. The Pesce report on 'problem suburban estates' points to the value of involving ethnic minority groups in community activities and of encouraging them to make their own specific contribution through the organisation of events.[35] It also indicates the importance of providing support services, to assist in a variety of fields from organising sporting and recreational activities to providing instruction in 'good housekeeping' for newly-arrived immigrant families.

A similar emphasis on a 'local' approach has been adopted in efforts to assist immigrants in their search for employment: advisory centres offer help ranging from guidance on filling out application forms to directing young people to vocational training schemes which hopefully might improve their longer-term employment prospects. This latter task is seen as critical for, as already discussed, it is in this section of the population and especially amongst those with North African parents, that the sense of disillusionment and rejection, due to the impossibility of finding work, is greatest. Self-help may also be an important factor in promoting understanding and integration, and has been encouraged by the freedom now accorded to immigrant groups to form their own societies and associations: typical of this movement is the 'Amicale des Travailleurs et Commerçants Marocains', with branches spread throughout France. Above all such associations provide immigrant communities with a vital means of expression, enabling them to articulate and express their views. That all of these initiatives are needed is not in doubt: this was forcibly demonstrated in 1983 with a march of immigrants to Paris, organised by young North Africans from Les Minguettes (Lyon), and inspired by the frustrations of these people and by their demands for equality of rights and an end to racial discrimination. Whether the measures currently in force and the commitment to them are adequate is more questionable.

A SOCIETY 'A DEUX VITESSES'?

For a society conditioned to expect a continuing rise in material well-being and accustomed to almost full employment, the onset of recession provided a rude awakening. In the years immediately following the oil crisis a lack of realism still pervaded concerning the idea of lower rates of growth and fewer jobs; such trends were seen as essentially short-term, transitory features. But in the 1980s it became evident that these were far more durable characteristics of the country's development. Adjustment has often been painful, as living standards for many individuals and families have failed to improve, even declining in some cases, and far more people have had to accept the unpalatable fact that their chances of employment or re-employment are remote, at least in the immediate future.

In such circumstances it is perhaps of little surprise that French society should now appear less compassionate and more intolerant, a change demonstrated by the growing incidence of various forms of criminal behaviour and the heightened animosity directed towards certain of the ethnic minorities. Similarly, although society has long been characterised by certain basic inequalities, the recession would appear to have generated its own further set of unjust and divisive influences. Numerous workers have been affected by redundancy or early retirement, but the conditions under which they have left their jobs vary greatly; these range from those applying to some employees of major industrial and commercial concerns who have retired yet through enhanced pensions have virtually retained their former level of remuneration, to those who have been made jobless in small, bankrupted firms and provided with no financial security.

The country's economic difficulties have also had an unequal effect on different groups within society. Young people have been hit particularly badly; they enter each year in large numbers a depressed labour market in which, for many, their competitive position is greatly diminished by a low level of educational attainment and therefore a frequent lack of skills or qualifications, and by the absence of any work experience. Immigrants have also come under special attack and become labelled as a principal cause of many social ills: they now represent a popular target on which society can focus those feelings of frustration and bitterness generated by a depressed economy and the rigorous application of deflationary policies. In these conditions young immigrants would seem particularly disadvantaged – resented, disorientated and jobless.

Such inequalities lead to the idea of the emergence of a 'dual' society. A wide gulf might be seen to exist between two opposing groups – those secure in their jobs, whose incomes have continued to rise, who sometimes profit from other privileges and benefits, and for whom the recession has had little effect; and those who have no such advantages or protection, and for whom the present economic crisis has meant demoralisation, a loss of opportunity and in some cases impoverishment. Moreover, although this notion of French society 'à deux vitesses'[36] could be seen as applicable to different occupational groups, it also has a geographical dimension; it is in depressed industrial regions such as the 'Nord', the inner cities of large urban areas and the bleak postwar, working-class housing estates that are found France's most vulnerable members of society. Hope for them must be in a revitalised economy, but as the subsequent chapter indicates, for this to occur restructuring and modernisation are essential, processes which in the short-term may continue to cause casualties rather than benefits amongst the country's traditional industrial work-force.

3 Restructuring the Economy

The sluggish performance of the French economy during the early 1980s and the problems which this engendered, notably in the form of unemployment and balance of payments deficits, make it difficult to imagine that little more than a decade ago France boasted one of the highest rates of economic growth amongst the world's advanced industrial nations, taking second place only to Japan; moreover this pattern of expansion had been sustained over an extended period, led by an exceptionally dynamic industrial sector. With the accompanying substantial rise in earnings and living standards, it is with some justification that the period from the end of the Second World War until the mid-1970s has been referred to as the 'trente glorieuses'.[1] Indeed so strong was the impetus for growth that it was confidently predicted just prior to the oil crisis of 1973 that by the following decade the size of the French economy would have outstripped that of its neighbour and rival, West Germany.

Even during the mid and late 1970s France appeared to withstand the negative forces of recession better than many of its major competitors, with the value of output still growing more rapidly than in other European countries such as West Germany, Italy and the Netherlands and only effectively challenged by the United States and Japan (not that France's relative 'success' was necessarily appreciated at the time judging by the general disapproval shown for the economic policy pursued by the then Prime Minister Raymond Barre!). Since then and following the 'deuxième choc pétrolier', there has been a deterioration of France's position. During the 1980s the economy has expanded only slowly, at a rate well below that achieved in the USA and Japan: even within Western Europe the recent performance of the French economy might be regarded at best as only mediocre (Table 3.1)

Yet whatever the country's problems, its economy still portrays a number of considerable strengths, not least in the troubled industrial field. France is the world's fifth major economic power and its fourth largest exporter, while within the EEC the level of per capita income is second only to West Germany. The country's reputation in high-technology fields such as armaments, nuclear energy, aerospace and telecommunication systems remains undiminished, with a number of

Table 3.1   Increases in gross domestic product

| | Mean annual rate of increase (%) | | | |
	1970–73	1974–79	1980–84	1985
France	5.6	3.1	1.2	1.0
West Germany	3.9	2.4	0.9	2.3
Italy	3.9	2.6	1.0	2.4
Great Britain	4.2	1.3	0.7	3.4
Japan	8.1	3.7	4.3	4.8
USA	4.7	2.7	2.2	2.3

Source: Ministère de l'Economie, des Finances et du Budget, *Le Budget Economique de la France pour 1986* (1986).

spectacular successes such as the Ariane rocket and the country's digitised telephone system attesting to this strength. At the same time, however, certain key pillars of the economy which have formed the foundation of postwar growth have lost part of their earlier momentum, notably the car industry, although France still retains its reputation for inventiveness in design and development in this activity. Thus, despite the record of past and current achievements and the radical transformation that the country's pattern of activity has undergone, there is evidence that France has been unable to consolidate and effectively sustain this progress. The 1980s have shown the French economy to be still vulnerable, particularly to a series of external forces.

THE IMPACT OF RECESSION

The virtual quadrupling of oil prices in the latter part of 1973 had an initial sharp impact on economic growth in France, although this might be seen as of little surprise in view of the country's then high dependency on imported crude oil as a source of primary energy; in 1973 France imported 135 million tonnes of oil, and two-thirds of the energy that was consumed originated from this source. Obviously national resources had to be transferred from investment elsewhere to pay for the increased cost of oil, resulting in the lower rate of overall growth apparent in 1974 and 1975. However, the effect appeared short-lived and by the following year the economy was again expanding at a rate comparable to those recorded in the early 1970s. Indeed the idea of any lasting recession was rapidly dispelled by various leading politicians, including Valéry Giscard d'Estaing who claimed in 1977 that by the end of that year the 'crise' would be overcome.[2]

Yet the grounds for such optimism proved unfounded; on the contrary the economic situation continued to deteriorate during the latter part of the decade, aggravated by the further sizeable jump in oil prices which occurred in 1979 and 1980. By now it had become clear that the breakdown in the previous pattern of unimpeded expansion was due to a series of basic structural weaknesses in the capitalist economic system. Such a position was not unique to France, but replicated in the other major industrial nations of the western world. Signs of disruption of the previous pattern of uninterrupted growth, which had been a feature of these countries for much of the post-war period, are now generally agreed to have become apparent by the end of the 1960s. First the rate of increase in productivity began to slow down and the returns on invested capital started to fall; then in 1971 as the Americans abandoned the gold standard for the dollar this had a longer-term destabilising effect on the other major world currencies, contributing to a disruption of trade and rise in inflation. These factors, together with the negative effects of the oil crisis, became mutually reinforcing, contributing to lower growth rates and reduced demand.

Progressivly these unfavourable tendencies became more pronounced. Firms invested less as their profits fell and as the cost of borrowing rose. Lower investment contributed to a falling level of increases in productivity as machines became more outdated and less efficient; moreover, it had been far easier to achieve rapid gains in productivity as demand and output were rising, but with this no longer the case, maintaining a comparable rate of increase became more difficult, implying the need for greater investment. The downward trend in demand continued as growth rates fell and investment decreased, with firms consuming less in terms of machinery and equipment: similarly, as households' incomes stabilised or declined in value, failing to keep pace with inflation, related consumption was also reduced.

Restrictions on home demand have encouraged firms to export, a strategy also considered essential to compensate for the much higher costs of imported energy products and raw materials (despite a fall in the value of the dollar and the first effects of a decline in oil prices, even in 1985 France's trading deficit in energy products amounted to

181.5 billion francs). However, as most of the developed countries have adopted a similar policy of promoting exports competition has become severe. Nonetheless, French industry now exports 31 per cent of its output, with certain branches such as arms, aircraft and electronics selling the bulk of their production in markets outside France: with the major exceptions of household appliances and certain textiles (and, of course, energy products) the country has a strong positive balance in its exchanges of industrial goods. While it might be tempting to attribute this favourable situation to the success of French exporters, it also reflects a much wider trend towards the increasingly international character of production activities and world-wide exchange of components: as a result imports into France have also risen sharply.

Many of the world's less developed countries have pursued vigorous and aggressive strategies of industrialisation, to become strong and damaging competitors for the traditional manufacturing nations. Similarly multinationals have not been slow to shift investment to these countries, particularly for the manufacture of standardised items, benefiting from much lower production costs and fewer constraints on their activities: such products are then imported back into the domestic markets of developed countries. In general, however, France still has a strongly positive trading balance in manufactured goods with less developed countries, their products accounting for approximately 10 per cent of the value of such imports, a situation which has altered little over the last decade.[3] Instead the strongest competition originates from other major industrial nations, especially West Germany, with which there is a marked negative balance in foreign trade. Overall more than 28 per cent of industrial goods sold in France are represented by imports, almost twice the level pertaining in the early 1970s. Part of the explanation again lies in the increasingly global scale of manufacturing activities, but it also reflects a growing preference amongst French consumers for foreign goods, whether they be German cars or machine tools, Italian electrical appliances, Japanese videos or American data-processing equipment. Such behaviour by consumers lends support to the contention that French manufacturers have lost some of their former competitiveness, a position further confirmed by the country's deteriorating foreign trade balance during the early 1980s.

Amidst these complex changes in trading and market conditions, manufacturers in France (as elsewhere) have had to contend with a major technological revolution linked to advances in microelectronics. Moreover, the force and impact of this change has arguably been greater in the 1980s than in the previous decade; with French manufacturers having lagged behind their major foreign rivals (USA, Japan, West Germany) in the use of robots and other computerised production techniques, there has been increased pressure to modernise.[4] While this is essential to enhance the long-term competitiveness of French industry, in the short-term the process of implementing change has itself provoked restructuring and reorganisation, often with attendant job losses, in many cases serving only to accentuate cuts resulting already from a reduced level of demand. There have been other important implications of this transformation, not least the need for far greater emphasis on retraining programmes and a more flexible use of labour. Thus for more than a decade, the French economy has been faced with the need to accommodate two major forces of change, although by the mid-1980s there were growing indications that the resulting adaptation of economic activity had brought a reversal of previous negative trends.

One of the major consequences of these combined processes of change has been the substantial reduction in the demand for labour. In part this has been expressed by the inexorable rise in unemployment, but it has also been seen in the reduction of those people in work. When the jobless total first started to rise sharply from the mid-1970s, there was still an increase in the employed population, so that between 1975 and 1982 the level of employment increased by an average rate of nearly 0.4 per cent each year (Table 3.2). Progressively, however, even over this period, the actual rate of growth was slowing each year, with the result that by the early 1980s total

Table 3.2   Changes in the employed population

Sector of activity	Mean annual rate of change (%)		
	1975–82	*1983*	*1984*
Agriculture	−2.4	−0.8	−0.9
Industry	−1.4	−2.8	−3.0
Building and civil engineering	−1.1	−6.7	−5.3
Services	+2.1	+0.9	+0.5
Total	+0.4	−1.0	−1.1

Source: Economie et Statistique, no. 171–2, November/December 1984; *Economie et Statistique*, no. 176, April 1985.

employment in France had begun to fall, a trend which was to intensify over following years: in 1983 and 1984, for example, there was a net reduction in the number of people employed of 214 000 and 234 000 respectively.[5]

The recent fall in jobs is largely a reflection of the losses in manufacturing and the building and civil engineering industry, confirming a longer-term trend towards a reduction of employment in the secondary sector which first emerged in the mid-1970s (Table 3.2). Now the decrease has become far more substantial; in manufacturing industry alone, jobs fell by an average of over 120 000 each year between 1980 and 1985, and the rate of loss has more than doubled since the late 1970s. In contrast, there is still a net increase of employment occurring in the tertiary sector, but over recent years the growth has eased significantly; indeed, within this sector certain activities, such as transport services, and car sales and repair, are now experiencing an overall decline in manpower. The 'knock-on' effects of reduced industrial activity, together with reductions in spending power and lower levels of consumption, have exerted a considerable depressive impact on the generation of jobs.

Change in agriculture

A reduction in manpower has also been a continuing feature of change in the agricultural sector. Over the last decade the labour-force in this activity has shrunk by up to 60 000 people each year, so that by 1985 there were little more than 1.5 million workers employed in farming, representing only half the total at the beginning of the 1970s. Over the years of recession, however, the rate of decline, somewhat paradoxically, has become lower. This is explained by the worst cases of over-manning having been eliminated, and by the present difficulties of finding employment in other sectors of the economy helping to dissuade members of the farming community from seeking an alternative occupation.

However, the counterpart to a declining work-force has been very substantial increases in output and productivity, trends which have been maintained throughout the recession. Agriculture and related food and drink industries play a significant role in the French economy. Even over recent years this sector has continued to generate a large trading surplus, amounting to 31 billion francs in 1985; agriculture and agro-industries now account for over a sixth of the country's export earnings. But although the strength of France as a farming nation is still widely recognised, certain trends suggest that change, accompanied by the recession, has also produced its casualties. In real terms farm incomes have shown a tendency to stabilise or decline, the rate of new investment has been falling and the extent to which the farming sector is indebted has risen. Many farmers might be seen as trapped between the need to continue to invest so as to remain competitive and the growing difficulty of repaying an increased burden of loans. In recent years the discontent aroused by these conditions has been heightened by the depressed state of the economy. High levels of inflation, particularly in the late 1970s and early 1980s, produced a substantial rise in costs, as did a weakened franc and its repercussions on the cost of many essential imported inputs such as livestock feeds and fertilisers. At the same time the outlets for many products had become restricted and agricultural policy within the EEC had become increasingly dominated by the need to restrain rather than augment prices.

As manpower continues to be reduced, albeit slowly, a parallel might be drawn between such changes in agriculture and the process of restructuring which has been affecting various branches of manufacturing industry. But the comparison is limited. In the latter case the outlook is often sombre, with any major revival of activity unlikely; for agriculture, however, the future appears far more secure with a considerable potential for growth, although this may not occur without further change. Certainly the implication behind the notion of agriculture representing France's 'pétrole vert' was of an 'industry of the future' rather than of an activity condemned to a gradual demise.

It has been forcibly argued that to maintain and develop further a strong agricultural sector it is essential that a widespread change of attitudes occurs amongst farmers.[6] Agriculture needs to be organised and operated much more as a commercial business, involving a move away from the idea that farmers should be continuously and artificially supported by high guaranteed prices and government aids. In seeking to promote a new attitude to farm management there is an associated desire to bring more young people into the profession. The success of such a policy might be seen to depend partly on the availability of financial assistance to help overcome the initially high cost of setting up a farm business. With this in mind a policy of providing grants to young farmers (dotation aux jeunes agriculteurs) has been in operation since the early 1970s, from which over 64 000 people benefited in the period 1973–82 alone.[7] Low interest loans (below 6 per cent in 1986) distributed by the Crédit Agricole are also available to assist young entrants to the farming profession. However, if such people are to be given the opportunity to successfully develop their holdings by applying new production and management techniques, then it is also essential that better training facilities should be offered, for their provision has long been inadequate.

Increasing the role of agriculture in the economy also depends on the more efficient use of the sector's output as a raw material for manufacturing activities. Already there is a strong relationship with the food processing industry and approximately two-thirds of agricultural production undergoes some form of further transformation before being marketed. The present aim is to increase such integration and to develop new outlets for this production, so raising the sector's value-added. Ample scope for this to occur would appear to exist, for compared with Britain, France has a much smaller food processing industry yet a considerably greater output from agriculture.

Further opportunities also exist to develop the use of agricultural products as raw materials for the chemical industry; during the period when oil became progressively more expensive such output became an attractive alternative base product for the petrochemical industry. Glucose, for example, is used not only to produce 'intermediates' (e.g. ethylene) for the manufacture of items such as plastics and synthetic rubber, but also to provide essential ingredients in the products of various industries, including brewing, biscuit making, cosmetics, paints, detergents and pharmaceuticals. Maize is used extensively as a raw material, a factor which partly explains its increasingly widespread growth in France; over 10 million tonnes of grain are now produced each year.

It is not only potential cost advantages which have encouraged the above trends. Agricultural products have other advantages. They are renewable and offer the realistic possibility of adapting each year's output to demand; they are biologically degradable so reducing problems of waste and pollution, and they are relatively easy to handle. Their increasing use has resulted in a new highly significant agro-chemical industry and the growth of a major research field associated with genetic engineering. However, one cause of concern for the French is the extent to which foreign capital plays a significant role in the control of these industries. This reflects a much wider tendency for farming to be governed increasingly, in terms of both the location and techniques of production, by the dictates of multinational business.

The transformation of agriculture continues but certain trends in the 1980s appear contradictory. Export earnings have risen, suggesting an inherent dynamism, yet farmers' incomes and the amount they have invested have stagnated. In addition agriculture has been faced with a growing demand for the reform of its support system under the CAP; overproduction (as in the case of milk, a particularly serious problem for many of France's small dairy farmers now that quotas have been introduced) threatens the continued existence of this policy. Hence the view that French agriculture is currently 'dans l'impasse'. Change has become even more critical and is now designed to reinforce the country's role as a major agricultural exporter and to develop further agriculture's industrial and capitalistic organisation. But the need for the activity to obey an increasingly economic rationale also produces social consequences as agricultural communities find their way of life transformed. Governments have therefore often trod wearily in instigating reform, for despite its diminished size the farming population retains a powerful political lobby.

OVERHAULING INDUSTRY

The changing face of production and consumption

In the early 1980s French industry presented a bleak picture. Apart from the substantial loss of jobs, industrial output has stagnated actually falling for three consecutive years between 1981 and 1983; this represented a remarkable contrast with the situation in the 1970s when between 1970 and 1973 production rose by an average of over 6 per cent each year.[8] Similarly, the rate of new investment was well below its level a decade earlier and continuing to decline. Reflecting these weaknesses, a growing number of the country's major industrial groups were making considerable losses. At first this feature was confined principally to certain basic industries such as steel, chemicals and oil refining, but subsequently many of France's largest and most prestigious multinationals experienced a similar fate, including Peugeot, Michelin, Renault and Creusot-Loire. Even in branches of advanced technology industry where France had become a world market-leader losses occurred, with Aérospatiale slipping into the red in 1982 and 1983. It is of little surprise, therefore, that *Le Monde* should have suggested that France had 'une industrie sérieusement malade'.[9]

Stable or contracting domestic sales, more intense competition in both home and foreign markets, higher energy costs and an underlying tendency towards a delocalisation of industry and disinvestment in this sector provide the backcloth to these changes. French industrialists would doubtless contend that they have had to face other difficulties. In the late 1970s when the recession first started to bite, many companies were ill-placed to respond effectively, as they were already in the process of reorganisation through recent take-overs and mergers: concentration of ownership has occurred more recently in France than in countries such as Britain and the United States. Past modernisation has led firms to resort to borrowing the necessary capital to effect change, but with low growth and higher interest charges indebtedness has often become a serious burden. Other financial problems have arisen as successive governments' policies to restrict expenditure have limited the availability of credit; similarly the need to pay for the socialist government's 'social progress' (a shorter working week, a fifth week's paid holiday, and a substantial rise in the minimum wage) has further depleted companies' resources. Moreover, faced with higher charges, firms have argued that they have been unable to pass on fully these additional costs to consumers due to government controls; prices were frozen for $4\frac{1}{2}$ months in 1982, while it was not until the summer of 1985 that a partial lifting of long-running restrictions on price increases for industrial products occurred.

Governments have viewed the situation rather differently. Both left and right wing parties, while seeking to blame the policies of each other for contributing to French industry's problems, are generally agreed that industrialists themselves have been partly responsible for their own misfortunes. Companies have been slow to modernise, reluctant to export and unwilling to increase expenditure in vital areas such as research and development. Certain firms have also been seen as more prepared to invest in foreign countries than in France. Even Renault, once seen as the flagship of state-run enterprises, has substantial investments abroad; for example it is Argentina's major car manufacturer, employing 5000 workers. But in 1985, as the company tried to ease its serious financial problems by cutting its French work-force, the practice of producing cars in countries such as

Spain and importing them for sale in France, brought harsh criticism from the unions.

Yet this position appears to contrast strongly with the performance of French industry during the latter part of the previous decade, when industrial output and economic growth generally were still increasing at rates comparable with those achieved in countries such as the United States, Japan and West Germany. Since then, however, a noticeable gap has emerged between France and its rivals: growth has picked up only slowly, investment has only increased belatedly, and foreign trading activity has remained persistently in deficit. So from having one of the most dynamic industrial economies in the EEC, France became characterised by a much less impressive pattern of development, prompting speculation as to why this has occurred. It seems likely that a number of factors contributed to this modified picture.

Changes in international trading conditions might be seen as one cause; for example, the high level of inflation in France at the beginning of the present decade, particularly compared with West Germany, rendered many of the country's industrial products less competitive, leading to lost markets – the franc was devalued three times between 1981 and 1984 to help overcome this constraint. It has also been suggested that in the latter stages of his presidency and prior to the presidential elections in 1981, Valéry Giscard d'Estaing was unwilling to take the necessary but painful measures (in terms of their social effects) to expedite the restructuring of key branches of activity. Similarly, early socialist economic policies have been seen as counter-productive; apart from the ill-judged reflationary measures, the nationalisation and reorganisation of major sectors of industry further delayed modernisation and new investment plans. But the deterioration in France's position has also been attributed to the complacency alluded to above, and to the reluctance of all the 'agents' involved in the process of economic growth to accept that continuous adaptation is necessary: too many had failed to accept that France's dominance in many markets could be challenged. Such an outlook is understandable for a population accustomed to a continuous rise in real incomes and living standards; but it also implies that in the long term, if France is to adopt successfully to a new economic climate, it is not just investment programmes that need to be modified but attitudes as well.

A new strategy for modernisation

Once in power the Socialists rapidly made it clear that the modernisation of industry was their priority for improving the country's economic health. The term 'modernisation' was seen as having a far wider application than under the previous government; Valéry Giscard d'Estaing had set in motion an ambitious programme of restructuring based on the strategy of concentrating resources in key growth sectors and partially withdrawing from production activities where France could no longer be competitive.[10] But now the process was designed to apply to the economy as a whole, embracing those industries in decline or in difficulty as well as those capable of generating growth. The underlying aim was to enable France's industrial structure to adapt to the current technological revolution; this would allow the country's industries to participate more fully in the manufacture of related products, particularly in the field of microelectronics, as well as ensuring that the benefits of new technology (robots, automated processes, new materials) would be utilised to a far greater extent in the process of manufacturing without recourse to the import of these products. Such a strategy was deemed essential to enable the economy to generate more jobs, a further key objective for the Socialists.

To assist this process a new system of contractual planning was introduced which required the country's major industrial groups to produce a detailed plan of their development programmes, with the expectation that these would conform with the objectives and priorities set out in the National Plan, such as saving energy (particularly important in the case of Pechiney and its production of aluminium) and developing new products (notably the position for companies such as Rhône-Poulenc and its research into the biotechnologies). Once formulated these plans were submitted to the government for negotiation and approval, forming the basis of a contract which on signing (this took place in 1983) committed each partner to a specified investment strategy.

This structured approach was given a wider dimension through plans prepared by the government itself (in consultation with relevant interested parties) to cover the reorganisation of specific industrial branches deemed as 'sensitive' due to their difficulties (e.g. steel, machine tools, shipbuilding) or growth potential (e.g. electronics components, computers). Although these plans involved industries where nationalised companies were strongly represented, this was not exclusively the case. They were also intended to act as a framework for the private sector and such direction indicates the way that successive governments (not just the Socialists) in France have taken an active role in seeking to guide the pattern of the country's industrial development and investment. As a further aid to modernisation, additional financial resources (outside of direct government funding) to assist with modernisation were also planned and in 1983 a special industrial modernisation fund (fonds industriel de modernisation – FMI) was created, its resources deriving from a new personal savings account (compte pour le développement de l'industrie – CODEVI), also launched by the government. The money thus made available was to be lent at low rates of interest, particularly to firms investing in high technology equipment.

However, for the Socialists the key to the successful rejuvenation of the economy and to the revival of industrial activity was its programme of nationalisation. This aspect of the government's policy was much contested, but after extensive parliamentary debate the bill nationalising five major industrial groups (Rhône-Poulenc, Pechiney-Ugine-Kuhlmann, Thomson-Brandt, St Gobain and Compagnie Générale d'Electricité – CGE), two powerful financial institutions (Paribas and Suez), and 36 banks, became law in the early part of 1982. With the steel industry already effectively nationalised (Usinor and Sacilor) and the government's further acquisition of a majority holding in companies such as Matra and CII-Honeywell Bull, the enlarged public sector was accorded a much more dominant role in the economy. Nationalised firms now produced 22 per cent of total value-added, accounted for 31 per cent of investment in industry and employed 21 per cent of the industrial labour-force;[11] in addition the government had virtually complete control of the major lending banks (those banks not nationalised were essentially small local organisations), giving it a powerful monopoly in a highly influential sector of the economy. Similarly with the industrial groups now in its ownership (including those previously nationalised such as Renault), the government could directly influence policy in a series of strategic industries – heavy metals, cars, electronics and microelectronics, chemicals, telecommunications and aerospace.

The impact of modernisation

By 1986 there were indications that restructuring was beginning to produce positive results, although the extent to which this was directly attributable to government policies is questionable. Manufacturing industry, now a much slimmer body having shed over 600 000 jobs between 1980 and 1985 (Table 3.3), appeared considerably more efficient. Productivity had started to rise again (although this was partly due to the effect of job losses), the downward trend in investment had been reversed, and spending on research and develop-ment had increased. Output was also now rising (by 1.0 per cent in 1985), although it had still only reached its level of 1980; and the scale and rate of job losses had fallen, with roughly 120 000 jobs disappear-ing in 1985, compared with a loss of around 150 000 in each of the two previous years. In addition many of the large public sector groups such as Rhône-Poulenc, Pechiney and Thomson-CGE had returned to profitability.

The cost of modernisation, however, in a period of recession had been high. Many branches of activity had seen their position as producers and employers considerably diminished, questioning their long-term viability. Steel, shipbuilding, textiles and paper represented just some of the industries which experienced substantial contraction, despite initial attempts by the government to protect their position. But the Socialists were forced to accept, as previous governments had done, that as long as France remains open to the effects of interna-tio-nal competition and global changes in the organisation and location of industrial activity, disinvestment from such sectors is likely to continue; in a capitalist society part of the process of modernisation and improving competitiveness inevitably involves the transfer of investment to the most productive activities. However, while this might respond to economic logic, it also implies certain social costs in terms of lost jobs, certainly in the short-term; herein was the Socia-lists' dilemma.

The latter part of 1983 and much of 1984 proved a particularly sombre period for industry, with the announcement of major cut-backs in employment; coal, iron and steel, and shipbuilding were expected to lose 50 000 jobs over the following three years, with a further reduction of 30 000 workers anticipated for the car industry alone.[12] Modernisation, for all its benefits, had now become a source of conflict and upheaval, leading to angry and at times violent reaction; one notable example was the march of over 30 000 demon-strators at Paris on 13 April 1984 (a Friday!) in protest at the cuts announced for the steel industry.[13] Discontent was not confined to the industrial sector; earlier in the same year exasperated farmers, hit by falling incomes, expressed their disenchantment by blocking roads and railways, and attempting to prevent imports of foreign produce.

Table 3.3   Employment change in manufacturing industry, 1980–85

Branch of activity	No. of wage-earners ('000)	
	1980	1985
Total	4746	4139
of which		
Heavy metallurgy	665	549
Textiles and footwear	665	536
Electrical engineering and electronics	562	551
Mechanical engineering	534	445
Vehicles	523	423

Source: INSEE, *Division Emploi, Paris* (1986).

2   *Industrial decline – counting the cost*
Pierre Mauroy (Prime Minister 1981–4) 'rowing against the tide' of rising unemployment. Despite numerous government measures to lessen the negative effects of industrial restructuring, these failed to stem the inexorable rise in unemployment.

In many cases the adverse consequences of job losses had been amplified by their localised impact – the mining settlements of northern France, the grey, anonymous steel towns strung out along the valley floors of Lorraine and the dockland communities of towns such as La Ciotat and La Seyne. Indeed in recognition of the seriousness of this problem, a series of 15 special development areas (pôles de conversion) was designated in early 1984 to pin-point and hopefully increase the efficiency of additional government aid.

As the reorganisation and rationalisation of industry occurred, so the attitude adopted by the Socialists to this issue became modified. A perceptible change occurred with the appointment of Laurent Fabius as Minister for Industry and Research in March 1982, which continued during his period as Prime Minister. Far greater belief was shown in market forces determining industrial strategy rather than government intervention, a change of emphasis which coincided with a more general re-orientation of economic policy. Largely gone were the ideas of comprehensive planning, backed by contracts with the government, determining the policies of different industrial sectors or of the nationalised industries; even when first announced this approach had been greeted with some scepticism, for one interpretation was that in a period of worsening unemployment, here was a thinly veiled attempt to commit major and influential groups to a policy of maintaining jobs. The guiding role played by the National Plan had also faded, despite original claims that this would not occur. Instead a new operating environment for industry had been created, offering companies greater freedom of action. This change responded to the criticism of excessive state interference in industrial policy, but less intervention also brought a further and, for some, less welcome reappraisal of attitudes; no longer was the government prepared to intervene automatically to save ailing firms and their related jobs. Further evidence of the government's altered approach was seen in its attitude to the nationalised industries.

From nationalisation to privatisation

The introduction of a programme of nationalisation had been partly a consequence of the Left's ideological stance and the importance attached to ownership of the 'means of production': indeed communist support for the government had been very much conditional on such a programme. However, in selling the idea to the nation, nationalisation had been justified rather in terms of offering the means by which the government would spearhead its policy of modernising and revitalising French industry. As such it was expected to achieve various objectives, including the restructuring of certain basic industries, the strengthening of the country's position in the field of advanced technology, and the creation of a new social climate with improved relations between management and the work-force. The nationalised industries were also expected to create jobs and were, therefore, seen as having a strategic role to play in the reduction of unemployment.[14] Finally state firms were intended to give a strong lead to the private sector, notably in terms of investment strategy. To help further these aims it was proposed to reorganise production around a limited number of groups which would act as technical development 'poles' for their particular range of activities. The large size of these organisations would provide them with the necessary critical size to support essential research, while overall they would hopefully act as 'national champions', making the challenge of French industry against international competition more effective. Finally, through its control of the principal banks, the state ought, theoretically, to be able to direct financial resources in the manner most appropriate to the attainment of these goals.

Predictably there was considerable opposition to these policies from right wing politicians, but the decision itself to nationalise also brought some undesirable consequences. The costs of nationalisation proved exceptionally high. Acquisition of the various companies was estimated to have involved an outlay of over 35 billion francs (1982 prices),[15] while the majority of these firms were making heavy and in some cases unexpected losses; similarly certain of the existing nationalised groups were also in considerable debt (Table 3.4). The inevitable result was that nationalisation produced a sizeable financial burden for the government and, therefore, for the country's taxpayers, making the policy appear to some as potentially a political liability. Not only was it necessary to cover the debts of these companies, but also (and far more significantly) to provide the resources necessary to fund reorganisation, re-equipment and research, all vital if the aim of modernisation was to be achieved.

The government had little option, therefore, but to invest heavily in the nationalised industries particularly as many appeared to have been underfunded for a number of years, a situation not unrelated to the prospect of nationalisation: assistance rose substantially over the years 1982–5 to total more than 50 billion francs. However, there has

Table 3.4 Financial results of nationalised industries, 1981–85

Company	Activity	Financial results (billion francs)				
		1981	*1982*	*1983*	*1984*	*1985*
Sacilor	Steel	−2.9	−3.7	−5.6	−8.1	−4.5
Usinor	Steel	−4.2	−4.6	−5.5	−7.6	−2.0
CdF–Chimie	Chemicals	−1.2	−0.8	−2.7	−0.7	−1.0
EMC	Chemicals	−0.3	−0.9	−0.2	0	+0.1
Rhône-Poulenc	Chemicals	−0.3	−0.8	−0.1	−2.0	+2.2
Pechiney	Non-ferrous metals	−2.5	−4.6	−0.4	−0.5	+0.9
Saint-Gobain	Various	+0.6	+0.4	+0.7	+0.5	+1.5
Thomson	Electronics	−0.2	−2.2	−1.3	−0.1	+0.5
CGE	Electronics	+0.6	+0.6	+0.7	+0.7	+1.0
Bull	Electronics	+0.5	−1.4	−0.6	−0.5	+0.1
Renault	Vehicles	−0.7	−1.3	−1.6	−12.6	−11.7

Source: Regards sur l'Actualité, no. 112 (1985); Ministère de l'Economie, des Finances et du Budget, *Economie et Prévision,* no. 70 (1985); *Le Monde,* 28 February 1986.

been some concern expressed over the distribution of this investment. Each year between a third and a half of the available resources have been consumed simply by the two steel groups Usinor and Sacilor (in 1985 this amounted to 5.8 billion francs), indicating the extent of this industry's financial difficulties. The chemical and non-ferrous metal industries have also been heavy consumers of government funds, with the result that the three electrical engineering and electronics groups (CGE, Thomson and Bull) have benefited comparatively little from direct state assistance; but given their potential for growth, allied to the high cost of research in these industries, a case could be made for higher funding. However, in a period of financial constraint (since 1983), particularly on public expenditure, according greater priority to this sector could only be achieved by reductions elsewhere, a decision the government was reluctant to take, not least due to the adverse implications this would have for jobs in basic industries.

Substantial restructuring has occurred in certain industries. Pechiney, for example, has withdrawn from the manufacture of chemicals to concentrate exclusively on non-ferrous metals, while Rhône-Poulenc has shed its interests in fertilisers to specialise to a greater extent in the production of fine chemicals. Much of the rest of the chemical industry has become centred on the two companies of CdF-Chimie and Atochem, the latter being a newly-formed subsidiary of the oil group Elf-Aquitaine. In the general field of electronics a rationalisation of activities has been effected between Thomson and CGE, with the former group concentrating on professional and household goods and electronic components, and the latter specialising in telecommunications. Reorganisation itself has prompted little criticism, but by carrying this out in conjunction with the process of nationalisation and the associated replacement of management teams, a lengthy period elapsed during which these companies were not operating to full efficiency. Furthermore, restructuring has not created a series of large, dynamic and highly influential groups capable of exerting a major directional force in the economy. Companies such as Thomson and CGE partly fulfil this role, but remain heavily dependent on state contracts.

As generators of new employment, public sector companies have singularly failed. In contrast, substantial cuts in jobs have occurred: in 1985 alone, jobs in the nationalised industries fell by 30 000, representing a decline of nearly 4 per cent compared with the previous year.[16] Rarely, however, has this resulted in enforced redundancies. A panoply of measures has been introduced to alleviate the impact of reductions in manpower, including early retirement schemes, social 'compacts' between the government and employers, retraining courses and redeployment of workers. While it may have proved increasingly difficult to preserve jobs, more progress has been achieved in modifying (and hopefully improving) relationships between management and their work-forces. The aim has been to provide the latter group with more opportunities to express opinions on company policy, and the measure has raised few objections. But this action and attempts to minimise the impact of redundancies, represent only a modest advance towards the goal of making the nationalised companies 'laboratories' for innovation and improvement in the social climate within firms.

Nevertheless, by 1986 the Socialists were claiming some success for their strategy, as most of the nationalised companies (with the principal exceptions of Renault, CdF-Chimie and the steel firms) were again making profits (Table 3.4). While this could be interpreted as a benefit of state ownership and direction, a more realistic view needs to take account of changing external factors such as growth in overseas markets and cheaper raw materials – Pechiney's 'redressement', for example, was greatly assisted by the fall in the price of bauxite. Despite the positive aspects to the balance sheet of nationalisation, right wing parties have maintained their opposition to the policy, and were thus committed to a programme of denationalisation when they were re-elected. However, prior to that, even the Socialists showed themselves not unopposed to some modification of their legislation, representing a significant shift in their approach to economic management, although financial motives also influenced this changed attitude. A growing consensus developed within the party that some private capital could be introduced into public sector companies, but with the state still maintaining a majority share, and in 1985 certain subsidiaries of the nationalised campanies such as St Gobain-Emballage were partly sold off or floated on the stock market. The Communists vigorously opposed such moves, but a number of leading Socialists, such as Laurent Fabius and Michel Rocard (for once in agreement), saw this as an acceptable and pragmatic strategy, for it was one effective means of increasing the capital of these firms in a period of tight monetary constraint.

However, this should not be interpreted as support for large-scale denationalisation. To this the Socialists remained firmly opposed, not least because of apprehension over the potential loss of French control of major companies if this should occur. But this did not prevent the new government of Jacques Chirac, as one of its first actions, presenting a bill to enable the privatisation of public companies, covering in theory a total of 65 enterprises, predominantly in the banking, insurance and industrial fields. But even the right wing, despite its rhetoric, has expressed certain reservations over denationalisation. It is questionable whether the relatively weak Stock Market in France could support the simultaneous flotation of a series of large companies, and considerable opposition even amongst the government's own ranks, particularly in the Gaullist party, has been voiced at the idea of selling-off firms such as Renault, nationalised prior to 1982. Given the relatively healthy financial condition of many of these companies by 1986, the desirability of their sale was also questioned, although at the same time the government was in urgent need of additional sources of finance to fund economic and social policies. Thus, as the Chirac government prepared to legislate on this issue, it seemed that following a limited programme of denationalisation, the pace of privatisation might slow.

Related issues

The debate over the nationalised industries has tended to focus attention on large companies, concealing the influential role played by small and medium-sized businesses. Despite the dominant position of major groups, over recent years they have displayed at least one essential drawback – they are no longer creating jobs. Conversely, small firms have in general demonstrated far greater dynamism and resilience in the face of recession. Between 1975 and 1983 companies employing over 500 workers experienced a fall in their share of total employment from 21 to 17 per cent; in contrast, firms with under 50 employees saw their share rise from 43 to 49 per cent, with the level of jobs in companies between these extremes remaining roughly stable.[17] Small firms also often possess the advantages of flexibility and adaptability and in many cases are associated with a high level of technical innovation. However, much of the growth amongst such businesses has been in service activities rather than manufacturing. Moreover, the majority of new firms are created either in the country's major urban centres or in the 'sun-belt' regions of the south; arguably neither of these areas possesses the same need for new jobs as many of the traditional heavy industrial districts.[18] There is, nevertheless, an increasingly widely held view that small firms are the key to future employment growth, although often they are relatively fragile concerns.

An important factor in any company's success is the quality of its management, and in the troubled economic climate of the 1980s strong leadership might be considered especially significant. Forceful direction has been given to Peugeot, for example, by its managing director Jacques Calvet who, in the quest for improved productivity, adopted a firm stance with unions, reminiscent of Sir Michael Edwardes' attitude while at British Leyland. It is difficult to quantify the impact of such factors but at least the Peugeot group was again making profits by 1985. Effective leadership is equally significant for the country's smaller companies, and the remarkable growth over recent years of the firm Bolloré might be seen to exemplify this feature. Bolloré was an old-established family concern in Quimper (Brittany) which specialised in the manufacture of cigarette papers. However, failing to modernise and adapt to a changing market rendered the firm increasingly unprofitable and it was eventually sold off to a group of financiers in the early 1970s. But, the losses continued. Then in 1980 Vincent Bolloré, a member of the family of the original owners, became a major share holder in the company and set about its revival. The result was an ultra-modern factory specialising in the manufacture of thin polyurethane film used in condensers, a field in which the company has become a world leader. Alongside continues the production of filter papers for cigarettes and sachets for tea bags. Between 1980 and 1984 the firm's turnover more than doubled from 208 to 500 million francs; the company now has an American subsidiary and is expanding its operations in Japan, a market area in which it is seen vital to be present to gain awareness of the rapid rate of technological changes. Overall Bolloré now employs more than 800 people.

Success has been attributed to the strategy of specialising to a high degree in the manufacture of a product with the potential for strong growth and in the use of advanced technology. Considerable emphasis is also given to research and development. Equally important have been the efforts made to mobilise and involve the labour-force in change. Employees are regularly consulted on the firm's policies, work only a 32 hour week (yet are paid on the basis of 40) and take a share of company profits. In return management has benefited from a flexible and co-operative work-force. Thus, the strategy of Bolloré offers a useful model for many other companies (both large and small) of how to effect a successful revival of an ailing concern and to restructure an industry, and indicates the importance of modernising management techniques as well as production methods.

THE REALITIES OF RESTRUCTURING

Finding the energy to go on: a nuclear success story?

In a relatively short section of the Rhône valley, south of Lyon, the contrasting fortunes of two complexes of power stations provide a revealing insight into the peripatetic nature of France's energy policy over the last twenty years. On the right bank of the Rhône just south of Givors lies an imposing monument to the age of modern coal-fired power stations. First opened in 1965, the massive 'centrale de la Loire' was designed to burn local coal originating from mines in the St Etienne area and to supply power to nearby Lyon. Then with the opening of a refinery a short distance to the north and the era of cheap oil, the power station was converted to run on fuel oil, a process completed in the early 1970s. Ten years later the conversion was in the opposite direction, back to coal, but no longer brought from the valleys behind; mining here had become uneconomic (or even more uneconomic than before) and ceased. Instead imported coal unloaded at Fos was brought up-river by barge, but even this source of supply was not to last as the government's policy of restricting imports and promoting indigenous energy resources led to coal being supplied, mostly by train, from mines (which are heavily subsidised) at Blanzy. Now the plant has been declared largely redundant, although it is capable of being brought back into service to meet peak demand. The 'culprits' (or at least two of them) responsible for the 'Loire's' present ignominious position are not hard to find. They lie approximately 25 kilometres downstream, this time on the left bank, wedged between the two small settlements of St Alban-du-Rhône and St Maurice-l'Exil. Here in 1985 and 1986 two 1300 megawatt nuclear reactors entered service, following seven years of construction involving up to 2200 workers and 185 subcontracting firms, and costing around 13 billion francs. This is very much the 'age of the nuclear power station'.

The recession revealed a major weakness in the pattern of supply of French energy – an excessive proportion originated from abroad, amounting to over three-quarters of total consumption in the early 1970s. As prices rose sharply the heavy reliance upon imported crude oil became an unacceptable burden for the country's now more vulnerable economy. Since this period, therefore, French energy policy has been dominated by the desire to free the country from the constraints imposed by a high level of imports. The solution has been to give the development of nuclear power absolute priority. This decision was first taken under Giscard d'Estaing; but despite changes in government, in the world energy market and in the attitudes and strategies of the oil exporting countries it has been pursued relentlessly, even ruthlessly, ever since, with only minor modification. Although François Mitterrand and the Socialists publicly opposed the 'nuclear option' before assuming power, even their protests became muted once in government. Certainly over recent years there has been a marked slow-down in the programme (with only one or two new reactors being commissioned each year compared with five or six in the mid and late 1970s), but this has been due to the current and predicted reduction in the growth rate of the demand for electricity rather than to a fundamental rethinking of policy. Even the sharp fall of oil prices in the early part of 1986 was expected to have little short-term impact on energy policy for it only produced a limited erosion of the substantial price advantage enjoyed by the nuclear power industry; it has been estimated that a sustained fall of prices to well below 10 dollars a barrel would be necessary before the nuclear option was seriously challenged.

Three principles underlay the revised energy strategy introduced in France following the first oil crisis – the economy of the use of energy and particularly a reduction in oil consumption; the development of new energy resources; and the diversification of production methods. Expanding the output of nuclear power responded to all these requirements. It would reduce the use of oil and cut imports, such a programme could be based partly on France's resources of uranium (and ultimately its capacity to produce enriched uranium), and it would give a broader base of production, both for electricity and for energy as a whole.

The need to reduce the reliance upon imported oil had become crucial by the early 1980s due to the destabilising effect produced on France's foreign trade balance. Imports were costing considerably more due to the two rounds of OPEC price rises, but as the franc started to depreciate rapidly against the dollar (the currency of oil dealings) France's bill soared even higher. In 1979 the exchange rate between the dollar and the franc stood at around 4 francs to the dollar: yet at one stage in 1985 over 10 francs were required to buy one dollar! The result was that as the world price of oil first started to fall again (particularly in real terms) during the period 1982–4, in France it continued to rise. Hence the strong interest, even for a socialist government, in maintaining the nuclear programme.

By this stage comparisons between the costs of producing electricity from nuclear sources and from conventional oil or coal-fired power stations were also showing a considerable advantage in favour of the former, with a difference of up to a third in the price, deriving essentially from lower fuel costs. This was used as further proof of the wisdom of the nuclear strategy. Other advantages have also been claimed from this choice. France has invested heavily in the pressurised water reactor, developed originally by the American Westinghouse Corporation. The French company Framatome took charge of this programme, originally producing reactors under licence, but then developing its own refinements to the design. By 1985, fifty-two such plants were in operation or under construction, with the long production run enabling the realisation of considerable economies of scale. At the same time France has become a world leader in the development of this technology, spawning a sizeable and valuable industry, estimated in 1984 at employing directly around 75 000 workers,[19] as well as providing jobs for a similar number of people in various dependent activities, amongst which the reprocessing of nuclear waste and the enrichment of uranium have proved particularly lucrative.

The advantages accruing from nuclear development have an important regional dimension. Building such a power station is a major undertaking, employing several thousand construction workers, and extending over a number of years. Frequently this provides local communities with the benefits of new jobs, and additional income for traders as part of the sizeable wage bill is spent in local shops, cafés and restaurants. With many plants having been built in areas where alternative employment opportunities have been declining or are limited (such as the Rhône valley to the north of Avignon or Gravelines near Dunkerque) these features have often been seen as particularly advantageous, counterbalancing opposition provoked by the noise and disruption caused by development: indeed because of its beneficial implications for jobs, the nuclear policy has been supported by the major left wing union, the CGT. The municipal councils of communes affected by nuclear power stations have often found themselves in an awkward dilemma, caught between the temptation to resist such development on the grounds of environmental damage and the potential threat to safety, and the desire to benefit from the substantial local tax revenue generated by plants of this scale; with jobs in generally short supply and budgets severely stretched, most have opted for the latter course of action.

Not that such a decision has always solved all the problems of local communities. The arrival in a short space of time of a large number of construction workers (and in many cases their families) means an urgent need for new houses, schools, roads and other services; yet the generally small rural councils in the areas where reactors were built were completely incapable of funding such building, let alone under-taking its organisation. Hence the belated recognition by the govern-ment and EdF of the need for new measures to assure the co-ordination and adequate financing of such operations. But a further problem remained. What was to happen when construction was complete and the related work-force departed? The permanent jobs of people working in a power station are relatively few in number and without special measures to induce alternative growth, the local economy, 'artificially' expanded over a number of years, risked a severe collapse. After much negotiation, EdF agreed to assist in a continuing programme of economic development in these areas, a decision partly explained perhaps by its desire to maintain a favour-able public image, for its financial commitment to nuclear energy is now huge. Consequently in 1985 it took a new initiative, signing a tripartite contract with the government and general council of the department of Isère, agreeing to help finance over 5 years the creation of an anticipated 2600 jobs in areas adjacent to three of its power complexes – the two nuclear sites at St Alban – St Maurice-l'Exil in the Rhône valley and at Creys-Malville (the location of France's first commercial fast-breeder reactor which entered service in 1985), and the hydro-electric plant at Grand-Maison.[20]

Public awareness of the importance of France's nuclear industry was revived in the mid-1980s as for the first time it began to make a significant impression on the country's pattern of energy consumption. It takes up to ten years to build and test a power station, so that the ambitious programme of development launched in the mid-1970s did not start to have a major impact until the following decade. By 1985 around 65 per cent of all electricity consumed originated from nuclear sources (compared with 31 per cent in West Germany and 19 per cent in the United Kingdom), and France had become an important net exporter of current, notably to Switzerland and Italy. Claims of too much power being produced were also countered during the period of intense cold experienced in the months of January and February 1985 when, without the huge investment in nuclear plant, the country's electricity grid would not have been able to withstand the very substantial increase in demand. France now benefits from the cheapest electricity amongst major industrial rivals in Western Europe,[21] and largely due to the nuclear programme (and measures to economise energy) it has cut considerably its dependency on external energy sources: imports of crude oil have fallen from 135 million tonnes in 1973 to 75 million tonnes in 1985.

But these advantages have to be balanced against certain costs and unwelcome side-effects. EdF became heavily in debt, its policy of persuading the French to go 'tout électrique' (to help dispose of the vast reserves of power becoming available) has not met with universal approval (particularly when power cuts occur), and many conventional power stations whose building costs have not yet been fully amortised have been mothballed. For those who appreciate huge cooling towers adding a new dimension to the landscape the policy has been a great success, but for others (with a more discerning gaze?) the massive scale of construction and its unattractiveness represent an unacceptable destruction of the countryside: at the Gravelines site on the western outskirts of Dunkerque six reactors each of 900 megawatts installed capacity (representing the largest development of this type in Western Europe), are now in operation, although in this case their presence might go relatively unnoticed amidst the vast complex of industry which exists alongside.

The nuclear programme has certainly not proceeded unchallenged in France, with the government and EdF being forced, for example, to back down on plans to build a plant at Plogoff in Brittany. But generally the opposition has been less forceful than in other parts of Europe, notably West Germany. Strong commitment by the establishment to the nuclear option and the determination of EdF to pursue this policy would appear partly responsible, as would the less well-organised and more easily demoralised character of the protest movement. After their triumph of Plogoff and violent protests against the fast breeder reactor at Creys-Malville, much of the opposition appears to have evaporated. But not all pressure groups in France have been opposed to development; the question of jobs has brought support from unlikely quarters, such as the Communists and CGT. Moreover, despite the imposed character of the nuclear option in France and the 'hard sell' approach adopted by EdF, a generally favourable public perception of the industry has been created, in marked contrast to the position in Britain; the fact that up to half a million people visit nuclear power stations in France each year may help explain this difference.

There is little question that France has been remarkably successful in developing a powerful nuclear industry and providing the country with a vital 'independent' source of energy supply. In such conditions it seems reasonable to assume that the targets set for 1990 will be met – 75 per cent of electricity and 30 per cent of total energy consumption from nuclear power, and imports of energy accounting for only 50 per cent of consumption. However, the main current issue concerns the future of the nuclear industry as the present programme of construction is wound down. Jobs, dependent activities and, above all, France's technical lead in this field are all at risk; indeed an important factor influencing the decision to continue building at least one reactor in France each year, even if current demand does not justify this additional capacity, is the desire to limit the extent of this damage. Originally it was thought that part of this difficulty could be overcome by exporting French technology, not least to potentially rapidly developing markets in areas such as China, Hong Kong, South Africa and South Korea; providing a 'ready-made' nuclear plant to one of these countries is estimated to represent 30–40 million hours of work for French manufacturers.

This policy still exists but as demands for energy have eased, as oil regains some of its competitiveness and as countries' budgets have been squeezed, the export market has proved far less buoyant than was anticipated. It has also been depressed by a widespread change in the perception of the nuclear power industry. Although France has retained a strong commitment to this source of energy, in many other countries the Three Mile Island accident in the United States in 1979 triggered new doubts about the industry's safety record, further reinforced by the Chernobyl catastrophe in May 1986. Moreover, as the demand for energy has eased, the pressure to find alternatives to oil has similarly moderated. Adapting France's nuclear industry to a new phase in its development presents, therefore, a demanding challenge; but it is one that is already under way as Framatome, for example, pursues a policy of diversification aimed at developing new growth sectors such as robotics.

No more lame ducks

As the recession began to take an increasing toll of French companies, it appeared to have become accepted practice that the government should intervene to initiate or participate in some form of rescue operation, particularly where large or strategically important businesses were concerned. Then, at the end of June 1984 the unthinkable happened when Creusot-Loire, one of the country's major industrial groups, went into liquidation, an event described by *Le Monde* as 'the greatest bankruptcy in France's industrial history'.[22] Creusot-Loire was created as a company in 1970 with the merging of two firms, the Société des Forges et Ateliers du Creusot based at Le Creusot and the Compagnie des Ateliers et Forges de la Loire concentrated at St Chamond near St Etienne, but its ancestry is much deeper. The company was a subsidiary of the Empain-Schneider group which in turn had grown out of the extensive business interests of the Schneider family, originally one of the 'guiding forces' behind France's early industrial development in the nineteenth century and a family which came to dominate life in Le Creusot.

Creusot-Loire specialised in heavy metallurgy and mechanical engineering and controlled Framatome amongst its subsidiaries. Many of its markets were overseas and the company was seen as an influential ambassador for the promotion of French technology and industrial goods. Yet throughout much of the 1970s the firm made losses, which by 1983 had risen to 1.8 billion francs for that year alone.[23] The factors leading to the downfall of Creusot-Loire were by no means unique to this company, and might be seen to apply equally to a number of other major industrial concerns. Similarly the nature of the restructuring programme set in motion following the collapse reflects policies applied elsewhere in France. However, the government's attitude towards Creusot-Loire and its unwillingness to bail out the company reflect a significant change in industrial strategy as it appeared that lame ducks could no longer be tolerated. Moreover, the government's agreement to the need for job losses as part of the restructuring proposals also marked a belated and reluctant acceptance that this would have to be part of the price to pay for the effective modernisation of French industry. Thus the approach adopted to tackle the problems posed by Creusot-Loire highlights a significant change in the Socialists' economic policy.

Creusot-Loire's financial difficulties had already begun to generate speculation about its future viability in the early 1980s, reflecting the similar problems experienced by its parent group. By 1983 the position had become particularly serious, with the company's managing director, Didier Pineau-Valencienne, who had been expressly appointed to redress the situation following his earlier success at Rhône-Poulenc, seeking substantial government aid as part of a rescue programme. Officially the cause of the firm's difficulties was attributed largely to its steel-making activities which, as elsewhere in France (and Western Europe), were loss-making but had never been subsidised as had been the case with the major steelmakers Usinor and Sacilor with their effective nationalisation in 1978. Similarly Creusot-Loire had become disastrously linked to the Phoenix Steel Corporation in America, also heavily in debt and on the verge of bankruptcy. Finally, markets had shrunk as firms had cut back on re-equipment programmes and exports had been severely affected as many developing countries had been forced by the recession to curtail ambitious development projects.

However, there were also claims of poor management by Creusot-Loire, especially in the 1970s. The company's expansion had lacked direction and had been too disparate resulting in the accumulation of loss-making activities such as machine tools. Investment had been inadequate and although the company was considered over-manned, insufficient measures were taken to prune the labour-force; above all no effective rationalisation occurred following the formation of Creusot-Loire to eradicate the duplication of activities produced by the merger of two similar companies.

At the end of 1983 the government finally agreed, although with some misgivings, to assist the company, sanctioning a loan of 2.1 billion francs. In turn Creusot-Loire was to sell off most of its steel-making activities to Usinor and Sacilor, the Commissariat à l'Energie Atomique was persuaded to take a 50 per cent share in Framatome, and Empain-Schneider agreed to inject more capital into the company. The problem appeared resolved. Yet by the following April (1984) Pineau-Valencienne was demanding further government aid, claiming the previous measures were inadequate and that the failure of markets to pick up was leading to a progressive deterioration of the company's financial position: monthly losses were now running at 100 million francs.[24]

Over the next three months a trial of strength ensued between government ministers and Creusot-Loire's managing director. The latter assumed that ultimately the government would cede, unwilling to bear the cost of the company's collapse or to sustain the damage this would inflict on France's image as an industrial power. However, despite an apparently strong hand, his bluff was called; the government refused to meet the company's demands and consequently at the end of June Creusot-Loire went into liquidation. A number of attempts were made to seek a compromise but these failed; government proposals that Empain-Schneider should increase its own investment in the company or that the nationalised banks should take a majority holding in the Schneider group itself were unacceptable. Both sides had shown themselves remarkably intransigent, producing an unsatisfactory conclusion to the matter. While the government justified its decision as 'responsible' in the prevailing economic conditions, it would seem reasonable to assume that it was also motivated by the unwillingness of a socialist administration to bail out a former 'champion' of private enterprise, particularly in view of the stance adopted by its managing director.

While the government had stood back and allowed Creusot-Loire to go bankrupt, it could hardly ignore, however, the consequences of this action for the company employed nearly 30 000 workers. As a result it played a central role in orchestrating a remodelled structure for the group. Certain peripheral activities were sold off to private buyers, but the bulk of the group's interests were split between two new companies – Creusot-Loire Industrie which was to form a subsidiary of Usinor and concentrate on the production of special steels and armaments (notably armoured vehicles at the St Chamond site), and Framatome which retained its former nuclear interests as well as taking over a number of related engineering activities such as the manufacture of turbines. Ironically the company's railway engineering section Jeumont-Rail, a profitable activity involved in the

TGV programme, was sold back to Empain-Schneider, helping to dispel suggestions that the former parent company had suffered a considerable set-back by the break-up of Creusot-Loire. On the contrary, the principal losers were those people who lost their jobs, and the government (and, therefore, taxpayers); certain of the employees due to be made redundant expressed their bitterness at the outcome by suggesting that they had been the victims of 'capitalists without capital and politicians without a policy'.[25] As for the government, its final bill was estimated at between 6 and 8 billion francs, considerably more than the loans originally sought by Didier Pineau-Valencienne.

The reaction of the work-force to the group's disintegration and to the above solution was hostile, reflecting fears that redundancies would be an inevitable consequence of restructuring and subsequent rationalisation. Marches, demonstrations and the blocking of railway stations and motorways were amongst the measures employed to convey disapproval. With the company's break-up it is hard to estimate accurately the overall number of job losses caused by the collapse, but at the two sites of Le Creusot and Chalon-sur-Saône, it was announced that the labour-force needed to be reduced by 2600 workers. However, under the barrage of protest the government agreed on a number of special measures to alleviate the impact of this loss. It was expected that up to half this total would be absorbed by early retirements and that for a large number of the other workers some form of retraining could be offered for a period of up to ten months during which they would continue to receive up to 70 per cent of their former wage. Furthermore, this same region had already been accorded priority to assist in the process of restructuring when designated one of the government's 15 special development areas in February 1984 (Figure 3.1).

These zones had been selected for preferential treatment due to the problems caused by the rundown of basic industries such as coal, steel, shipbuilding and textiles, and the recognition that such decline tends to be highly localised in its impact, reflecting the inherent nature of the distribution of these activities. In these 'poles' job losses were considered to have been particularly severe, leading to an above-average rate of unemployment. Hence the need for speical remedial action, which has been designed to take two forms – first, a series of schemes to try to avert redundancies as such, aiming instead to encourage workers to retire early, follow training courses or take on a temporary job; second, the availability of additional financial re-

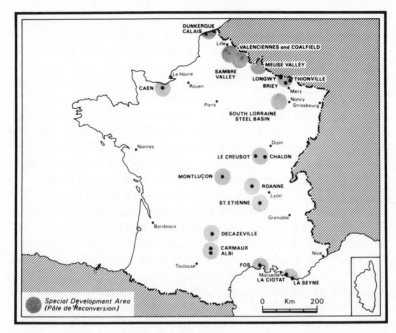

Figure 3.1   Areas of priority development for industry

sources and powers to waive certain fiscal obligations of firms in an attempt to persuade new investors to locate in these areas. The aim is that the Commissaire de la République of the departments in which these 'poles' lie should be responsible for setting up and co-ordinating these measures: in his task he is assisted by a small team of government civil servants, specialists in fields such as labour retraining and the audit of firms, seconded for this purpose. Viewed from the regions concerned the process does not always appear so straightforward. It took some time for this machinery to be set in motion and despite the Commissaire's co-ordinating role there is frequently a problem of duplication of services and sources of funding, rendering the operation highly complex particularly for firms seeking to invest. In particular the need to refer applications to relevant ministries in Paris (several of which might be involved) can cause further delay and complication, despite the efforts of the DATAR to expedite matters. Yet this problem is not new; it has been a constant criticism of regional planning over numerous years, which even the recent measures of decentralisation appeared to have failed to overcome.

Despite such shortcomings Le Creusot has benefited from its designation as a 'conversion pole'. It was within this framework, for example, that agreement was reached between the government, unions and management to limit the effects of job losses: indeed by the summer of 1985 no worker at Le Creusot had actually been sacked. But limiting or preventing redundancies represents only part of the problem; the other is to attract new employers. In Le Creusot this was seen as crucial. At the time of Creusot-Loire's collapse the firm employed approximately 6000 local people (Le Creusot has just over 44 000 inhabitants). Overall the town's employment structure remains dominated by industry – 56 per cent of the work-force is employed in this sector, compared with a proportion of only 31 per cent at a national level; in addition over two-thirds of the workers in industry are employed in heavy metallurgy and directly related activities. Thus, not only was Creusot-Loire a major employer itself, but its presence dominated the employment structure of the town and supported a host of much smaller subcontractors. This dominance was further illustrated by the importance of the company's contribution to the town's finances. Around 70 per cent of the local business tax (taxe professionnelle) paid to Le Creusot came from Creusot-Loire and its subsidiaries, representing 40 per cent of the town's total budget. Here is a remarkable case of over-dependency upon an extremely narrow range of activities, where even before the recent crisis jobs were slowly declining in the principal activity; already between 1965 and 1983 the company's work-force had been halved. It was considered imperative, therefore, to bring in new activities and to broaden the employment structure.

The problem for the town has been how to react most effectively to this challenge, particularly as after an extended period during which the Schneider family, and subsequently Creusot-Loire itself, had represented a source of security for the work-force, the company's bankruptcy had produced an important adverse psychological and demoralising effect. Certain options have been available to the local authority (the 'urban community' of Le Creusot-Montceau which includes the adjacent town of Montceau-les-Mines itself adversely affected over a number of years by the decline of the local coal industry). It has the possibility of buying up much of the now disused industrial land and providing ready-built factory space for new firms; similarly, to encourage such investment it also has the power to offer various incentives such as the waiving of local taxation for a specific period, or the sale or lease of land at below market prices. But to be able to do this implies that the necessary resources are available. However, the decline of Creusot-Loire has had a depressant effect on the town's income, making this strategy more difficult to implement.

Funding does exist from other sources, notably the government, and has been increased under the 'conversion pole' strategy, thus helping to alleviate one problem. However, attracting new firms is not only a matter of offering grants and loans; it is also related to other features of the area concerned, such as the quality of accessibility and educational training facilities, and the degree of attractiveness of the environment. In these respects Le Creusot might reasonably claim to be well placed, particularly concerning accessibility. The TGV which now serves the town means that Paris is reached in one and a half hours and Lyon in thirty-five minutes: any firm located at Le Creusot, therefore, has rapid access to the country's two major business centres. Such advantages, and doubtless some arm twisting by the DATAR, have produced one notable 'coup' for the town – the decision of SNECMA, the nationalised company renowned for its precision and advanced engineering and engine manufacture, to invest in a new plant at Le Creusot, employing 200 workers. The jobs themselves are vital but so too is the enhanced image the presence of such a company gives to the town and the positive effect this is likely to have in attracting other firms, an important consideration after the events of recent years.

Two further problems stand out. Attracting new investment has become a highly competitive business, particularly as local authorities now have greater powers (following decentralisation) to offer various incentives to firms: even between the various conversion poles competition is intense. This raises the issue of the extent to which it is desirable that councils should seek to outbid each other in this manner. Secondly there is the question of the competence of local authorities, particularly in small and medium-sized towns, to mount an effective promotional policy. This demands a very different style of approach in dealing with companies compared with councils' more traditional functions and requires high quality marketing skills; their acquisition may take time and above all can be expensive. Nevertheless, in the difficult process of restructuring the local economy, Le Creusot would appear to have certain advantages. Also, despite the trauma of Creusot-Loire's demise and a local rate of unemployment approaching 12 per cent (late 1985), the town's prospects might be seen as far healthier than those of similar industrial areas of northern and north-eastern France. Le Creusot has not yet been ravaged in the manner that Longwy has suffered, and still retains the appearance of a relatively prosperous community, set in pleasant surroundings.

The troubled car industry

The demise of Creusot-Loire, rather than representing an isolated case of industrial collapse, epitomised the debilitated state of wide sections of French industry. Certain features of this problem had been evident for a number of years, notably the declining performance of many of the country's basic industries. But the realisation that once flourishing growth sectors within the economy were no longer able to sustain their former momentum offered a particularly sobering reminder of the weakened competitive position of French manufacturers. This was the case of France's car manufacturers as during the 1980s they faltered in the face of an increased challenge to their formerly dominant position. However, while this industry illustrates the process and adverse consequences of decline, it also offers an example of the means employed to revive production and regain competitiveness, not least through heavy investment in new technology.

Since 1980 alone the number of people employed in the industry has fallen on average by approximately 16 000 each year,[26] reducing the work-force to a current total of around 400 000. Output, having increased continuously throughout the 1970s (except in 1974 and 1975 following the first oil crisis) to reach a peak of 3.2 million vehicles in 1979, has also slumped in the 1980s (Table 3.5). The same deterioration has also been apparent in exports, which in 1985 were at the same level as in 1970. Nevertheless cars remain a major export commodity for France, earning 43.8 billion francs in 1984 which represented 5.4 per cent of the total value of exports. But while foreign sales have declined, imports have increased, and in an almost stable home market have been accounting for a larger share of new car registrations. In 1980 they took just over 20 per cent of total sales, yet by 1985 this had risen to nearly 37 per cent. This failure of French manufacturers to maintain their market share underlies the current problems of the French car industry; not only has demand been depressed by the recession, but consumers have shown a growing preference for the products of foreign competitors. The loss of confidence in the 'home product' has been set against the background of a troubled industry. For much of the first half of the 1980s both

Table 3.5 Output in the French car industry

	Production		New vehicles registered	
	Total	Exports	Total	French component
			(millions of vehicles)	
1970	2.2	1.2	1.3	1.0
1979	3.2	1.7	2.0	1.5
1980	2.9	1.5	1.9	1.4
1981	2.6	1.4	1.8	1.3
1982	2.8	1.5	2.1	1.4
1983	3.0	1.6	2.0	1.4
1984	2.7	1.1	1.8	1.1
1985	2.6	1.2	1.8	1.1

Source: Conseil Economique et Social, *Le Devenir de l'Industrie Française de l'Automobile* (1984); *Bulletin Mensuel de l'Industrie du Pétrole*, no. 290 (1986).

Renault and Peugeot were making substantial losses; this period was also marked by a protracted series of disputes and strikes, disrupting production. The Peugeot subsidiaries were the worst affected, with the main battleground their Parisian factories.

In common with other major European manufacturers the two French giants have had to adapt to fundamental changes in the market. Apart from its currently depressed state, reflecting the results of an essentially short-term squeeze on consumption, there has also been an underlying flattening of demand as ownership levels have risen. Over 73 per cent of French households possess at least one car, therefore restricting market growth to replacements of these vehicles or to additional sales to families already owning a car. Consequently increasing efforts have been made to encourage exports, with a continuing interest being shown in investment in manufacturing plants abroad where production costs are often lower than in France. Companies have also had to accommodate rapid changes in technology. Automation has long been a feature of the industry, but developments in microelectronics, computerised systems and robotics have enabled the applications of this practice to be vastly extended. In addition this represents an essential means of improving productivity and thus competitiveness. Increased pressure has also been applied to manufacturers, not least by consumers, to improve their vehicles so that they comply with new expectations (and regulations) in matters of durability, safety, pollution, economy and fashion. Design has, therefore, become a more complex process, and itself has undergone substantial change through technical advance.

However, developing revised models, attacking new markets and adapting to the latest technology all imply the need for heavy investment; but it is here that French manufacturers appear to have fallen behind their competitors, with the inevitable result that the industry has become less efficient. Confirmation of this was given in 1984 when François Dalle, the former managing director of the cosmetics firm L'Oréal, who had been asked by President Mitterrand to head a commission of enquiry into the problems facing car manufacturers, reported his findings; he stated that 'while Renault and Citroën require 8000 workers to produce 1200 vehicles a day, Fiat only employ 6000 and the Japanese 4000.[27] However, a further vital factor in improving competitiveness has been the level of employment in the industry, which appeared not to have been adjusted sufficiently to take account of falling output and changed production processes. But in attempting to adapt to rapidly changing manufacturing and marketing conditions, Peugeot and Renault have been restricted by their own indebtedness and by an initial government reluctance to authorise cutbacks in the labour-force.

The need to reduce manpower to improve efficiency developed into a highly contentious issue between government, unions and management, although the Dalle report had clearly indicated that this measure was essential; it estimated that between 1984 and 1989 around 50 000 jobs would need to be lost from the industry. Yet from the early 1980s both Renault and Peugeot were already seeking to reduce substantially their work-forces. The area worst affected by these measures was Paris. In part this was an inevitable consequence of the concentration of manufacturing in this area and of the comparatively old age of certain plants. Equally there was a case for suggesting that production costs were higher in this region. However, the unions made a rather different interpretation, arguing that the desire to diminish the importance of Parisian factories was a deliberate policy to shift production away from strongly unionised areas. But whatever the cause, cuts have been substantial; over two-thirds of the job losses in the industry in the early 1980s were concentrated in the Paris region, and between 1980 and 1985 the proportion of total French production originating here fell from nearly 52 per cent to under 30 per cent.

A significant test for the industry on this issue came in 1983 when

Peugeot announced it wished to reduce its labour-force by nearly 7400 workers, with a major part of the loss concentrated in the Talbot plant at Poissy which had a notorious reputation for poor labour relations and had suffered from inadequate past investment. The unacceptable element of the management's proposals was that nearly 3000 of these losses were to be achieved by dismissals. There followed an ugly but predictable confrontation. The government finally agreed to sanction a reduced number of sackings (1906), with concessions from Peugeot (such as offering retraining courses) to help attenuate the impact of its cuts. However, this compromise was rejected by the unions, with the CGT heading the opposition and in the latter part of 1983 violent clashes occurred at Poissy leading finally to police evacuating striking workers occupying the factory. The issue was further complicated by the presence of a large proportion of immigrants amongst the work-force, who were to form the majority of those sacked, and for whom a special payment was to be offered to encourage them to return to their country of origin. Calm slowly returned in the early part of 1984, only to be followed by a similar dispute at Citroën's Aulnay plant in northern Paris when the firm announced in March the need to reduce employment in the company's factories by up to 6000 workers, of which nearly half would be made redundant. Six months later agreement was reached on 1950 redundancies together with a programme of retraining for most of these workers lasting up to a year. The resolution of these two disputes may be seen as particularly significant for, as in the case of Creusot-Loire, it indicated the government's revised attitude to modernisation; there was now an acceptance that a reduction in manpower was frequently an inevitable part of this process.

Further shocks for the industry came in 1985 when Renault announced its record loss of 12.5 billion francs for 1984 (since followed by a further loss of 11 billion francs in 1985), leading to the premature departure of its managing director Bernard Hanon and his replacement by Georges Besse who had previously encountered considerable success in re-establishing the profitability of Pechiney.[28] Part of the prescription of the new 'patron' to revive the company was a considerable reduction of employment estimated to involve over 10 000 workers for each of the next two years. Renault's disastrous financial situation and substantial overmanning were seen as an embarrassment to the government; not only did this imply inefficient management of a major nationalised company, but it also further highlighted the limitations of the Socialists' early policies of avoiding

forced redundancies through alternative strategies such as redeployment. Meanwhile, Peugeot had returned to profitability, arguably
partly as a result of a more ruthless policy towards overmanning.

These negative aspects of the car industry might be counter
balanced by a number of more positive features. In a recent report by
the Conseil Economique et Social it was indicated that France has a
number of factories which technically are amongst the most efficient
in the world:[29] Renault's plant at Douai and Peugeot's at Mulhouse
are but two examples. In the latter case despite the extensive use of
robots on the production lines, the factory has maintained its labour
force, which currently stands at around 13 600. The impact of this
particular plant, ideally located adjacent to two branches of the
national motorway network on a vast site to the east of the town in
southern Alsace, is considerable: it is estimated that it provides
employment directly and indirectly for nearly 50 000 people. Its
ability to maintain employment is largely due to production of one
particular model, the 205, which has also been of vital significance to
the group as a whole; two-thirds of Peugeot's sales in 1985 were
accounted for by the 205, leading to the potential problem of
overdependency by the firm on a single model, and it is therefore
hoped that the more recent 309 will prove equally successful and
provide greater balance to the pattern of production. But other
factors have played important parts in Peugeot's revival – tackling
overmanning where it has been a problem, investing heavily and
reorganising production processes to produce greater coherence
between the different subsidiaries and plants within the group; in
particular the company has sought to create a far larger number of
components common to various models. As such there is an increasing interchange of parts not only between the group's different
factories in France, but also with its plants in Spain; parts are
supplied as well to foreign manufacturers such as Mercedes. In part
this produces economies of scale, while co-operation with other
companies helps to reduce the now substantial sums required for
research and development. Moreover, by using a continuously operating supply system, stocks are reduced to a minimum, leading to a
considerable saving in overheads.

The French car industry has the potential to regain the ground
recently lost to other car manufacturers, but this implies the need for
continuing change. Productivity remains too low by comparison with
major competitors, yet its increase depends on tackling manning
problems, promoting investment and ensuring that more factories

operate at full capacity. The task is not impossible as has been shown elsewhere in Europe by Fiat's remarkable revival.

WHICH WAY FOR GROWTH?

Changing patterns of consumption and demand, a continuing redistribution of activity between the world's industrialised and industrialising nations to the detriment of countries such as France, and a reduced efficiency in certain branches of French manufacturing have combined to limit the scope of conventional industries to generate increased wealth and, above all, additional employment. In a parallel movement, as the economy has matured, it has spawned a growing need for a greater number and more diverse range of services. Given these two tendencies it is only natural that the tertiary sector should perform the role as the principal generator of jobs.

At the same time mobile investment capital has been attracted increasingly towards new sectors of the economy, hopefully offering a much higher rate of return than more traditional activities. In particular this movement has been associated with the development and application of new manufacturing techniques and materials. It has also involved greater emphasis upon those industries featuring a high added-value in the manufacturing process, frequently achieved by the use of advanced technology. Within these growth areas, activities linked to the storage, processing and transfer of information have taken on a special significance, as they become increasingly essential to the efficient functioning of modern society.

France has an impressive record of achievement in many of these fields and various examples might be cited. Over the last decade it has confirmed its position as a world leader in the building of nuclear reactors and aerospace equipment, linked in the latter case with prestigious projects such as the Airbus and the Ariane rocket launcher. The reputation of related manufacturing firms, including Framatome, Aérospatiale and Matra, has been built on the success of these undertakings. Similarly companies such as CIT-Alcatel and Thomson (now linked together) have contributed to and benefited from the very considerable progress achieved in the development and installation of telecommunications systems, a field again in which France has become an established world leader. In the associated area of microelectronics the country has also become renowned for products such as Bull's 'smart card', developed originally in the mid-

1970s by Roland Moreno. The card contains a minute microprocessor and apart from its versatility has the great advantage of a high level of security. Currently a major programme to launch the card is underway.

The manufacture of advanced weapon and defence systems is another of the country's most dynamic industrial sectors, reflecting the priority given to related research and development ever since de Gaulle sought to establish France's technological independence in this field. French successes in this field are many, including the Exocet rocket of Aérospatiale, a series of Mirage fighter planes (of which the 2000 is the most recent) originating from the Dassault company, and radar equipment manufactured by Thomson-CSF. Whatever the objections on moral grounds to such production, a factor which has always been a problem for the consciences of some Socialists, in economic terms it has been a very important money-earner for France. Certainly this was the view taken by Charles Hernu who strongly defended the industry during his term of office as Defence Minister (prior to his departure from the government over the Greenpeace affair). Arms sales account for around 2.5 per cent of France's gross domestic product and manufacturing activities employ around 300 000 people. Above all the industry is a major exporter, producing an income of 62 billion francs in 1984,[30] largely as a result of contracts won in the Middle East in such countries as Saudi Arabia and in Gulf States such as Abu-Dhabi. Further confirmation of the industry's strength and of the vital role played by exports was given in November 1985 when it was announced that the Americans were to buy the French communications system RITA to equip their armed forces (in preference to the rival British Ptarmigan system); the contract was worth 8 billion francs to Thomson-CSF, the French manufacturer.

This is far from a comprehensive list of French achievements and could be extended to take account of the lead given in various other diverse areas such as computer software and languages, equipment for underwater exploration and the production of sophisticated transport systems, centred in the latter case around the development of various forms of metro network and of the commercially highly successful TGV. Behind these advances lies a considerable effort in research, reflected in the existence of a number of prestigious laboratories in fields such as nuclear science, electronics and telecommunications. France too has become renowned for certain areas of medical research related to the work carried out by organisations such as the

Insitut Pasteur, which in 1985 achieved much success and world acclaim through its identification of the AIDS virus ahead of American teams engaged in similar work.

The need to continue to promote research and to increase the importance attached to this activity has not escaped the attention of governments, with the Socialists seeking to attack this problem along various fronts; financial aid to the nationalised industries was designed partly to help achieve this goal, while to encourage the more general search for innovation and technological advance, strong backing was given to the state's research development agency (ANVAR). Part of the appeal of this organisation is its decentralised character, with offices in each of the country's regions; in 1984 over 1600 companies received financial assistance from the ANVAR, amounting to 800 million francs.

France appears, therefore, to display an impressive record in advanced technology, a feature of vital significance given its link with inducing and sustaining economic growth. Yet there is still evidence of inadequate progress in the development of certain new technologies and uncertainty over the future pattern of expansion. The French, for example, have been spending a lower proportion of gross domestic product on research and development than many of their major competitors, notably the United States, Japan and West Germany. Key areas of 'high-tech' remain underdeveloped in France, including such contrasting fields as biotechnology and the manufacture of computer systems. As far as employment is concerned, the rate of growth has been relatively low, failing to match the pace of decline in many more traditional branches of the economy; indeed in fields such as telecommunications and electronics components jobs have been cut, reflecting changes in the pattern of demand and intense competition from foreign manufacturers.

Changing patterns of growth in the tertiary sector

Uncertainties about employment prevail elsewhere. France may have entered the era of the post-industrial society, but the ability of its service sector to continue to generate jobs on a large scale now appears increasingly in question. Gone are the years (at least in the short-term) when tertiary activities were producing a net yearly increase of up to 200 000 jobs, as in the late 1970s. More recently the service sector has managed to create barely a tenth of this total each year. However, such generalisation can be misleading. The problem of making reference to the tertiary sector as a whole is that it covers such a diverse range of businesses and administrative organisations, many of which have experienced very different patterns of evolution; it is also increasingly questionable whether in many cases the distinction between manufacturing and non-manufacturing activities is still valid, particularly with reference to the so-called 'high-tech' industries where research and production are highly interlinked. Certain services have ceased to generate substantial numbers of jobs, as was the case a decade ago. This trend has become particularly evident in the field of banking and insurance, where it is attributed to changes in working practices and organisation following the widespread computerisation of transactions, and to a downturn in activity during a period of recession. A similar pattern of declining growth is now apparent in education, related in part to the underlying trend towards a smaller population of school age as birth rates have fallen as well as to efforts to reduce the level of public expenditure in this field. Other areas of previously high growth, such as local government and health and social services, have also experienced a slowing in their rate of expansion, although the tendency has been less pronounced than in the above examples: in the former instance decentralisation is likely to sustain a further increase in jobs, while in the latter case improvements in the standard of care and a growing level of consumption of these services by an increasingly more affluent population have continued to foster relatively strong expansion.

Business services continue to flourish, not only in traditional areas such as advertising and media consultants and legal advisors, but more particularly in a growing series of 'cabinets de conseil' related to computing and data processing. But even in this general field reverses have occurred, illustrated recently by the difficulties encountered by the firm Technip, France's leading consultants in the design and construction of industrial plant. During 1984 and 1985 the firm shed nearly 1000 jobs, leaving a total work-force of little more than 2000. Redundancies were bitterly contested, with the CGT and CFDT arguing strongly that the incompetence of management was the basic cause of the company's problems. Much of Technip's work derives from foreign contracts and it would appear that in a highly competitive market too many of these were negotiated at an unrealistically low price. This led to severe financial difficulties for the firm which it became unable to support in a period of depressed business. Such problems were then further aggravated by the acquisition of the ailing subsidiary of the former Creusot-Loire group, Creusot-Loire Enterprise, which although specialising in a similar field of activity and therefore offering theoretically the opportunity to strengthen Technip's operations, was also handicapped by an underlying lack of profitability.

Recent trends in retailing

Conversely, in certain other areas growth has held up much better, a trend which may be illustrated by reference to certain aspects of retailing and leisure activities and tourism, although in neither case have these branches as a whole displayed a particularly high rate of expansion. In the case of retailing the continuing investment in superstores has led to a substantial rise in related employment; between 1977 and 1984 jobs increased from nearly 71 000 to over 166 000 contrasting markedly with the losses occurring amongst the ranks of the small shopkeepers and traders.[31] Despite attempts to restrict their development, hypermarkets remain a major area of expansion. France now has nearly 600 such stores, accounting for 12 per cent of all retailing turnover.[32] In 1984 the Euromarché chain alone created 1000 new jobs. Part of the hypermarket's appeal relates to continuing efforts to enhance its image; no longer is it a utilitarian and purely functional shopping area with the emphasis purely on size but increasingly it is linked to an associated, diverse range of shops and services, the whole complex designed to offer a far more attractive environment in which to shop. Furthermore hypermarkets are no longer to be found exclusively on the outer fringes of the urban area; an increasing number are now located in town centres, often acting as influential anchor stores in new shopping complexes. In the latter part of 1984 Euromarché opened a hypermarket at la Part-Dieu in Lyon, one of the largest enclosed commercial centres in the central areas of West European cities, relying for its success on the centre's pre-existing appeal and its proximity to a dense area of inner-city population and therefore, potential customers. Other examples of this trend are found in cities such as Paris, Bordeaux and Rouen. It is this willingness to be innovative and take calculated commercial risks that set many of the hypermarket companies apart from older established retailing chains. Nonetheless doubts exist about even their ability to continue to expand as the market for such stores becomes increasingly saturated, as the proportion of families' income spent on food and on furnishing their homes declines, and as purchasing power has tended to remain stable during the early 1980s.

Judging by the number of track-suited joggers now gracing France's pavements and parks, sport is becoming an increasingly popular pastime for many French families. This impression is confirmed by more rigorous analysis. It is now estimated that 52 per cent of men and 40 per cent of women participate in some form of sport, compared with proportions of 41 per cent and 28 per cent respectively in 1973.[33] Such trends form part of a wider movement of growth in leisure and cultural activities, which now account on average for around 8 per cent of households' expenditure, representing more for example than is spent on clothing. More free time, greater affluence and changing lifestyles have all contributed to this movement. Over 57 per cent of French people now go on holiday at least once a year and tourism earns France a substantial income, with receipts exceeding outgoing expenditure by 27.6 billion francs in 1984. Not surprisingly there has been a corresponding expansion of linked employment, covering areas such as travel agencies, the hotel and catering trades and various forms of administrative, managerial, and teaching and training activities.

The development of sport and of recreational pursuits has other important implications, not least for related industries. Sales of sportswear and sporting equipment now represent a market with an annual turnover of over 50 billion francs, offering a considerable potential for French manufacturers.[34] Regrettably for France, however, home producers do not always appear to have responded effectively to this challenge: for example two-thirds of the 48 million pairs of sports shoes sold in 1984 were imported. Similarly a number of the major manufacturing groups in France, such as Adidas, are the subsidiaries of foreign-based multinationals. Trends and fashions change rapidly in sport, requiring manufacturers to be innovative and versatile. Thus as many have expanded their operations they have also diversified their production. Adidas now produces not only footwear but a wide range of other items including swimwear and tennis racquets. Such manufacturers have also benefited from the vogue of wearing sports clothing for everyday use, which has considerably widened their market and led by way of response to the addition of a more glamorous range of products. It is not only manufacturers which have sought to capitalise on sport's popularity, but also retailers, and not least some of the superstore chains, further testifying to their dynamism and aggressive marketing techniques. Thus Auchan has launched a series of Décathlon stores and Darty (specialising originally in home electrical goods) now runs a chain of Sparty sports shops, based on the same self-service selling technique.

New forms of tourism

Traditionally the benefits which accrue from the expansion of tourism have been linked with resorts in coastal regions and in selected inland locations offering attractive surroundings as well as the potential to undertake various recreational and sporting activities, particularly winter sports. However, it has become increasingly recognised that tourism can also play an important role in the urban economy, and not just in capital cities such as Paris with the obvious attractions of their historical and cultural inheritance, and wide range of entertainment and retailing facilities. Indeed, as more conventional components of the urban economy such as industry and offices are either losing employment and generating less revenue, or growing more slowly, increasing efforts have been made to foster alternative forms of development. Tourism, as a growth industry, is seen as offering numerous potential advantages, including the generation of jobs, the ability to induce expenditure in other activities, the provision of a new option for the re-use of derelict sites and buildings and the creation of a means by which to promote a city's image and vitality. Certain of these assumptions, however, might be challenged; for example, although tourism induces new employment, many such jobs require few skills, are poorly paid and may only be temporary or seasonal in nature – this is hardly injecting new dynamism into the economy. Such possible shortcomings have done little though to deter interest in this field and the search for appropriate development strategies.

Precise measurement of the role played by toursim in cities is rendered difficult by a frequent absence of appropriate statistics, but where estimates have been made they suggest that its influence is considerable. At Lyon (1.2 million inhabitants) tourism is calculated to produce an annual revenue (1984) of approximately 1.7 billion francs, roughly equivalent to the yearly operating budget of the commune of Lyon (450 000 inhabitants); moreover, in relation to the city's size this level of expenditure does not appear exceptional. Apart from providing an important return for local hoteliers and restaurant and café owners, there are also other significant spin-offs for transport operators, retailers and numerous other smaller organisations such as printing firms.

Business tourism, relating to visits to firms, conferences, exhibitions and seminars, has been shown to exercise a particularly influential role in urban areas. In the case of Lyon, cited above, two-thirds of the turnover of the city's hotels derives from these activities. Yet within this market changes are occurring. Expenditure deriving from the routine visits of businessmen to branches of their organisation or to meet clients is tending to diminish as improved communications (e.g. more internal air services, the TGV) have decreased the need for an overnight stay. Conversely the conference and exhibition business, despite some decline in activity and ever-increasing competition from new venues, is seen as a very lucrative market. Conference delegates are highly sought-after visitors, for their average level of daily expenditure appears to be at least double that of the conventional tourist. It is estimated that participants at conferences in provincial cities spend around 700 francs each day on accommodation, transport and meals, a figure which rises to over 1000 francs in the capital. Paris is the world's leading conference centre, hosting 274 international events in 1985.

Despite the potential benefits accruing from the staging of conferences and exhibitions, offering such facilities can involve considerable risks. Related centres are expensive to construct and equip, and incur high running costs, often leading to a deficit on the operating budget. Yet this has not deterred the continued launching of ambitious development schemes, justified on the basis that the indirect benefits which are generated for the wider urban community far exceed any operating losses. Thus in recent years a major purpose built exhibition complex (Eurexpo), rivalling Britain's National Exhibition Centre, has been opened on the eastern outskirts of Lyon; similar facilities have been provided at Villepinte in the northern suburbs of Paris. In the field of conferences, new centres have recently been opened at Cannes, Monte Carlo, Nice, Angers and Lille, while by 1987 Toulouse will also have joined the ranks of cities equipped with ultra-modern complexes. With the aim of ensuring maximum profitability, many of these centres have been designed to fulfil a dual or even multi-purpose role, combining conferences with musical events, and catering as well for small exhibitions and seminars: considerable emphasis has also been placed on the provision of a high-quality and sophisticated 'product', not least in response to the demands of an increasingly exigent clientele. The prestigious and sumptuous Acropolis convention centre at Nice, opened in 1985 having cost over 400 million francs, highlights these various features. But the scale and cost of such ventures also implies that the number of urban centres able to enter this expensive and highly competitive arena is limited.

A very different but potentially similarly lucrative form of tourism is represented by the creation of a growing number of theme parks (parcs d'attractions), based loosely on the model of Disneyland in the United States. Although such developments are not restricted to city areas, in recent years two ambitious projects have been announced which are specifically designed to give a significant boost to the urban economy of the regions in which they are located. As one of numerous initiatives to regenerate economic activity in Lorraine, a large amusement park is to be created in the midst of the region's traditional steel making districts; it is based on the strip-cartoon characters the Stroumpfs (Smurfs). The aim is to produce up to 3000 jobs within ten years, with benefits for related businesses particularly in the hotel and catering trades.

A much larger undertaking is now programmed for the Paris region with the decision (taken provisionally in late 1985) of the Walt Disney Organisation to set up a European Disneyland on a site at the eastern extremity of the new town of Marne-la-Vallée. Proximity to a huge local market, allied to the French capital's existing function as a major tourist centre and its high quality of accessibility make development in this area a particularly attractive possibility. The park itself is likely to cover 200 hectares and, apart from the profits it would generate for the parent company, is seen as capable of bringing substantial benefits to the surrounding area; for in the longer-term it is planned to develop an associated commercial complex including offices, conference facilities, sports amenities and hotels. In all 23 000 jobs could be provided by the early 1990s. Despite the extremely ambitious scale of this scheme, given the strong commitment to its development by both the American parent company and regional authorities in Paris, as well as the favourable location, its success appears assured. The main problem is likely to be controlling related speculative investments. In the case of Lorraine, however, the spin-off is unlikely to be so significant; the project is smaller, the region does not have an established reputation for tourism and, if visitors come only on a daily basis requiring no overnight accommodation, the opportunities for generating jobs and income in related businesses remain limited.

HIGH-TECH AND THE COMPUTER AGE

Space-age France

Given the extensive news coverage accorded in France to the Ariane rocket, it might seem reasonable to imagine that this is an entirely French project. But this is not the case. Ariane is the fruit of a European collaborative effort, set in motion in the early 1970s under the guidance of the European Space Agency. However, it is the French who have played a leading role in this organisation, contributing almost two-thirds of the development costs. Furthermore, in 1980 a new private, French based company was created (Arianespace) to take charge of the project and above all to promote sales of Ariane; its headquarters are in the new town of Evry (in the southern outer suburbs of Paris), adjacent to the offices of the Centre National d'Etudes Spatiales (CNES), an organisation which has made an important contribution over a rather longer period to the development of France's aerospace industry. These two form the nucleus of a rapidly growing business which covers not just the construction and sale of rocket launchers, but also the production of satellites and the manufacture of associated ground equipment to receive, decode and retransmit their signals. The harnessing of space for peaceful purposes in fields such as telecommunications and surveillance presents manufacturers with a major technical challenge, to which European firms and governments are anxious to respond positively in the face of strong competition from the United States. It also offers an appropriate shop window for French high-tech industry to display its capabilities.

Although the aerospace industry has become synonymous with the application of advanced technology, its importance as an employer and as a generator of income is still limited. In 1984 turnover amounted to around 7 billion francs and employment totalled approximately 8000, figures which are very considerably below those recorded by the aeronautical industry of 65 billion francs and nearly 128 000 employees.[35] Yet the two activities are closely linked, a feature illustrated in the common use of production techniques, in the similar location patterns and in the high level of government funding which has been essential to support the huge cost of the necessary research input. Four large companies dominate the industry (Aérospatiale, Matra, Société Européenne de Propulsion – SEP, and Alcatel-Thomson Espace), complemented by around 40 other key firms most of which are relatively small concerns, representing overall a highly concentrated activity. Many of these companies were related originally to the aeronautical industry and although this link still remains strong, the importance of the aerospace sector is growing; in the case of Aérospatiale it now accounts for approximately a third of the company's turnover.

The Ariane programme has generally been considered highly successful, despite a limited number of failures, the most notorious occurring during a visit of François Mitterrand to the launching site at Mururoa in September 1985. For a President who at that time was being widely criticised in international circles for the Greenpeace affair and who was seeking some revival of national prestige through a successful launch, the sight of Ariane plunging towards the sea, rather than disappearing into the sky, must have been particularly depressing. Setting aside this fiasco, however, the long-term commercial prospects for the rocket appear promising, allowing a return substantially above the 12 billion francs already estimated to have been spent on development. In the field of satellite launching, Ariane is in direct competition with the American space shuttle, but it has the advantages of lower cost and greater precision and, as each successive generation of the rocket enters service, of constantly improving technical qualities, enabling for example the launching of much heavier satellites. The aim is to take around a third of the world market, which current results suggest is feasible. Indeed following the tragic accident to the American space shuttle Challenger in the early part of 1986, and the setback this represented for the launch programme of the United States, Ariane seemed poised to achieve a commanding position in this field, only to be temporarily grounded by its own technical problems.

The manufacture of the satellites themselves represents a further potentially important market, particularly for companies such as Aérospatiale and Matra. However, development costs are high and this has resulted in various collaborative schemes between European manufacturers. Matra also works in association with the American Ford Aerospace concern, as on the Arabsat project, which resulted in the launching of the first satellite in February 1985 designed to provide the basis for a telecommunications system to link 22 Arab States. Satellites offer numerous possibilities for development in fields such as weather forecasting (e.g. Météosat), survey and reconnaissance work (e.g. Spot 1), the relaying of television programmes (e.g. TDF 1) and telecommunications (e.g. Télécom 1A). The launching of

Spot 1 (by Ariane) in February 1986 represented a particular success and a significant technical achievement for the French aerospace industry. Not only was the satellite designed by the CNES but it was largely built by French companies under the guidance of Matra, with Belgian and Swedish firms also contributing to the programme. Now Spot 1 produces images of a superior quality and offering a higher degree of resolution than its American rival Landsat 4, destined for uses which range from the provision of basic data for map production to the monitoring of crop growth. Not surprisingly its commercial success appears assured.

The wider spin-off from such developments is considerable and again highly varied. Just as there is a rapidly growing market for the supply of related ground equipment| (of particular interest to firms such as Alcatel-Thomson Espace), satellites are providing new opportunities for their users to greatly extend their services. Thus Télécom 1A is designed to provide far greater capacity for the PTT for telephone traffic between France and its overseas departments and to offer a new channel for the transfer of computer data, a field in which demand is exceptionally strong and where reliability is essential. French initiatives form part of a wider European movement (Eutelsat) aimed at promoting and co-ordinating satellite developments. Its headquarters is at Paris, further reinforcing the French capital's role as an influential centre of the aerospace industry. Yet despite the industry's rapid development, certain expectations have not been fulfilled. The benefits for other branches of activity remain limited and the high-level of concentration which characterises production and results in a small number of companies dominating the industry, is also reflected in the pattern of location, with a clear focus on the two 'poles' of Paris and Toulouse.

The computer revolution

It may by gratifying for the French to learn of the successes of their aerospace industry, but few would probably argue that this directly influences their lives. Yet the vast progress made in the fields of electronics and especially microelectronics which have underlain such development has given rise to a much wider and profound transformation of the country's society and economy. France is currently immersed in the revolution induced by the micro-chip. Its ramifications are numerous, ranging from the rapid expansion of the market for personal computers for businesses and the home, to the continued growth of the use of robots in fields such as difficult environments (e.g. nuclear reactors and underwater exploration), medicine and in the manufacture of industrial products.

Advances in microelectronics have provided the possibility of obtaining increasingly rapid access to information, of greatly accelerating its processing and of widening considerably the opportunities for its transfer and exchange. In responding to these changes new industries have emerged. The marriage of computer systems and telecommunications has produced 'la télématique', epitomised by the Minitel service; and the similar application of computerised techniques to office equipment has given birth to 'la bureautique', centred on facilities such as word-processors, small desk computers, sophisticated copiers and facsimile transmission services. Above all the market for microcomputers and accompanying software, whether for the office or the home, has shown substantial expansion. Such interest is stimulated by intensive promotional campaigns; it is not just cars, alcohol, perfumes and other 'good things' in life that the French are being persuaded to consume, but also a growing range of micros and their accessories: thus, according to the publicity of one manufacturer (Apple) all that has to be done to find paradise is to 'croquez la pomme' (crunch the apple)! Whatever the techniques used to generate sales, the steadily growing interest in this field is indicated by the increasing range of specialised magazines and periodicals which have appeared on this subject.

Not only is the data processing industry expanding rapidly, but it has also come to represent an activity with a substantial turnover and labour-force. By 1985 annual sales of French firms exceeded 50 billion francs, having more than doubled since 1980; jobs have grown less rapidly, but by the same year had risen to over 51 000. However, the industry has a considerably wider impact, resulting from the spectacular growth in related service activities – specialised advisory and consultancy firms, servicing agents, sales organisations, training specialists and promotional experts. In common with these trends, the number of computers in use has grown with great speed; for those systems valued at over 50 000 francs (1985), which excludes many micros, the annual rate of increase averaged more than 21 per cent between 1975 and 1985.[36] It is in the field of microcomputers, however, where explosive growth has been taking place: in 1980 fewer than 20 000 such systems were used for business purposes, but by 1984 the number has already increased to over 300 000, with the likelihood that it would exceed 2 million by 1990. The past increase is already reflected in a substantial rise in the number of small businesses equipped in this manner. Between 1980 and 1985 the proportion of firms employing between 10 and 200 workers possessing a computer rose from 19 to 70 per cent.[37] As for smaller home computers, it was estimated that over 400 000 were sold in 1984 alone.[38]

The market for computer products, therefore, has proved highly buoyant in the 1980s, but it could be argued that French manufacturers failed to capitalise fully on this advantage. Part of the growth in demand has been met by foreign production as France has become an increasingly important net importer of data processing equipment, so that in 1985 the value of imports exceeded 30.6 billion francs compared with export sales worth just over 20.5 billion francs.[39] Part of the explanation for this discrepancy relates to the substantial increase in the value of the dollar (and therefore the cost of imports) during the early 1980s, but it also testifies to a worrying lack of competitiveness in a key growth sector of industry. Further evidence of the comparative weakness of French computer manufacturers is given by the extent to which IBM (through its French subsidiary) dominates the domestic market. The company accounts for approximately half of the industry's sales, although the French firm Bull takes a further third of this total. IBM's presence is particularly marked in the field of large mainframe systems, whereas other manufacturers offer a much more effective challenge in the market for personal computers. Apple is a strong rival in the supply of micros for the business world, but again the company is American. It is only in the sale of home computers that French companies exert any major influence, with Thomson the market leader. But this is a highly competitive field which has not expanded to the extent that has occurred for example in Britain and in which there are now signs of an easing of demand. One area in which French firms do lead, however, is in the production of computer software and packages, and in related consultancy. Dominating this activity in France, and the leading such company in Western Europe, is the firm of Cap Gemini Sogeti which has recently been responsible for programming the PTT's electronic telephone directory to cover the whole of the country. Such developments might be interpreted as implicit recognition that the most effective strategy for the future growth of the French data processing industry is to specialise in those areas where American competition is least effective.

IBM's pre-eminent position amongst French based computer

manufacturers is indicated in Table 3.6, which also demonstrates the highly influential role played by American companies. Not only does IBM have easily the largest turnover, but it is also a highly successful organisation, with profits exceeding 2.5 billion francs in 1984, making the company the second most profitable industrial group in France after Elf-Aquitaine. The firm is also a major investor, with investments totalling 2.9 billion francs in 1984, and major expansion is currently under way at its sites at Montpellier and particularly Corbeil. This pattern of investment illustrates a more general (and for some) problematic feature of the computing industry in France – its excessive concentration in a restricted number of areas. The Paris region is the prime focus, accounting for 56 per cent of all employment and 60 per cent of the salaries bill; next, but a long way behind is the region of Languedoc-Roussillon (reflecting IBM's presence at Montpellier) where jobs and wages each amount to 6 per cent of the respective national totals. Thus, as in the case of aerospace (and other 'high-tech' sectors) the potential advantages accruing from their growth, in terms of jobs and the multiplier effects from wages and subcontracting, are generally available only in a limited number of areas, many of which already benefit from a relatively prosperous economy.

Bull's position, in comparison with IBM, appears far less favourable. Not only is it a much smaller manufacturer, but the firm has also been making heavy losses, although with the help of government aid its investment programme has greatly increased: 4.5 billion francs were promised to the company between 1983 and 1986. The present

Table 3.6   Major companies in France specialising in the production of data-processing equipment, 1984

Company	Turnover *(billion francs)*	Employment
IBM-France	33.2	21 799
Bull	13.6	26 435
Hewlett-Packard	3.4	2 693
Burroughs	2.7	2 289
Texas Instruments	2.1	1 332
Digital Equipment-France	1.8	1 588

Source: Le Nouvel Economiste, Les 5000 – Classement des Premières Sociétés Françaises et Européennes, November 1985.

Bull group, which is nationalised, was formed in 1983 when the former CII-Honeywell Bull company merged with three smaller concerns to form a new flagship for the French computer industry. But this might be seen as only the latest stage of a long series of restructuring operations inspired by successive governments seeking to establish an important and independent French presence in this key industry. Arguably it has been the constantly changing patterns of organisation, ownership and strategy associated with this process that have previously compromised the group's commercial success; for example in the mid-1970s it had been decreed that the then CII-Honeywell Bull group should not be involved in the production of microcomputers, yet this was already seen as an area of rapid growth and one in which the French industry could mount an effective challenge against its foreign-owned competitors. Now the company appears to have a more coherent structure and strategy, in the latter case designed to ensure its presence in all sectors of the market; with its enlarged range of Micral micros the firm has substantially increased its sales of such machines. And, as an indicator of the firm's improved performance, it returned to profitability in 1985.

Other dimensions to growth

Expansion of the computer industry, whether in the French or foreign-owned sector, has been fostered by the vast extension of the applications of computerised systems and techniques. Such growth has in itself been rendered possible by two fundamental changes which have affected the product – miniaturisation and reduced cost. But to these general processes may be added a number of more specifically French influences. The popularisation of the computer was at first relatively slow in France and the public's awareness of its potential, whether for use in the business or the home, appeared to remain low. Even the number of people skilled in the use of computers (technicians, analysts, programmers) was (and still is) considered inadequate to match demand. Consequently various initiatives have been sponsored by the government aimed at rectifying this situation (not forgetting, of course, intensive publicity campaigns by the manfacturers to generate interest). One such initiative has been launched by the National Agency for Data Processing (Agence de l'Informatique) set up by the Socialists in 1981. It has helped create a series of regional centres providing instruction in the use of computers; these have to meet certain requirements in terms of their activities and equipment. To help promote the idea they are grouped together under the label 'centres X2000' and it is planned to set up at least 1000 of these centres by the end of 1986.

A further significant lead was given in January 1985 when Laurent Fabius announced his 'plan informatique pour tous'. In this case the prime aim was to equip schools (and to a lesser degree other educational establishments) with micros to familiarise children and students in their use. This was seen as a positive response to a major gap which had been perceived in educational programmes. Consequently during the remainder of the year schools and colleges were equipped, while their teachers were dispatched to special training courses run in the Easter and summer vacations to discover for themselves the mysteries of the computer. The whole operation was directed by Gilbert Trigano, of Club Méditerranée fame, who had already experimented with setting up computer facilities for young people in his holiday centres and who had been given a special brief by the President and Prime Minister to co-ordinate the programme. Now that the systems are in place it is expected that schools will also offer their services to the general public: whether this will prove popular (not least with teachers) has yet to be established. In total the 'plan informatique pour tous' has led to the purchase of nearly 122 000 micros valued at nearly 1.2 billion francs and herein lies the major interest for the French computer industry, for the government (not surprisingly) has opted to buy French. The Thomson group has benefited most, but Bull and Matra, as well as some of the smaller firms such as Exelvision have met part of the order.

Other examples exist of government policies designed to have a beneficial impact on high-tech industry, notably in the related area of telecommunications. In 1982 the decision was taken to equip France with a series of local cable networks, aiming to offer to the populations thus served programmes from local television stations (for which the go-ahead was given in 1985) and a range of information services, as well as access to transmissions beamed by satellite. The original plan was to use the technically superior fibre optic cables in establishing these systems, particularly as this would provide a valuable stimulus to the development of related French technology; and to help promote the idea an experimental network was established at Biarritz. Since then, however, proposals have been modified, partly due to the high cost of employing such materials; initially greater emphasis is being placed on the use of traditional co-axial cables which are considerably cheaper, although less efficient. Difficulties have also arisen over agreeing the exact conditions under which these stations could operate and over their commercial viability, at least in the short-term, particularly with the launching of two new national channels. Nevertheless, despite some initial hesitation, an increasing number (over 60 by 1986) of urban centres have reached agreement with the PTT on establishing a cable network. In December 1985 Cergy-Pontoise became the first town under this programme to inaugurate its cable network, bringing an important element of credibility to the venture. Whatever the problems, however, the Socialists' ambitious 'plan du câblage' has created a new and important challenge for the telecommunications industry, as well as having a much wider ramification on other sectors of activity – even the process of installing the necessary cables represents an extremely valuable business.

The success of Minitel
The major successful venture of both the telecommunications and data processing industries in the mid-1980s might be seen, however, as the introduction of the Minitel, giving access to the country's electronic telephone directory and a rapidly growing range of services offered by Télétel, the French videotex system similar in conception to Britain's Prestel service. The Minitel comprises a screen and console linked to the telephone which gives access to computerised data banks; entry to the system is made by dialling an appropriate telephone number. Experiments began in 1981 at Vélizy in the Paris suburbs using the Télétel services; then in 1983 the electronic directory was tested in the department of Ile-et-Vilaine in Brittany. Subsequently Minitels have spread rapidly throughout the country, equipping both homes and businesses. By the beginning of 1986 1.4 million were already in use, with this figure expected to double by the following year. Originally (in the late 1970s when the project was set in motion) it was intended to replace all paper telephone directories by this system; at the same time it was anticipated that the resulting large base of clients would act as a vital factor in the development of related information services. The Socialists then decided that the 'electronic directory' should be optional. While this will slow the extension of the system, the still sizeable and rapidly increasing number of users has already assured the growth of a substantial range of information services. The basic model of the Minitel is issued free of charge, but more sophisticated versions offering a wider range of operations are available for purchase or lease. Apart from simply providing information, the system also now allows various commer-

cial transactions to be carried out such as hotel, rail and airline bookings and credits and debits to a bank account.

For the PTT the system represents a considerable cost saving over the traditional methods of providing directory information: it is far more efficient, being capable of rapid updating and saves on conventional directory enquiries. From the public angle heavy usage suggests the Minitel is popular. Indeed so heavy has use been that it has caused over-loading problems for the Transpac data transmission network that relays the enquiries and information and is used extensively as well by businesses for their needs. The Minitel programme also represents a considerable commercial interest for the manufacturers of telecommunication equipment, although the current lack of export contracts might limit this potential. Nevertheless, with this exception the development of France's videotex industry represents a remarkable case of state-led success in the creation and commercialisation of a product.

Credit is also merited for the radical and long overdue modernisation and extension of the country's telephone service. Although this programme was completed under the Socialists, its origins again lie with the previous administration of Valéry Giscard d'Estaing. The fruits of this effort are now in evidence – a telephone service based on the most advanced technology (digital switching) and a vast increase in subscribers: their number rose from 4 million in 1970 to 23 million in 1985 with 88 per cent of homes by then equipped with a telephone. Public booths are now widespread, but as their number has risen so too has the problem of vandalism. In the centre of Paris a stage was reached where in any one month up to 40 per cent of the 7800 public call boxes were out of service for this reason, costing in a full year (1984) 15 million francs to repair.[40] Yet this situation has in itself produced a new response as card telephones, using the principle of Bull's smart card, are being introduced extensively in high risk areas – try telephoning from an area such as the Gare de Lyon without one!

Even a dynamic sector such as telecommunications, however, has been obliged to reorganise and reduce manpower. In part this is a response to the rapid pace of technological change, but it also reflects the completion of major investment projects such as the updating of the telephone service. But telecommunications, as well as the electronics branch as a whole, is seen to represent a key strategic industry for the country, and as such has received various forms of government financial support, although the need to subsidise heavily many basic industries where job losses have been high, has faced the government with a difficult choice of priorities. In 1983 approval was also given for a fundamental reorganisation of activities between the two major French companies in this field – Thomson and CGE. The former was to concentrate on military equipment, household goods and components, the latter on the 'communications' industry. In this respect the essential change was to link the telecommunications branches of the two groups in a new subsidiary, Alcatel-Thomson, under the control of CGE. Justification for this reorganisation stemmed from the need to create a French company of sufficient size to mount an effective challenge in a highly competitive market, but reorganisation has proved extremely disruptive and been associated with job losses. Restructuring, therefore, with its associated benefits and drawbacks is not just a feature of the country's traditional industries. Nor is it a process which has ended. This became apparent when the new Chirac administration with its liberalising philosophy considered breaking the monopoly held by the PTT in the provision of telephone services and giving its approval to a link between CGE and the American company ITT.

The high-tech regions

As the modernisation of French industry has become synonymous with technical innovations, this has implied the need for much greater emphasis on research and the associated development of new materials, products and manufacturing processes. This in turn has led to the growing recognition of the vital importance of the symbiotic relationship between universities and tertiary level education, research institutes and 'high-tech' industry. Thus the means by which sustained growth within the economy can be engendered and the manufacturing sector rendered more competitive has been equated increasingly with the development of these activities. At a local level this has been translated into the desire to foster an environment conducive to such expansion. Twenty years ago the creation of an industrial estate was considered the essential passport to growth; then the modified concept of an activity zone, incorporating not just manufacturing plants but also warehousing, offices and retailing was seen as a more realistic model. Now the accent is very firmly upon the science park, bringing together research laboratories and related production units; but while this is perceived as the most effective (and fashionable) strategy to pursue in the quest for new firms and jobs, all areas obviously do not possess the same potential for this form of development.

The dominant role of Paris

Already there are pronounced regional contrasts in the distribution of the country's 'matière grise' and only a restricted number of cities have succeeded in branding themselves with the label of 'high-tech'; for despite an apparently footloose character, in practice these activities display a high degree of spatial concentration. One measure of this uneven distribution is provided by the location of research centres. Paris dominates in this field, housing over half of the country's research workers, while behind the capital, a distant second, comes the region of Rhône-Alpes with just under 12 per cent of the total, suggesting that the notion of 'Paris et le désert français' still has considerable significance in an area vital to the process of economic growth. Even in the Paris region there is a far from equitable spread of research activity and related educational institutes; it is to the south-west of the capital that their presence is most marked, concentrated in an arc now extending for almost 40 kilometres between the new towns of St Quentin-en-Yvelines and Evry. Here are situated approximately 60 per cent of the country's 'grandes écoles' and 40 per cent of its research laboratories.

Activity is focused on the triangle of towns created by Orsay, Saclay and Palaiseau where the now vast complex of science-based establishments began to emerge in embryonic form almost 30 years ago. Amongst the original and most influential creations in this zone were a major research centre of the Commissariat à l'Energie Atomique, the huge science faculty (Paris XI) of the University of Paris, decentralised from its congested accommodation at the Sorbonne, and the prestigous Ecole Polytechnique. Alongside these dynamic leaders are now grouped a wide range of similar institutions which include the CNRS, Ecole Supérieure de l'Electricité, INRA, and the Institut d'Optique. Research laboratories of industrial companies, including those of large multinationals such as Thomson and CGE are also strongly represented, with over 50 per cent of the country's research potential in this field concentrated here. The existence of these activities has in turn attracted an extended series of dependent industries, estimated to number around 8000. Growth has been largely spontaneous with much of the area's appeal deriving from its high level of accessibility (including proximity to Orly airport) and an attractive outer suburban environment.

As part of its development strategy the new town of Evry has shown particular interest in deriving maximum benefit from its location at the eastern extremity of this 'high-tech' belt. Evry has been one of the more successful of the Paris region's new towns, and in seeking to maintain a high rate of growth, a policy of promoting the town as 'a centre of advanced technology' has been pursued increasingly actively since the early 1980s. Those responsible for the new town's development would no doubt claim substantial progress in realising this goal. Evry has been successful in attracting the French headquarters of the two prestigious American computer manufacturers Hewlett-Packard and Digital Equipment and also houses the head office of Arianespace. Their presence, and that of other data processing firms such as IBM, Bull, Micro-Contrôle and Logabax, which have production or distribution facilities in the new town, have greatly contributed to the creation of a high-tech image. To assist in the growth of this sector a 'technological park' is now under development (Parc d'Activités Bois Briard) based around Hewlett-Packard, and increasing emphasis is being placed on establishing the 'right' environment for high-tech firms and their personnel, involving such diverse action as landscaping and the building of executive housing. There is also now a substantial base of higher-educational and training facilities, geared to advanced technology industries, such as the Centre d'Etudes Supérieures Industrielles and the Institut National des Télécommunications. From this has grown a specialisation in the manufacture of electronics components, and equipment for the data processing and robotics industries, aided by such initiatives as the creation of ADECIR (Association pour le Développement à Evry du Centre de l'Informatique et Robotique), an organisation designed to foster co-operation amongst firms and to provide advice on development problems. Evry is certainly not yet a science-based city such as Grenoble or Toulouse, and here the emphasis is upon production rather than high-level research, but out of the town's 18 000 private sector employees nearly 30 per cent are now employed in the electronics, robotics and data processing fields.

Following the new town's lead, there is now some attempt to promote more actively the capital's southern high-tech zone, partly to encourage the more widespread utilisation of the area's research capacity through publicising its activities, and partly to help resist competition for investment from other similar zones equally anxious to enhance their status. To co-ordinate this strategy a special 'mission' was created in 1983, while the area itself became referred to as the 'cité scientifique d'Ile-de-France sud'. This choice of title, giving the impression of a cohesive unit, might be seen as assisting in the region's promotion, particularly in response to the challenge from other 'science parks', but for an area of extensive and discontinuous development, encompassing various other activities having little direct relationship with advanced technology, its appropriateness is questionable.

The number of provincial cities with a sizeable research sector and accompanying range of higher education establishments is limited. Toulouse, Bordeaux and Strasbourg are amongst some of the larger centres which fall within this category, but none challenges the leading position held by Grenoble where 10 000 people out of the city's work-force of 172 000 (1984) work in the research field. In this respect Grenoble far exceeds the importance of Lyon, its much larger and close neighbour; nearly 40 per cent of those employed in research in the region of Rhône-Alpes work in Grenoble. The city's reputation in this field was already established in the 1960s following the arrival of research units such as CENG (Centre d'Etudes Nucléaires de Grenoble), which depends on the CEA and from which itself grew the highly renowned Laboratoire d'Electronique et Technologie de l'Informatique (LETI), considered one of Western Europe's most eminent centres of research into microelectronics. More recently this strength in the development of silicon chip technology was reinforced with the setting up in 1978 of a major government research unit for telecommunications (CNET – Centre National d'Etudes des Télécommunications). Such laboratories are backed by three universities, grouping around 30 000 students and a series of 'grandes écoles' including the Institut National Polytechnique de Grenoble, the Ecole Nationale Supérieure d'Ingénieurs Electriciens and the Ecole Nationale Supérieure d'Electronique et de Radioélectricité.[41] Numerous links exist between these institutions, of both an informal and formal nature, illustrated in the latter case by the Centre Interuniversitaire de Micro-électronique opened in 1983. The bias towards training and research in electronics and microelectronics is also reflected in the city's manufacturing activities; Grenoble is a major centre for the production of electronics components, notably integrated circuits, with the electronics industry as a whole now employing nearly 9000 people in the city.

But Grenoble no longer displays the dynamism which underlaid its remarkable expansion in the 1960s and early 1970s. Less than a decade ago the idea still prevailed that while the recession might adversely affect the economies of other cities, this could not happen here: after all the industries upon which Grenoble depended were those of the future. Yet in recent years growth has slowed considerably, tarnishing the city's image of success. The rate of increase of the city's population has slowed markedly (as the number of newcomers is now exceeded by those leaving the city), the total level of employment has been increasing only slowly, with jobs having been lost at a high rate in industry (Table 3.7). Part of the explanation would appear to lie in factors influencing the pattern of growth in the country generally, such as lower birth rates, a reduction in immigration and a restructuring of industry in favour of capital rather than labour; also increasing decentralisation and suburbanisation, provoked by the constrained site of Grenoble, tend to give an exaggerated impression of a loss of dynamism in the city itself. However, there is also a feeling that during the years of rapid expansion insufficient emphasis was placed on attracting manufacturing activities compared with research, leading to a relative weakening of this sector of the economy. Whatever the cause, following an extended period of sustained expansion, adapting to a different and less attractive model of development has proved difficult for the inhabitants and their municipal authorities. The need for the city to capitalise fully upon its assets as a centre for high technology now appears of critical importance.

Table 3.7   Grenoble: changes in population and employment, 1975–82

a. *Employment*

		Total		*Mean annual rate of change (%)*
	1975	1982		1975–82
Industry	67 365	57 456		− 2.1
Services	89 160	100 832		+ 1.9
Total	157 365	158 288		+ 0.1

b. *Population*

	Total		*Mean annual rate of change (%)* 1975–82		
	1975	1982	Total	Natural	Migration
	387 353	390 849	+ 0.1	+ 0.9	− 0.8

Source: INSEE, *Recensement Général de la Population* (1982).

Science parks in fashion

At Grenoble, as elsewhere in France, the pursuit of this goal has become intimately linked with the development of a science park, referred to variously under such names as 'cité scientifique', 'parc technologique' and 'technopôle'. Whatever the subtleties implied by different forms of description the basic philosophy underlying these zones remains the same – the association of research, higher education and innovating industries. The 'model' for such growth is essentially American in origin, deriving from the extremely successful 'high-tech' industrial park which grew up spontaneously around the University of Stamford, leading to the creation of the so-called Silicon Valley. Similarly the 'science city' at Tsukuba in Japan is also regarded as an influential pioneer development in this field. Such experience suggests that for the creation of a successful science park certain essential features need to be present. The mix of activities indicated above is considered vital due to their supposed close interdependence and interaction. A site offering a high-quality environment is also deemed essential, representing part of the 'package' offered to attract investors and highly trained and skilled (and therefore highly sought-after staff). Proximity to major transport infrastructure such as an international airport is also important given the multinational character of many of the targeted companies and the importance of the exchange of information which occurs at this level. Interaction on the site and its general appeal are also enhanced by the provision of various common facilities such as a canteen, bars, sports facilities, seminar and conference rooms and hotels.

Much of the attraction of these areas, however, is seen to relate to image. High-tech implies an 'up-market' appearance with emphasis upon a working environment and lifestyle of quality. Firms investing in a science park might be likened to members of an elitist club, with the aura of sophistication and quality being to their mutual benefit. The ability to attract a number of major 'names' is also important, for their presence serves to enhance the credibility and desirability of such a location. In reality the situation appears considerably more complex. Innovating industries are inherently unstable organisations requiring to take risks. Just as there are 'winners', there are also 'losers' and selecting firms which form part of the first category is itself a challenging task. Furthermore, for a firm to be able to commence operations it frequently requires access to external funding, implying the need for a capital market prepared to underwrite projects where the potential gains are high but the risk element is also elevated. Here the French have displayed a certain hesitation in developing a system capable of generating a strong supply of venture capital, emphasising that the successful realisation of a science park is not only dependent upon the nature of the site and the complex itself but also on a much wider set of factors including attitudes to investment and development.

Over recent years the number of science parks, either under development or proposed, has multiplied rapidly, now totalling more than twenty (Figure 3.2). Given the concept's fashionable character and increasing evidence of the success of certain pioneering schemes, it is hardly surprising that local politicians and planning departments in the country's leading cities have sought to include such a project in their development strategies. The term science park, however, has come to cover a wide range of developments, not always corresponding very closely with the principles outlined earlier; similarly the extent of their realisation is highly variable. It is also somewhat questionable as to what exactly constitutes 'high-tech', with the result that precise definition and categorisation of these zones is difficult.

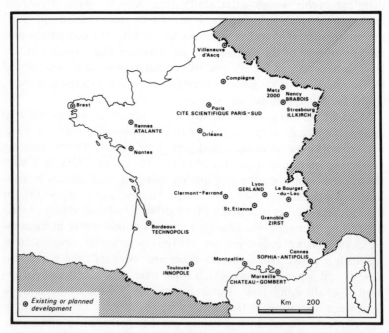

Figure 3.2   Science parks and zones of high-technology industries

Nevertheless certain generalisations might be made based on the state of present development and potential for future growth. Many of the 'technopôles' still exist only in embryonic form, as at Metz, Brest and Marseille, with little more than the site designated. Strong candidates for future expansion, but where there is still relatively little evidence of development, include Strasbourg, Montpellier, Nantes, Toulouse and Bordeaux. Rather more substantial progress has been achieved in a limited number of cities such as Nancy, Rennes, Lyon and Lille; but the two leading sites are clearly those at Grenoble and Sophia-Antipolis (Antibes) where development has been under way for more than a decade.

The Brabois science park at Nancy provides one illustration of a relatively small but increasingly successful initiative, established in an attractive wooded area to the south of the city. Over 40 hectares are currently available for development and the zone already has a growing mix of 'high-tech' ingredients – university and research centres and advanced industries such as ECM (Electronique Centrale Mesure) specialising in various electronic fields including robotics. While the Brabois park's future seems assured certain doubts remain about Metz 2000 and Lorraine's ability to support two such poles; cynics might even remark that the principal reason for the launch of the latter project was to challenge Nancy, continuing a long history of rivalry between the two cities. Lille has been less fortunate with its plans. From the early 1970s with the decentralisation of the university's science faculty to the eastern outskirts of the city and parallel creation of a new town (Villeneuve d'Ascq) it was envisaged that these two operations would provide the necessary stimulus for a 'science city'. But this has never fully materialised, despite the transfer of a large number of industries to the new town; indeed it is arguably the area's industrial rather than scientific image, and its associated working-class connotations, which have prevented Villeneuve d'Ascq realising its ambition.

Until recently it seemed that Lyon too had failed to capitalise on its potential for attracting 'high-tech' firms. Despite the stength of the city's facilities in higher education (three universities and a series of 'grandes écoles', and the presence of various research centres (e.g. Institut Mérieux, Rhône-Poulenc, SEPTEN, Elf-Aquitaine) specialising in fields such as medicine, pharmaceuticals and biotechnology, a significant multiplier effect bringing related science-based activities had not emerged. However, with the decision of the Ecole Normale Supérieure to transfer part of its teaching and research in the technical and scientific fields to a new complex in the district of Gerland on the southern fringes of Lyon's inner city, there is a strong expectation (at least amongst the city's politicians and planners) that this situation will change. Gerland is being extensively redeveloped and the Ecole Normale Supérieure is seen as the key element in the creation of a major scientific and technical complex. A number of laboratories already exist in this zone providing a further base for such development, but even if their number increases it is not immediately evident that this will lead to the intimate relationships between high-level teaching, research and innovating industries implicit in the concept of a 'science park'. In addition the area's present character is much more associated with that of an industrial zone (reflective of its proximity to Lyon's port area) rather than an environmentally attractive tertiary activity park, which may compromise its future. Nonetheless the plans for Gerland are ambitious involving considerable changes in its appearance, and the provision of extensive leisure and recreational facilities. But the project's biggest hurdle is likely to be the problem of finding the necessary resources and enthusiastic investors to support such development, especially as it is hoped to develop two other 'technopôles' on the city's northern and western fringes.

However, these various developments appear relatively insignificant compared with the science parks established at Sophia Antipolis, located at Valbonne on a low plateau in the Maritime Alps behind Antibes, and at Meylan on the eastern outskirts of Grenoble. Both are now regarded as highly successful operations, yet when first launched also raised doubts about their longer-term viability. Sophia Antipolis was the brainchild of Pierre Laffitte, former director of the Ecole des Mines and now a senator representing the department of Alpes-Maritimes, who saw the potential for reproducing in southern France the formula responsible for growth in California's sun-belt. In 1969 he set up a special association to promote this idea. Now a 'high-tech' park extends over 140 hectares, and includes more than 130 firms and organisations which have created directly in excess of 5000 generally highly paid jobs; it is estimated that a further 12 000 people are employed elsewhere in the local area due to the existence of this complex. The potential for future growth is vast, with 2000 hectares available for development. Companies attracted to the area range considerably in size and include a number of significant leaders in their respective fields, making an important contribution to enhancing the park's general image: Dow Chemicals has its French headquarters at Sophia, Digital Equipment has a manufacturing plant and technical centre, and Rohm and Haas and Dow Corning have major research laboratories on the site. Organisations in the public sector include bodies such as the CNRS and BRGM, while the Ecole des Mines represents the presence of higher education facilities.

Sophia-Antipolis has become much more, however, than simply a zone of economic and research activity. It has grown into an identifiable and apparently thriving community. The population of the commune of Valbonne increased from around 2200 in 1975 to just under 4000 seven years later, with residential development and related services based around the mushrooming village centre of Les Bouillides. Emphasis has been laid on the organisation of festivals and events with the aim of generating a sense of belonging, an ethos which is also intended to underlie the behaviour of the various companies present; the interchange of ideas is encouraged and actively promoted through regular seminars and discussion sessions.

Various explanations have been offered to explain the area's success. It undoubtedly benefits from an exceptional site, set amidst pine and mimosa forests and offering extensive views of both the coast and rugged mountainous terrain inland. The climate is equally appealing, while the area's natural attractions have been enhanced (for the businessman and Sophia's work-force) by a range of ancillary services, including an hotel and an up-market sports complex, the Sophia Country Club, with a particular focus on tennis. Proximity to Nice international airport and to the city's university represent further attractive features. But one vital additional influence might be seen as the efficient and innovative manner in which the complex has been managed: illustrations include the provision of a nursery zone to help small firms become established, and the creation of a consultancy service, 'Technopôle service', whose personnel use the experience of Sophia to advise on the varied aspects of establishing and managing a science park. Sophia has undoubtedly taken off, but growth has still not matched certain expectations (when first launched the government talked of 30 000 jobs by the end of the 1980s comparing the scheme's growth potential with that of Fos) implying that even high-tech is not immune from wider economic trends; or more likely that it is inherently not an activity conducive to large-scale employment creation.

A similar history of development applies to the science park at Meylan, known as ZIRST (Zone pour l'Innovation et les Réalisations Scientifiques et Techniques). This project first became a reality in the early 1970s when the municipal authority (of Grenoble) decided to create a special industrial zone designed to accommodate exclusively innovating industries and firms committed to the use or development of advanced technology. The aim, as elsewhere, was to capitalise on the city's very considerable potential in 'grey matter' – University, Institut National Polytechnique and a series of public and private research laboratories (e.g. CEA, CNRS, Air Liquide). A site adjacent to the Grenoble-Chambéry motorway was selected as an appropriate location for the scheme, lying amidst a relatively affluent residential district (Meylan) and close to the main university campus. Much of the basic thinking in this design was inspired by the Boston highway 128 model.

By the mid-1970s development was fully under way, led by a private company (Prozirst) formed specifically to promote the zone and its expansion. Policy was determined by certain principles which lay behind the conception of the Zirst. First, only specific types of firm would be accepted: they had to be engaged in research and development, producing advanced prototypes or offering a specialised service to high-tech companies. Overriding emphasis was placed on the soundness of the enterprise's capacity for research. Second, development was to be achieved in the context of the maintenance of a high quality urban environment. Firms had to agree to comply with various requirements concerning the design and presentation of their premises (relating, for example, to position, size and colour schemes), while the area's wooded and parkland character was to be preserved wherever possible. Third, the zone's development plan was kept 'flexible' to enable the accommodation of as wide a range and size of activities as possible; and fourth, communal services such as a restaurant complex were to be established to the mutual benefit of all firms in the 'park'.

On the 65 hectare site there are now over 140 firms providing nearly 3500 jobs. Most of the companies are relatively small in size, with 80 employing less than 10 workers, but there are a number of larger concerns such as Merlin-Gerin and CNET (Centre National des Etudes des Télécommunications), employing respectively over 300 and 1000 workers. The range of activities undertaken in the Zirst is also extremely varied, although approximately three-quarters of the firms are engaged in research or development related to the field of electronics; hence the view that this zone has come to constitute a 'mini' Silicon Valley.

Amongst the smaller enterprises two processes of development have emerged. Many firms have remained highly specialised in research work, and if involved in manufacturing, have limited their activity to the production of a restricted range of prototypes; once the product has been commercialised, research is switched to the search for different applications or the development of new ideas. This is the case, for example, of the firm Delphia which is concerned exclusively with research into advanced computer languages. Conversely other companies have sought to develop the manufacturing side of their business having conceived and tested an original range of products. X Com has grown in this way. The company was started in 1979, employing only 5 people, seeking to devise equipment for 'conference at a distance' facilities. Now the main preoccupation is to manufacture and market this product, which has involved movement into a larger factory and the growth of the work-force to over 150 people, with branches of the firm at Rennes and Paris. Amongst the larger concerns Merlin-Gerin is engaged in research into robotics and in the development and limited production of automatons, while the CNET is concerned with advanced research in telecommunications, resulting recently in the perfection of the SMS (semiconductor, metal, semiconductor) transistor.

Many of the same factors which account for the considerable growth of Sophia Antipolis also apply to the Zirst at Grenoble – a particularly attractive setting amidst the Alps, proximity to the national motorway network, the high quality of the environment of the science park itself and an innovative organisation responsible for its management. In this respect Prozirst has come to represent a further pioneer of nursery or incubator units for small businesses in their early stages of development, and was also responsible for providing the first ready-built units available for renting; yet despite the now proven popularity of this latter idea, initially Prozirst was unable to persuade the banking sector to provide the necessary financial backing – the venture was considered too risky and instead it was finally the commune of Meylan which underwrote the project. Similarly, in accounting for growth, proximity to the university, a series of research centres and a range of innovating companies has provided a climate ideal for producing individuals with the desire to set up their own small laboratory or business enterprise.

This latter feature also represents an illustration of the risks associated with high-tech industries, making it perhaps surprising that both these science parks should have proved successful; yet relatively few deaths have been recorded, for example, amongst the many small enterprises in the Zirst. Growth, however, has not been without its problems. Initial development in both cases was slow, leading at the time to speculation that this type of project was not a realistic formula for attracting investment and jobs, but also suggesting (again due to the risk element) that the processes of launching such a venture and establishing its credibility were longer than had been anticipated. In reality the success encountered by the Zirst in attracting firms means that there is now relatively little space for future development. Therefore, to extend the zone expansion is currently taking place on a site in the neighbouring commune of Montbonnet, although this has not been without difficulty due to disagreement and rivalry between the different municipal councils of the two areas – but this is not uncommon in France.

Two other essentially negative features apparent at Grenoble might also be outlined. Despite the existence of functional links between enterprises in the science park and companies or organisations outside this zone, relatively little interchange appears to occur between firms actually located on the estate, questioning therefore the need for such spatial concentration. Of more fundamental concern is that the many research-orientated enterprises of the Zirst have not succeeded in spawning a range of dependent manufacturing activities. Thus while the science park in itself might be regarded as successful it has not acted as a stimulus for wider growth in the city's economy, and has not led to the creation of a more extensive zone of activity within this part of the city. Why this has not occurred is hard to determine. Possibly inadequate priority has been accorded to the Zirst by the municipal authorities, as competition from other locations within the city for investment has shifted interest away from this zone. For the firms located on the Zirst itself there is also the problem that the move from research organisation to production unit is often a difficult step to take, requiring a very different outlook for those involved. It is for this reason that Prozirst is seeking to act as an advisory service to assist in this process and it is this challenge which faces the Zirst in the future if its contribution to the city's economy is to be increased significantly.

WHAT FUTURE?

In view of achievements in areas such as aerospace and telecommunications France could justifiably claim an enviable record of successes in the research and development of new technologies. Yet there are other key fields such as biotechnology and microprocessing where, despite the capacity for innovation, the French have been unable to realise this potential. Obviously, therefore, scope exists to improve the country's performance in developing advanced technology; moreover, if this is assumed to provide the essential base for a competitive industrial sector and therefore increased national wealth and social well-being, then change is essential. But this provokes the question of what action should be undertaken and how this should be achieved?

One response is to increase spending on research, particularly as during the 1970s France appeared to fall behind its major competitors in terms of the amount of its annual budget devoted to R and D. The Socialists acted to increase expenditure, with the result that it rose to around 2.5 per cent of GDP in 1985, placing France in a similar position on the international league table with rivals such as West Germany and the United States. However, there is also the issue of how this money should be used and it has been argued that too much of French spending has been in the public sector. While this may account for the country's strength in fundamental scientific research, it might also explain a relative weakness in the applied field, leading to the suggestion that France has sometimes lacked the ability to translate technical advance into sound industrial and commercial applications.

Thus progress is likely to be achieved as much by a change of attitudes as by an increase in funding. Research and development need to be carried out along less rigid lines with more emphasis given to the marketable character of the results. The same problem is also a feature of the manufacturing sector, for it is often not just production techniques which require revolutionising but also the processes of marketing and distribution. Again this is a field in which France traditionally has lagged behind certain of its competitors.

Finally in an intensely competitive trading environment and given the huge costs of developmental programmes, it is questionable whether France (or any other West European country) has the financial capacity to proceed simultaneously and effectively on several research fronts. As a result there has been increased interest in the idea of transnational co-operation, pioneered in the industrial sector and now seen as critical to the development of advanced technology. The Esprit project, strongly supported by France, and designed to enhance research and development within the EEC into information technologies is a prime illustration of this form of collaboration. Launched in 1984, it has since been followed by the more ambitious, and again largely French inspired, Eureka programme established by President Mitterrand in 1985; co-operation is envisaged in areas such as microprocessors, robotics, telecommunications, biotechnologies and the development of new materials. The political will for such joint action now appears evident not least as a response to the American 'star wars' initiative, but whether this can be translated into the efficient combined working of different national research teams has yet to be tested. Nevertheless in backing this project there is some indication of a fundamental change in French attitudes.

4 Revitalising the City

AN URBAN CRISIS?

At first sight the idea of a growing malaise in France's urban areas may appear rather strange. After all it is only comparatively recently that the country has become strongly urbanised. Since the early 1950s the number of urban dwellers has increased by 15 millions, so that now three-quarters of the population is officially classified as living in a town or city. Urban growth was seen as an essential factor in the modernisation and economic advance of a previously predominantly rural nation. During the 1960s and even in the early 1970s, the country's urban centres and not least its major cities epitomised the new, dynamic France. Rapid population growth was frequently accompanied by a similar increase in jobs; even if there were contrasts in economic performance between different sizes of urban centre and different parts of the country, the towns and cities were seen as synonymous with the country's impressive industrial development. Equally urban centres became the focus of a wide array of imposing building projects; this was the age of the urban motorway, redeveloped town centres, vast new peripheral housing estates and the provision of an extended range of new municipal facilities from theatres to swimming pools.

Nevertheless by the early 1970s there were signs of strains within a number of urban areas. A rapidly rising population may help sustain and invigorate the local economy, but it also induces problems of managing this expansion and synchronising the arrival of new inhabitants and jobs with the provision of related services and amenities – the French record in this respect has not always been very impressive. Similarly certain towns were already experiencing the negative effects of industrial restructuring, and were faced with the need to adopt strategies to encourage rather than limit growth. Yet there was little general appreciation of an urban crisis; the problem regions of the country were still largely seen in terms of 'la France profonde' – rural areas of the west and the Massif Central, their economic vitality sapped by generations of out-migration. To these were added a restricted number of the 'old industrial basins', mainly located in the north and north-east, but these were seen as essentially of secondary importance. If anything, the urban crisis was one of excessive attracti-

163

veness and undue pressure on services – hence the widespread preaching of economic decentralisation, a central feature of government regional strategy at this time.

Yet the situation in the 1980s has become very different. No longer are the country's urban areas experiencing a rapid growth of population; on the contrary in the major cities the number of residents is now falling, notably in Paris. Not that France is exceptional amongst industrial nations in experiencing this trend of residential movement away from the major cities; the tendency, generally referred to under the broad heading of counter-urbanisation, first became apparent in the United States in the early 1970s, since when it has progressively become a feature of a number of European countries, not least Britain. But in France the particular interest of this feature is the rapidity with which it has occurred, coming so soon after a period of intense growth and therefore representing a brutal contrast with the situation in the earlier postwar period.

Thus on demographic grounds alone the loss of vitality exhibited by the country's larger urban areas is suggestive of a certain rejection of urban society which might now be seen to exist. Other changes, many directly linked to the modified pattern of population growth, lend support to this contention. No longer do the major urban centres represent expanding labour markets, but instead areas of stable or even declining employment. Paris is now losing over 12 000 jobs each year, while a similar trend is observable in the large provincial capitals such as Lyon. In these centres office employment has generally held up relatively well; it is the industrial sector that has been particularly badly hit. Viewed in the wider context of the strongly negative effects of the recession on manufacturing employment, this is of little surprise, particularly in view of the past build up of industry in metropolitan areas. Previously decentralisation had been widely encouraged, not just from Paris, but from other large urban centres to their outer suburbs or surrounding area; in a situation of strong economic growth this was seen as inevitable and beneficial. Moreover, in many cases this represented either the disappearance of already marginal concerns from inner-city sites which were rapidly taken over for more lucrative use in the form of apartments or offices, or the transfer towards the periphery of expanding firms whose previous premises had outlived their useful life, offering no further scope for expansion. In such cases, for the city as a whole, jobs were not lost but instead were often considerably increased in number.

By the 1980s this had progressively ceased to be the case. Deindustrialisation was hitting many urban areas particularly hard – and no longer just the inner suburbs. As major manufacturers cut back severely on their manpower requirements, often this affected large plants on the outskirts of the city, a feature which was clearly seen in the Paris region with the substantial reduction in the work-force of the Peugeot (Talbot) plant at Poissy. At Lyon the pattern has been repeated in the case of the city's major industrial employer, (Renault Véhicules Industriels). Not only is the size of employment loss high in each case but, due to the considerable influence exercised by such plants on the local economy, the wider negative multiplier effects are also often significant, leading to the loss of jobs or short-time working in an extended series of dependent firms, as well as a significant reduction in wages to be spent in the local economy.

The elevated level of employment losses in industry has produced altered attitudes to decentralisation and new policy initiatives from local authorities. Now the aim is to retain and expand wherever possible established elements of the industrial base, whether it be in the inner or outer suburbs. It is not quite industrialisation at any price, but it is a marked reversal of the stance adopted a decade earlier. Promotional organisations have been created to stimulate interest (and hopefully investment) while a plethora of new locational options has been devised, ranging from the broadly based activity park to the more sophisticated and specialised science park. None the less, despite such initiatives the urban economies of major cities have lost their momentum. Fewer industrial jobs and a generally lower level of demand for manual workers or the less well-qualified has been translated into higher levels of unemployment notably amongst the young. Not unnaturally such circumstances have fostered the notion of crisis in the urban economy.

The same sentiment has also become a growing feature of urban society. Urban living has long been seen as involving additional costs and providing increased stress, but more recently it appears as more and more synonymous with some of the least attractive aspects of French society. Many of the potentially divisive forces which have emerged over recent years relate to essentially urban based problems. This is reflected in rising crime rates, increased racial tension, and the growing number of people who are homeless or without adequate income. Paris, like a number of other major European cities, experienced a substantial increase in the number of squatters in certain of its inner areas during the early 1980s, reflective of this situation. Similarly, over the same period, the level of unpaid rents in large estates of social housing also increased significantly. Other problematic features are also associated with housing conditions in major cities. Despite a major effort to enlarge and thus modernise the housing stock through a massive building programme, particularly from the late 1950s until the early 1970s, there are still numerous examples of sub-standard accommodation. The bidonvilles which characterised the above period may well have disappeared but there remains a large and growing problem of renewing or rehabilitating inner-city properties, where much of the housing is often of a considerable age and has been poorly maintained over many years. As an example, in the central areas of the capital half of the 1.3 million dwellings were built before 1914 and over 14 per cent before 1871. The shortcomings of many of these were recognised in the recent Merlin report which stressed the factors of age, smallness, a high proportion of tenants and lack of comfort as key features of residential properties at Paris.[1] The implication is that many of the capital's inhabitants are poorly housed, a situation which affects most those with modest incomes and thus inadequate purchasing power to improve their living environment. Hence the recommendation by the above report for the need to encourage the building of an increased number of subsidised dwellings accessible to the less well-off. Similar conditions may be found in the country's other large urban centres.

More worrying is the extent to which the same features of multiple deprivation and social malaise are now becoming evident in some of the recent postwar suburbs. Homes that have rapidly deteriorated in quality, high concentrations of the less favoured in society, and an atmosphere characterised by depression, tension, stress and insecurity have all become identifying features for many of the interminable apartment complexes found on the peripheries of almost any French town or city. Here 'on vit mal' and the notion of living in the 'banlieue' has increasingly taken on a pejorative sense, not always implying such undesirable features as outlined above, but certainly a mundane, anonymous and often wearisome existence in an unattractive urban setting. There would seem to be a strong case for suggesting that it is in certain of the large satellite or dormitory suburbs that the main problem areas of French cities are to be found in the 1980s.

There is also a political dimension to the current urban 'crise', expressed in a variety of forms. At a basic level there are a growing number of problems which municipal authorities have been forced to face relating to a significant reduction in their resources. A much reduced rate of employment growth, higher unemployment, and the disappearance of many firms whether through closure or transfer all imply a lower level of income for the city. At the same time central government has also sought to control much more stringently its expenditure, resulting inevitably in a reduction of its allocations to urban development projects, whether they be schools, hospitals or major improvements to transport infrastructure. Naturally this generates frustration on the part of local politicians and population alike, leads frequently to the raising of local taxation (and the increased unpopularity of certain people amongst the ranks of the former group) and results in less ambitious projects of development and improvement, or their deferment or abandonment. Certainly the disappointing performance of the Socialists in local elections in many urban areas during the early 1980s might be interpreted as a vote against deteriorating conditions; similarly the relative success of the National Front in the major cities of Paris, Lyon and Marseille in the European (1984) and General (1986) elections could be seen as the result of a protest vote, inspired by growing concern over issues such as the breakdown in law and order which had become increasingly prominent features of large urban areas.

Yet the Socialists did not ignore the problems prevalent in urban society; on the contrary, as part of the IXth Plan the government adopted a priority programme of improvement for the country's cities, under the heading 'mieux vivre en ville'. A strong accent was placed on rehabilitating run-down suburban areas, whether in the inner or outer parts of the city, and this emphasis is reflected in the subsequent and more detailed appraisal of this policy which is contained in the present chapter. But government action to ameliorate urban living conditions was much wider, including a strong commitment to improving public transport. Certain aspects of policy, however, generated considerable polemic, not least the 'loi Quilliot', passed in 1982, which sought to reform the private rented sector of the housing market. The law was popularly held to have given excessive rights to the tenant, resulting in a widespread reluctance to let property and a corresponding shortage of supply in this sector of the market, posing particular problems in the larger cities where demand for rented accommodation is traditionally strong. It is of little surprise, therefore, that Jacques Chirac's government should have proposed the early repeal of this legislation to create a fairer (?) balance between landlord and tenant.

As in the economic field, a liberalising tendency was to become apparent in the Socialists' policy towards urban development. The government agreed to the sale of state-subsidised, rented housing (HLM) and gave continuing support to the promotion of home ownership, a policy which had been adopted by the previous administration. Such decisions might appear unusual for a socialist government, but reflected realistic responses to popular demands. By decentralising various administrative responsibilities in the fields of urban development and management the Socialists also sought to make these processes more democratic. However, much of the effective control over planning appeared to remain vested in government ministries at Paris, a situation which the Right has again pledged itself to alter.

URBAN CENTRES LOSE THEIR DYNAMISM

The pronounced slow-down in the rate at which the population in urban centres has been increasing is part of a much wider reversal of demographic tendencies in France, as growth generally has eased (Table 4.1). The trend has been most evident in the country's major cities (Paris, Lyon, Marseille and Lille) and in the older industrial centres, such as St Etienne, Valenciennes, Lens and Rouen, where former staple industries have seen their previous vigour and influence greatly eroded under the recession (Figure 4.1). The extent to which population growth has been checked is revealed by the fact that in many cases there is now an overall loss of inhabitants from these

Table 4.1   Variations in populations, 1962–82

	Mean annual rate of change (%)								
	Total change			Natural change			Migrational change		
	1962 –68	1968 –75	1975 –82	1962 –68	1968 –75	1975 –82	1962 –68	1968 –75	1975 –82
France (overall)	1.1	0.8	0.5	0.7	0.6	0.4	0.5	0.2	0.1
Urban areas	1.8	1.1	0.2	0.8	0.8	0.6	1.0	1.0	−0.4
Rural areas	−0.4	—	1.1	0.3	0.1	−0.1	−0.7	—	1.2

Source: Boudoul J. and J. P. Faur, 'Renaissance des communes rurales ou nouvelle forme d'urbanisation?', *Economie et Statistique*, no. 149 (1982).

169

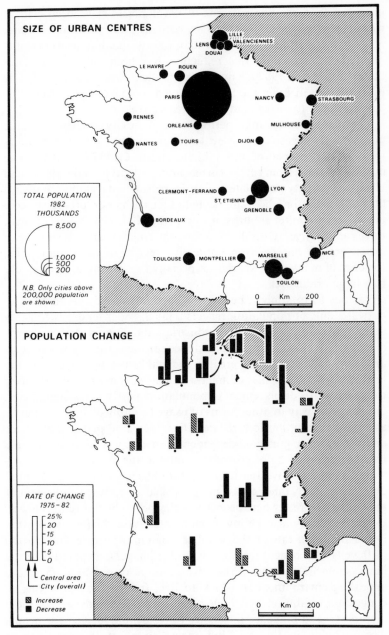

Figure 4.1   Major urban centres in France, 1982

urban areas. Changing patterns of development have been evident within the city as well. By the 1980s virtually all the central and inner zones of urban centres with more than 100 000 inhabitants were losing population: frequently this reduction has been substantial. Thus between 1975 and 1982 the number of residents in central Paris fell by over 130 000; in Lyon the loss amounted to 45 000 and in Marseille and Toulouse to 35 000 and 31 000 respectively.

The altered demographic performance of the city as a whole and the now strongly negative trends evident in inner areas are due essentially to a marked reversal of migrational patterns (Table 4.1): the strong drift of migrants from rural to urban areas, apparent in the 1960s, had given way twenty years later to an increasingly developing outward flow of population, the result being to focus urban or 'urban induced' growth on the outer suburbs of towns and cities or in adjacent small towns and villages. Overall, therefore, the counterpart to a slowing of urban growth has been an impressive revival of the demographic fortunes of many rural districts, especially those located in proximity to a large urban area.

Various factors might be seen to have influenced this trend. The outward shift of population reflects a much wider tendency towards decentralisation, with many industrial and commercial activities demonstrating an increasing preference for the periphery where costs are lower and accessibility greater. Inevitably as jobs move so do the related workers. Schemes of inner-area renewal have also contributed to the outwards displacement of population, partly as residential land use has given way to other forms of usage (notably offices) and partly as redevelopment has lowered densities. Increased personal affluence and a desire for greater independence on the part of young people have contributed to a growing trend for the various generations within a family to live apart. This in turn has helped lower residential densities in many inner areas, and provoked an outward movement of the young, to areas where property is cheaper to buy or rentals lower. Other costs may also be lower, with rates (taxe d'habitation) often levied at a lower rate on the periphery than in the centre. Outer areas of the city also benefit from a favourable image. Compared with the inner suburbs, the rural/urban fringe is perceived as a far more appealing environment in which to live, free of such problems as congestion, pollution and high crime rates. Not only do all these factors serve to influence the choice of residential locality for people already living in the city, but they also affect the decisions of newcomers.

The growth of home ownership

In the French case such general influences have been given an added impetus by two related movements – an official policy of seeking to extend the level of home ownership (currently 51 per cent of French householders are owner-occupiers) and a similarly government-led initiative of promoting the building of houses as opposed to apartments, the latter form of construction having dominated urban development in the 1960s and early 1970s. By the latter period, in response to growing criticism of the large estates on which apartment blocks were frequently concentrated, efforts were already under way to reduce their scale, and to modify their form and composition through the introduction of a wider variety of architectural styles and attempts to achieve a greater social mix of the residents. A parallel movement favouring the increased construction of houses as opposed to apartments was also developing, stimulated by a wide range of influences. Hostile reactions to apartment living, and changing preferences and aspirations on the part of potential residents concerning their accommodation were major factors. So too was the existence of a reorganised and more flexible building industry, facing less pressure to provide homes quickly and in great number as the problem of the housing crisis of the 1960s had diminished. Moreover, a lead was originally given by the innovative planning taking place in the country's then recently launched new towns. Since this period the amplitude of this movement has grown considerably so that by the mid-1980s two-thirds of all dwellings being built were in the form of houses rather than flats, almost reversing the situation which existed a decade earlier (Table 4.2). Considerations of land availability and cost have ensured that the greater part of this movement has taken place on the urban periphery.

For those tempted (and with the necessary means) to invest in a new property, the choice around the outskirts of virtually any French town or city is extremely wide. There is no doubt that the 'maison individuelle' is 'à la mode'. Originally relatively expensive, frequently built 'sur demande' in comparatively select locations and generally small numbers, it has now become a product of mass consumption. Estates (or lotissements) have mushroomed and with this trend densities have increased and individuality of design has been sacrificed for greater uniformity, as many such developments have come to resemble their British counterparts. The image portrayed by the home builders and house agents is very much one of the 'good life' – 'le bien-

Table 4.2   Changing patterns of house building

| | Dwellings completed each year | | |
	Houses	Flats	Total
1970–73 (average)	206 933	296 167	503 100
1980	250 200	128 100	378 300
1981	249 900	141 000	390 900
1982	218 600	117 700	336 300
1983	208 300	105 800	314 100
1984	181 700	89 100	270 800

Source: Ministère de l'Urbanisme, du Logement et des Transports, *Statistiques de la Construction* (1985); M. Pagès, *La Maîtrise de la Croissance Urbaine* (Paris: Presses Universitaires de France, 1980).

être accessible à tous' as one builder suggests. Tranquility, pleasant semi-rural surroundings, traditional building styles are all themes which are strongly developed, accompanied by the choice of names aimed to evoke these features – 'le hameau (de Crécy)', 'les campagnardes', 'les maisons du terroir' and 'les cottages (de Mions)' are all typical of this trait. The reality is sometimes very different; high land and building costs, and the desire to widen the market by facilitating entry to it (i.e. lowering the cost) have resulted in tightly-packed estates with few of the 'charms' outlined above. In addition shops and other services are frequently absent or inadequate in number and range.

However desirable it might seem to own a home, for many people this can only be achieved by contracting a sizeable loan. If such loans are expensive and not readily available then obviously the market for new houses is likely to remain relatively small. This was certainly the case in France until around ten years ago when a fundamental reform of the financing of house building and home ownership was undertaken, inspired by none other than Raymond Barre. The reforms (which took effect from 1977) had as their basic aim the transfer of a substantial part of state subsidies from the constructors to individuals: in addition they introduced a new system of state-backed loans to facilitate home ownership; these are known as the 'prêt aidé par l'état pour l'accession à la propriété (PAP)' and the 'prêt conventionné (PC)'.[2] The former is the most significant for it is subsidised by the state and therefore benefits from particularly low rates of interest; as such it is designed to assist those people with relatively low incomes or large families (or both), groups who previously were frequently excluded from the housing market due to the high interest rates applying to conventional bank loans. Both these new sources of mortgage finance also offer people the right to qualify for assistance with repayments from a further state subsidy, the personal housing allowance (aide personnalisée au logement – APL).

The importance of these loans has been seen in the reaction of the building industry, with a growing trend to provide properties conforming to the conditions laid down for obtaining a PAP or PC; thus, just as in Britain it is common to see homes on new estates advertised 'with mortgages available', so this is now a feature of many French 'lotissements' where houses are offered for sale with 'possibilité d'un PAP'. This movement may not constitute a 'revolution' but it marks a profound change in behaviour which, after a slow beginning in the late 1970s, has become far more evident in the early 1980s. Confirmation that the government has supported this trend has been provided by its efforts to increase the availability of PAP and PC loans, and to maintain highly competitive rates of interest. However, these measures might also be seen as a means by which to revive the flagging building industry which, with a substantial fall in demand, has been in constant difficulties throughout the 1980s.

Irrespective of these issues, it is possible to detect two important consequences of the decision to build more houses and to facilitate the access to home ownership. First, this has directed a growing current of first-time buyers towards peripheral housing estates, encouraging them in part to shun the more traditional apartment market. Second, for those people who in the 1960s moved into rented apartments at a time of housing shortage and perhaps relatively low personal incomes, there is now a tempting option to move to a house as their means have increased and the choice of home has widened considerably; for many the chance has been offered to leave behind the drab and increasingly undesirable environment of the large flat complexes for the quiet of the individual house. But such movement has only served to compound the growing series of problems now characterising these estates. There is a third and more unwelcome result which relates to the financial implications of these trends. From the individual's point of view the relative ease of obtaining a home loan has encouraged certain people to become over-committed, posing severe financial difficulties as the recession led to a cut in real incomes, while the fall in the rate of inflation meant that the burden of large loan repayments was reduced far more slowly. Viewed from the government's position all is not well either; the reforms of 1977 have proved increasingly expensive, relating to the growing popularity of the PAP and to the rise in the number of families encountering financial difficulties and becoming eligible for other forms of subsidy such as the APL, a problem not unrelated to the previous issue. The system requires further reform, a question the Socialists avoided, but as constraints on public spending continue, it seems increasingly inevitable.

Problems of the building industry

In the early 1970s over 500 000 new homes were being completed each year in France, yet by the mid-1980s this total had fallen to under 300 000 (Table 4.2). The marked slow-down in the country's rate of population growth would appear to have taken its toll. Undoubtedly this factor has been of major significance but other influences might also be seen to have played a role. During the 1960s and early 1970s there was an urgent need to respond to an accumulated shortage of homes, aggravated by a high rate of population increase and particularly by a heavy influx of migrants from outside France and by the strong movement to urban areas. This problem has now been resolved and indeed there are now nearly 2 million vacant homes in France. In such conditions it is only to be expected that the demand for new housing should fall, although there is some evidence to suggest that the effective slack in the market is much less than is implied by the above figure, not least due to the distortions resulting from the 'Quilliot' reform.

A more basic problem has been posed by the worsening economic conditions of the 1980s which have done much to slow the rate of house building. The high level of inflation has helped push up the cost of building land (which in many cases has also become in much shorter supply as land use controls and planning procedures have been made more stringent), while house building costs have also risen substantially, outstripping increases in personal incomes. Despite the existence of loans such as the PAP, generally high interest rates have further discouraged potential purchasers, while the government, as part of its policy of reducing public expenditure, has sought to diminish its level of funding of the public housing sector. Thus the early 1980s have also been marked by a housing crisis, but of a very different character. In this case it has not been a question of shortage;

on the contrary demand has been inadequate to meet supply, as high unemployment, greater insecurity of employment, and a stable or declining level of purchasing power have discouraged house purchase and investment in property. The consequences for the construction industry have been severe and in turn have had a serious effect on a series of dependent activities manufacturing products ranging from bricks to internal fitments. Moreover, this has been combined with a much wider cut-back in construction projects as private investors have hesitated and public purses have been squeezed.

Various indicators attest to the amplitude of the problems currently facing the building and civil engineering industries. Twenty years ago this activity was one of the most dynamic in the economy; jobs were increasing at a rate of over 4 per cent per annum, far outstripping expansion in the tertiary sector. Now the situation is very different. Between 1980 and 1985 the once buoyant construction industry was losing jobs at the rate of around 4 per cent each year while employment in services continued to grow at an annual rate of 1.1 per cent. During 1984, a particularly bleak year for the industry, the building sector alone lost 73 000 jobs, its turnover fell by 4 per cent and 2500 firms went out of business.[3] But despite such ravages the construction and civil engineering sector as a whole remains a major employer, still accounting in 1985 for 1.7 million workers.

Not surprisingly the amplitude and persistence of the industry's erosion have led to frequent demands for assistance from the government. Under the Socialists some positive response was forthcoming, aimed at encouraging home buying (and thus stimulating the building industry) and launching a number of new public works or infrastructural projects. Such measures culminated in the adoption in the early part of 1985 of a special and more comprehensive programme, 'le plan du relance du bâtiment et des travaux publics', to help revive the industry. For the house building sector this plan offered lower interest rates for those borrowing under the PAP system, as well as an increase in the amount of interest on home loans qualifying for tax relief; for the civil engineering branch it was proposed to encourage activity by releasing 700 million francs from the government's special fund for infrastructural works (fonds spécial des grands travaux). Theoretically the government also had the power to persuade some of the major public companies to increase their level of investment (e.g. SNCF, Gaz de France, Electricité de France) but this is often a delicate issue particularly at times of tight budgetary constraint or when development strategies imply less rather than increased investment (such as the reduction in the building of nuclear power stations). Within the industry these proposals were greeted with a certain scepticism: this was not the first time a government had produced a package of measures to stimulate activity, and previous experience suggested that the impact was likely to be limited. Doubts existed over the efficacy of the type of measures proposed. It could be argued that the housing market is unlikely to expand significantly until real incomes start to grow more rapidly and interest rates fall substantially, changes which are only likely to occur in the context of a general revival of economic activity. However, one encouraging sign for the industry (and partial vindication of government measures) was a much reduced rate of job loss in 1985, with employment falling by only around 1 per cent.

Even if economic recovery does induce renewed expansion in this sector, the scale of activity is unlikely to rival the situation ten or fifteen years ago; certain outlets for the industry have now disappeared, illustrated by the virtual completion of the country's motorway building programme. The limited impact of government measures, and the changing requirements of the country are among factors, therefore, which have encouraged the more dynamic firms to reorientate their activities. One option has been to seek contracts abroad, a path taken by many civil engineering enterprises. Their presence is now evident in numerous less developed countries, whether it be in South America, North Africa or South-East Asia, as well as in the Gulf States. But even here there are difficulties – a reduction in the number of major schemes being undertaken due to constraints on spending and as a consequence of these countries themselves becoming better equipped; a far more competitive market as a growing number of firms from other developed countries have adopted a similar strategy, and as local industries have increasingly attained the necessary level of competence to undertake the work themselves; and, in this latter context, the requirement specified in contracts that local sub-contractors should carry out a certain proportion of the work.

The need for adaptability may be seen in other ways. As house builders have seen their costs rise and the demand for their product fall, they face even greater pressure to secure sales; otherwise they risk going out of business, as has happened in many cases. But for those with sufficient initiative, flexibility or resources (or all three), the other alternative is to improve or vary their 'product', thus hopefully increasing its appeal. One of the easiest methods for the builder to reduce his outlay and not necessarily alter the basic attractiveness of the house is to complete it to a lower level of interior finish – surfaces and walls are no longer painted or papered; kitchens no longer 'fully equipped'. Over recent years this trend has become widespread and has been taken further with the idea of offering houses 'prêtes à finir', frequently providing the potential for an economy of up to 30 per cent on the price.[4] In these cases it is left to the purchaser to complete to a greater or lesser extent the interior of the house – from partition walls to electrical circuits and fittings. (It is tempting to suggest that the image of France as a nation of peasant farmers has been replaced by one of a nation of 'bricoleurs'!). It is still questionable whether there is a substantial market for such basic constructions, for the work to be completed represents a sizeable task, requiring a range of skills not all of which are readily learnt; moreover the cost of repairing any inadvertent 'damage' might well cancel out the original saving. None the less such developments illustrate again the search for diversification and inventiveness.

REHABILITATING INNER URBAN AREAS

Despite the large-scale of construction since the early 1950s, France still possesses a considerable stock of much older housing. Nearly a third of the country's 24 million dwellings were built before 1915 and in many of the larger cities this proportion is much higher, rising to over 50 per cent in the central area of the capital. This factor has frequently produced a growing need for the replacement or improvement of dwellings. In many cases apartments or houses no longer meet current safety or sanitary standards, or fall short of potential residents' expectations in terms of their restricted size or lack of facilities. The same quarters in which such accommodation is generally found have also often become associated with a range of social and economic problems, whose very existence and concentration in these areas further testify to the deterioration of the built environment. Here are concentrated groups of people who for one or a number of reasons have become less favoured members of society: the unemployed, those with few qualifications or skills, the elderly, immigrants and those with relatively low incomes. A number of other adverse characteristics are also often linked to these conditions, not least a comparatively elevated crime rate, and a reputation as an unsafe part of the city.

Obviously these are not features found throughout the urban area.

Originally they became particularly associated with certain inner districts of the larger cities where their incidence has often been aggravated by the decline of employment, notably in manufacturing activities; furthermore the rejection of such areas as a living environment has been reflected in a growing outflow of population. In the face of such conditions, the need for remedial action has long been recognised, resulting in the marked transformation of many central and inner quarters of the country's major cities. In Paris the redevelopment of the Italie quarter offers a classic example of large-scale renovation where the 'solution' to many of the problems cited above has been the complete demolition and replacement of the previous built-up area, accompanied by widespread restructuring with new road layouts, shopping centres and leisure and recreational facilities. Numerous other illustrations of this approach exist in the provincial cities: le Tonkin at Lyon, Alma-Gare at Roubaix in the Lille conurbation and the left-bank quarter of St Sever at Rouen represent but three examples.

As in other countries, renewal of this type has often attracted criticism, ranging from adverse comment over the unnecessary loss of many buildings of historic interest, to a similar reaction to the brutal character in which the previous population, of only modest means, has often been displaced. Partly as a result, the number and scale of such operations have diminished, although as the worst conditions have disappeared this has also had a natural depressant effect on schemes of renovation. Yet, even in the mid-1980s, this solution is still proposed in certain cases where there is an advanced state of physical deterioration and social malaise. Again it is in the capital where such problems remain most apparent. The scale of proposed intervention is more modest than before, but potentially the need is even greater, as the recession has accentuated the difficulties of the less favoured in society. The quarter of Goutte d'Or in the 18th arrondissement of Paris, lying to the north and east of the metro station Barbès-Rochechouart, highlights these conditions of squalor and deprivation.

Here in the space of approximately 6 hectares live around 8000 people, the majority of whom are foreigners.[5] Indeed one of the predominant features of this area is the cosmopolitan character of its population. Algerians, Moroccans and Tunisians, or people of such descent, are most numerous, but there are other distinctive racial groups from areas such as the French West Indies and Black Africa. Undoubtedly this brings further colour and variety to an area that has long had the reputation as a 'quartier chaud' and is renowned for the marginal character of many of its activities including prostitution and drug pushing. But this does not conceal the underlying features of poverty and decay which have prompted the decision to renovate. While this should ensure a far better standard of accommodation and the provision of long-absent facilities, it also implies the permanent disappearance of many of the district's inhabitants and of its traditional commercial activities. For a certain sector of the populaton, therefore, the project represents an unwelcome threat to their life-styles rather than the promise of a much better living environment. Even in the case of Goutte d'Or, however, it is not proposed to demolish and rebuild the whole quarter, as might have happened twenty years ago. Over half of the buildings are likely to be retained and improved, reflecting on a much wider scale the greater importance that is now accorded to rehabilitation rather than renewal.

Policy initiatives

The idea of improving rather than replacing buildings is not new. Ever since the early 1960s schemes have been launched (under the Loi Malraux) to restore and conserve a wide range of buildings of historic interest in numerous French towns. Subsequently the scope of such work was enlarged to cover residential property, particularly at the lower end of the market; it was in this sector that certain basic items of comfort were often lacking (e.g. bathroom, internal WC) or maintenance had long been neglected and therefore a state of dilapidation was most advanced. As this has occurred the philosophy behind urban renewal schemes has also been modified. While the demolition of dwellings might often have been seen as essential due to their excessive degree of deterioration, such operations frequently implied the replacement of a previously relatively poor population by a more affluent group of residents. Indeed this was often the implicit if not explicit aim of the scheme given the high value attached to inner area sites. Since such operations have been undertaken not only has there been an adverse reaction to the large-scale and questionable aesthetic qualities of the architectural style of many redevelopment projects, but also to the accompanying social change. Thus rehabilitation became seen increasingly as a means of avoiding many of these less satisfactory characteristics, particularly as it was envisaged that this would enable a far greater number of the original residents and owners of shops and small businesses to remain in 'their quartier'. More recently other influences have strengthened the trend towards improvement. These range from the emphasis now given to insulating buildings against heat loss, as part of the government's programme to conserve energy, to the desire to promote rehabilitation work as a means of absorbing some of the excess capacity currently so apparent in the building industry.

To encourage this movement both left and right wing governments have sponsored a number of measures to try to reduce the financial burden of improvement, to make such action more comprehensive in terms of the number of buildings rehabilitated in any one sector of intervention, and to co-ordinate this work with other 'environmental' improvements. In particular efforts have been directed towards the private rented sector, reflecting the predominance of this type of property in inner areas. Thus as early as 1971 the Agence Nationale pour l'Amélioration de l'Habitat (ANAH) was set up to administer and finance rehabilitation work; any landlord may apply for an improvement grant for a property built before 1948 and such subsidies usually cover between 30 and 40 per cent of the cost of improvement. Then in 1977 the idea of 'housing improvement areas' (opérations programmées d'amélioration de l'habitat – OPAH) was instituted, corresponding to a similar philosophy which led to the designation of 'general improvement areas' (GIAs) in Britain. In the same year the government established an 'urban development fund' (fonds d'aménagement urbain – FAU), replacing an earlier more complex system of financial assistance, to which local authorities could apply to help fund various accompanying social and environmental improvements (e.g. a crèche, improved road access) in rehabilitation areas. Over the same period measures were also taken to provide a system of grants for which owner-occupiers could also apply to help fund certain work and a similar subsidy (referred to as PALULOS) to enable the rehabilitation of apartments in the state subsidised sector of the market (HLM). Additionally various forms of low-interest loan became available to assist with the cost of repairs and modernisation; for example, the state-backed PAP and PC may be used for this purpose when a property is purchased, providing it is over 25 years old. In such a case, however, between a quarter and a third of the total cost of the operation must be represented by the outlay on improvements. Thus over a number of years an increasingly comprehensive system of assistance (although not always particularly generous) has become available to further the goal of generally improving the quality of older properties.

Of these various measures, one of the potentially most influential is that of the OPAH; under this arrangement it is the responsibility of a local authority to designate an improvement area and to negotiate a contract with both the state and the ANAH. This gives the right to landlords and tenants to qualify for a grant from the ANAH, at a higher rate than normal, and for low interest loans underwritten by the government to further assist in covering the cost of rehabilitation. Once the agreement has been signed, the work has to be carried out in a period of three years. Despite the official designation of an improvement area, there is however no obligation on the part of residents or the owners of property to carry out such work, although it is frequently strongly advised by the agencies responsible for carrying out such schemes. Under the arrangements of the agreements which govern these operations, certain conditions also apply to those who benefit from assistance. For example, the person to whom a grant has been made is allowed to raise the rent charged, but for a period of ten years after the completion of improvements the amount of the increase is limited by the state. At the same time the tenant is given the chance to apply for a government subsidy (APL) to cover at least part of the increased rent, and it was through this provision that it was anticipated that it would be possible to retain in an area a significant proportion of the original residents.

Examples of change

The above measures, changing attitudes to the remodelling of urban areas and a reduced availability of funds, both from the government and the private sector to finance major development schemes, have all combined to promote an increasing movement of rehabilitation. A substantial rethinking has also occurred in the design of a number of redevelopment schemes, a trend first seen on a large scale in Paris in the 1970s. This revised philosophy has been seen over recent years in a part of the 14th arrondissement known as the Guilleminot-Vercingétorix sector. Here, in a densely built-up area lying parallel to the railway tracks which converge on Montparnasse station, the lack of amenities and advanced state of deterioration of the housing, much of it dating from the last century, were particularly marked. But the original plans to remodel completely this quarter have been abandoned, including the idea of a major expressway leading to the outer suburbs, and although some renewal is still being carried out, emphasis has shifted to a policy of conservation and improvement.

In the provincial cities a similar evolutionary pattern is evident. At Lyon the run-down, left-bank quarter of Paul-Saxe Bert, lying to the west of the prestigious new central business district of la Part-Dieu, was scheduled for large-scale renewal in the mid-1970s, the proximity of the above centre adding greatly to the appeal of such an operation in the eyes of the private developers responsible for its realisation. Ten years later, following intense local opposition, a 'softer' approach is being pursued, focused on the progressive rehabilitation of certain residential streets and the limited replacement of the most insalubrious districts. A similar pattern is evident at Marseille in the Belsunce district to the north of the Vieux-Port; this is the city's kasbah, colonised and dominated by a population of North African descent and featuring the colour, culture and customs of these people; sixty per cent of the resident population are officially registered as foreigners. Many are still housed in appalling conditions. Over four-fifths of the dwellings were built before 1915, 90 per cent are in the private rented sector and 40 per cent have either no piped water or no interior WC. Moreover, at the last census (1982) nearly three-quarters of the residents were classified as living in a state of overcrowding, with over half in a severe condition. These might be seen as convincing statistics to justify renewal and this was the original intention. Yet although part of the area is being redeveloped, plans have been revised to favour rehabilitation. Such a decision might be seen as particularly enlightened given the area's undoubted character and its close-knit society; yet there is a racial dimension to the issue and given the large size of the immigrant community involved, a gradual approach to change might be seen as a pragmatic solution to the need to improve living conditions in a sensitive district of the city.

Assessing the impact

Now after a decade during which increased emphasis has been placed on rehabilitation policies, it would appear an appropriate juncture to evaluate this approach. In this respect, whatever the advantages of improvement as opposed to replacement, it is also possible to detect certain shortcomings. While there has been a continual increase in the number and value of grants given to assist in rehabilitation, particularly since the early 1980s, and in the number of officially designated operations (OPAH), of which over 400 were in progress during 1984, there is some evidence to suggest that the present scale of work is inadequate in view of the still large number of substandard properties. For example, in the Paris region (Ile-de-France) it is estimated that over 250 000 old apartments require improvement, yet at present only around 13 000 are being rehabilitated each year.[6]

It might be suggested that this reflects the relatively low level of financial assistance that is available and therefore a certain lack of incentive to improve. In the rented sector grants rarely exceed 50 per cent of the total cost of improvement and for owner-occupiers their value is extremely low; in this case the grants (prime à l'aménagement de l'habitat) not only have a very modest ceiling but are also means-tested. Moreover, these subventions are generally paid after the work is completed (or at least a certain part of it) resulting in an additional financial burden. There are also a number of other potentially dissuasive influences. Taking up a grant from the ANAH places a landlord under various obligations, which are perceived by some people as being counter-productive. An improved property may not be sold for up to ten years, the aim being to discourage rehabilitation carried out purely for speculative reasons; but this constraint also induces a degree of reluctance to undertake such work. Equally the requirement in the case of an OPAH that rents should be controlled for a similar period is also seen as a major limitation for there are too many memories of the difficulties which certain landlords have faced in trying to raise rents due to the controls of the 1948 Rent Act. Such considerations have led to a situation where if the demand for property is strong, there is often a reluctance to participate in an official programme of rehabilitation; this frequently implies a con-siderable financial outlay, but with few short-term benefits. In an OPAH, grants from the ANAH are accorded on the basis of certain specified work being carried out to a given standard, particularly in terms of amenities such as bathrooms and toilets; improvement, therefore, can be expensive but subsequent rent increases are limited. Thus, in areas such as central Paris the unscrupulous landlord would appear to have a considerably greater personal interest in undertaking the minimum amount of remedial work at his own cost (although still being able to benefit from low interest loans), and retaining the freedom to determine the level of rent he then wishes to charge. Certain practical problems have also arisen. Rehabilitation is not compulsory, even within the OPAH, yet in an apartment building sub-divided amongst several owners, where structural work is required, it is obviously essential to have the agreement of all parties; frequently this has not been readily forthcoming and hence has restricted progress.

Confirmation of the apparently limited efficiency of the state's initiatives in this field is given by the fact that, despite an increase in the number of improvement areas set up under the OPAH policy, the majority of rehabilitation work takes place outside of such structures; and the role of grants from the ANAH is similarly restricted. Evidence from Lyon suggests that only a third of improvements carried out in the city during the early 1980s was funded from this latter source, while at Paris the proportion has been even lower; nor has there been any sign of a more recent change in the situation. In general, therefore, it is the owners themselves of property who finance the greater part of improvement work. Presumably they are motivated by the investment potential which they feel their property possesses. Such a trend appears inevitable under present funding arrangements but it does raise certain questions about its desirability. If the profit motive is one of the principal determining factors in initiating rehabilitation, then certain run-down districts located away from the more fashionable residential areas would appear to be condemned for a considerable time to their advanced state of squalor. This suggests the need for a more flexible and generous system of grants, but in a period of financial restraint it appears unlikely that this will occur, at least in the short term.

Even within improvement areas not all of the intended objectives have been realised. One of the supposed benefits of rehabilitation (particularly compared with renovation) is that it provides a much greater opportunity for tenants to remain in their original dwellings: either the person stays put during the work or returns afterwards. In practice this has not always been the case. Often this is the result of the subsequent rise in rent, despite its control and the availability of allowances (APL) to help compensate for the increased cost; the latter form of assistance is means-tested and thus is not granted automatically. Those people with relatively modest resources and not qualifying for a rent allowance may find the increase excessive and therefore leave. Another problem has also arisen, particularly as local authorities' budgets have come under greater pressure. The temporary rehousing of residents while improvement is occurring requires a sizeable stock of alternative dwellings but this is an expensive undertaking and increasingly difficult to support, hence the slowing-down of the whole operation.

Reservations exist, therefore, over the efficacy of rehabiliation policy. This should not infer, however, that the improvements themselves are inadequate. Certainly in the case of work carried out in officially designated areas it is often of a high quality and of an extensive nature – replastering of the external facades, restructuring of the interior and often the addition of facilities such as bathrooms, toilets and central heating. Indeed, in view of the desirability of such modifications, efforts have been made recently to remove some of the difficulties outlined above; for example in 1985 the ANAH, in association with a number of banks (e.g. Crédit Foncier de France), offered a means of prefinancing the cost of the work for landlords through the introduction of a special system of low interest loans. In this case grants are paid directly to the bank concerned which then takes responsibility for their payment. Changes may also be detected in the nature and extent of improvement work; new formulae have been adopted recognising the tighter budgets with which many people have to live. One idea in the owner-occupier sector of the market is to improve simply the main structure of the building and ensure the adequate provision of essential services, leaving all internal changes to the charge of the individual owners based on their wishes and financial possibilities. As with new building, therefore, there is evidence of innovation and an amelioration of the product in the approach to rehabilitation.

There are other signs of a change in attitude in the 1980s. Increasingly it has become accepted by the government and municipal authorities alike that improving the living conditions and environment of people is not just a question of better housing, however important this may be. It is also dependent upon a series of other, interrelated features such as the availability of jobs, the adequate provision of public services, opportunities for recreational and sporting activities and a reasonable standard of accessibility and public transport services: not that efforts have never been undertaken to bring about changes in these fields, they have. The interest of more recent thinking, however, is that a much greater attempt is being made to co-ordinate such action. This is now the case in the central north-eastern and eastern quarters of Paris for which a special development plan has been drawn up by the city's administrators, under the direction of Jacques Chirac. The programme was agreed with the state which will contribute to the financing of certain operations.[7] Approved by the city's councillors in 1983, the plan (Plan Programme de l'Est de Paris) is scheduled to run until 1989. It covers the 10th, 11th, 12th, 13th, 18th, 19th and 20th arrondissements, housing over a million people and nearly a third of the jobs found in the commune of Paris; this is the traditional working-class district of the city which despite extensive renovation and transformation still retains much of its former image. For, even with such changes the area is still characterised by a comparatively poor population, a high proportion of immigrants, a declining industrial base and relatively high unemployment.

Now guided by the above plan, the aim is to enhance considerably the area's appeal through a number of inter-linked programmes. These include new homes, rehabilitated flats, new schools, sports and social facilities and libraries, additional leisure and recreational areas (notably in connection with the redevelopment of la Villette) and premises for small-scale industries and office activities: an ambitious plan. Whether all this will radically improve the attractiveness of the capital's 'east end' and produce a superior quality of life for its many inhabitants seems questionable. Already, despite the dynamic leadership of Monsieur Chirac, certain elements of the plan are proving difficult to realise; rehabilitation work has not advanced at the rate anticipated, largely for the reasons outlined above which have generally curtailed its introduction. Furthermore, although the cost of the five-year programme is considerable, estimated at 5.8 billion francs (1983 prices) for the municipality of Paris alone, transforming an area's character and the manner in which it is perceived by its residents or those wishing to live or invest there is an inherently long-term process.

Apart from encouraging such initiatives, the government has sought other ways by which to increase the effectiveness of its intervention. Since 1984 a special interministerial committee has existed to consider the nature of action to be taken in deprived urban areas (Comité Interministériel pour les Villes – CIV); its principal aim is to seek to co-ordinate investment decisions so that different ministries reflect the same priorities in their budgets.[8] The committee is also responsible for allocating a new urban social fund (fonds social urbain), which replaces the former FAU. It is designed to help combat the difficulties encountered in some of the worst affected areas, although particularly in the outer rather than inner suburbs. However, despite such attempts to improve the efficacy of central government action, the Socialists also proposed shifting responsibility in this field to local authorities, a decision corresponding with their policy of decentralisation. The aim, therefore, is that the bulk of financial aid to assist with environmental improvements in rehabilitation areas (e.g. resurfacing roads and the provision of play areas and sports facilities), part of which previously came from the FAU, should now be provided by municipal, departmental or regional councils from their budgets. This may be more democratic, but it could also lead to less priority being accorded to urban improvement as authorities seek to balance the competing demands on their resources.

LA BANLIEUE

In view of the advanced age of much of the residential property in the central and inner areas of cities, the limitations of its original construction and the associated presence of a range of manufacturing plants, warehouses and workshops, in many cases also in various stages of decline, it is of little surprise that schemes of renovation and rehabilitation are widespread. It is less easy to comprehend that many of the outer suburbs of France's major urban centres, often constructed less than twenty years ago, are now also in need of radical improvement as their built environment deteriorates rapidly and their population is now declining. These are but two of the adverse features which have come to characterise many of the vast apartment complexes (grands ensembles) rapidly built on the urban periphery, largely in the 1960s.

Twenty years ago there was an extreme demand for new accommodation. High birth-rates, a strong rural to urban flow of population, and a heavy influx of foreigners (notably from North Africa and directed principally to the country's main urban centres) were largely responsible for this pressure; added to this were the effects of renovation schemes in central and inner residential districts which started to produce an increasing displacement of residents towards the periphery, also in search of new accommodation. The response to this situation is well-known; extensive anonymous, high-rise estates, housing in the case of the largest, up to 20 or 30 thousand inhabitants: these are the 'grand ensembles'. Isolated on the outskirts of the town and poorly served by public transport, these residential districts also suffered from an absence of services, sports and recreational facilities and employment opportunities. The aim had been to build rapidly and cheaply; but this factor together with an inadequate level of subsequent maintenance of the buildings has led frequently to a premature and advanced state of disrepair. This problem has been further exacerbated by the nature of the resident population. Much of the accommodation is in the subsidised sector of the French housing market (generally referred to as HLM), built by companies specialising in this type of construction with the aid of government loans at low rates of interest. Thus these estates have come to house a population characterised by its relatively modest means, lacking the incentive or ability to contribute to the up keep of the area.

Over a comparatively short space of time these essentially single-class suburbs have become marked by other difficulties, the majority of which are social in character rather than directly related to the built environment.[9] For various reasons these areas often house many of the disadvantaged members of the community; thus it is common to find a high proportion of young people who are unemployed, of those qualifying for assistance from social security services and of immigrants who in many cases possess few qualifications and only limited manual skills. The pronounced presence of foreigners, or of second-generation immigrants, has meant that in the eyes of many French people the 'grands ensembles' have become synonymous with the country's racial problems. Add to this a relatively high crime-rate and increased difficulties in the maintenance of law and order, and it becomes possible to appreciate the poor reputation that many such estates have earned. This has been seen most recently by their increasing rejection as residential areas, particularly by the French; numerous flats are now unoccupied and in many cases there has been a substantial fall in the number of inhabitants.

The scale of these problems and the frustration felt by the areas' inhabitants were first brought to the notice of the majority of French people during the summer of 1981, when a number of violent incidents broke out in the 'grands ensembles' on the eastern outskirts of Lyon (notably in the estate of Les Minguettes). Subsequently the pattern was repeated elsewhere, including the suburbs of Paris where other similar estates such as the 'cité 4000' at La Courneuve, in the northern suburbs of the capital, acquired a similar notoriety. In certain cases the incidents were serious, involving not only severe clashes between the police and certain groups of residents, but also the shooting of a number of inhabitants; regrettably these latter events often had racial overtones with French people firing on fellow North African residents claiming, for example, they were making excessive noise.

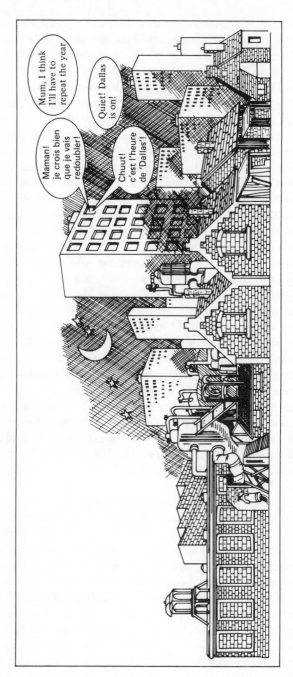

3 *Suburban malaise*. Low educational attainment amongst children has been one of the social problems which have come to characterise many large postwar estates.

Faced with such circumstances it was obvious that action needed to be taken, and rapidly. However, this should not imply that the problems of these suburbs had not been recognised previously or that remedial action had not been attempted. Already in the 1970s the 'errors' of earlier large-scale residential developments were recognised, with the passing of legislation in 1971 and 1973 to limit the overall size of estates and particularly the dimensions of individual buildings. Certainly in this field French architects would seem to have a great deal to answer for, with numerous 'excesses' committed, and not just in the major cities. Even much more modest towns such as Nancy and St Etienne feature their 'murailles de Chine'. In the former case two enormous horizontal blocks, respectively 300 and 400 metres in length, house part of the population of the estate of Haut-de-Lièvre. Their massive and overwhelming character is reinforced by the suburb's visual prominence which derives from a location in a dominating position on the plateau above the 'old' town of Nancy; over a third of the apartments in the two above blocks were empty by 1982. At St Etienne, in the southern suburbs of Montchauvet, there is a similar 'barre' dating from the early 1960s, 300 metres long, 16 storeys high and containing over 500 flats! By the late 1970s, however, more comprehensive efforts were being undertaken to improve such accommodation: rehabilitation had become just as much an issue in the outer suburbs as in older inner districts. It also formed part of the wider question of the need to modernise and improve a growing section of the country's 'social housing' stock; (it is now estimated that at least 600 000 HLM dwellings built since the end of the second world war are in need of improvement, the greater number located in the large estates which fringe the majority of French urban centres).[10]

At the same time, it has been recognised that improving the built environment alone in the 'grands ensembles' is unlikely to resolve many of their other serious deficiences which are essentially social in origin. It is in seeking to combat this aspect of the problem that action pursued in the 1980s might be viewed as particularly significant and innovatory. In the wake of the disturbances of 1981, the government set up a special interministerial commission (Commission Nationale pour le Développement Social des Quartiers)[11] to review the situation and propose a prescription for the future. It also immediately set in motion a series of projects designed to alleviate conditions in some of the worst problem estates such as at Les Minguettes and La Courneuve: sixteen such quarters were originally defined, situated in a wide array of towns including Marseille, Dunkerque, Grenoble, Strasbourg, Amiens and Dreux, indicating that the difficulties were by no means limited to the country's main industrial centres.

When the Commission first reported in the early part of 1983 it advocated strongly an integrated approach to rehabilitation.[12] While it recognised the need to improve the quality, design and management of the flats on these problem estates, it also argued that change was essential in other spheres. Improvements to the social environment were seen as vital, including better educational, recreational and leisure facilities. The inadequate number of local employment opportunities, especially for young people, represented a further area for priority action. Measures to improve relationships both within the communities of the 'grands ensembles' and between these people and other groups in society were also considered important. On the one hand this might involve prompting a more harmonious co-existence between the various racial groups on any one estate; and on the other fostering better relations with local police forces, hopefully based on mutual respect and understanding rather than on animosity and confrontation as had frequently become the case. However, while the Commission had identified the main strands of a remedial strategy to improve living conditions in the 'grands ensembles' and to ameliorate their tarnished image, it left the hardest task of devising and implementing appropriate policies to those directly involved with the problems at a local level.

Having set in motion this programme, the National Commission has seen its role and direct involvement in the problem diminish. It remains essentially as a 'think-tank', meeting two or three times each year to review policy.[13] Responsibility for overseeing the various rehabilitation projects has now been transferred to a series of regional commissions which direct and co-ordinate the various operations, and liaise with government ministries in Paris. For the planning and control of individual schemes within a particular region a local commission has also been created, comprising representatives of the various interested parties, such as local councillors and the owners of the property (HLM organisations). Such delegation conforms entirely with the decentralised administrative structures introduced by the Socialists; and it is with the same spirit that the onus of responsibility for obtaining government aid to assist with the rehabilitation of these 'problem suburbs' has been placed on the mayors of affected communes. Moreover, not only has there been a devolution of power but also an attempt to render more democratic the decisions which are taken. To achieve this the aim is to involve wherever possible the local inhabitants, both in the decisions which are taken relevant to their neighbourhood and in the actual work of transformation. But despite the attraction of the idea, in practice it has often served only to complicate the process, causing disagreement and delay.

While these organisational changes have taken place the import-ance generally accorded to this programme has been reinforced, indicated by the increase in the number of 'quartiers' forming part of the official list in receipt of government financial aid: from 16 in 1982 the total had risen to 120 by 1985. Moreover, provision for such a policy exists in one of the government's priority programmes included in the IXth National Plan; the section 'mieux vivre en ville' aims specifically to improve conditions in the large postwar estates of 'social housing'. Similarly the Socialists sought to launch various other initiatives to upgrade living conditions generally in the suburbs. These ranged from rendering the exteriors of buildings more attract-ive, to the provision of new shopping precincts or roads. Such action is grouped under the banner 'Banlieues 89' and is animated and co-ordinated by two architects, Roland Castro and Michel Contal-Dupart specially delegated by President Mitterrand. Indeed two further indications of the importance attached to the problems of the suburbs are given by the fact that the socialist government placed the 'Commission Nationale' directly under the responsibility of the Prime Minister's office and that François Mitterrand has expressed con-siderable personal interest and commitment to the policy; indeed he has gone 'into the field' himself to witness conditions and the changes being made; as he declared 'je préfère voir par moi-même'.[14]

Les Minguettes

Laudable as these expressions of intent are, the vital issue is, of course, the extent to which the above initiatives and policies are leading to an improvement in living conditions and a change in the character and image of these quarters. Attempting such an analysis presents certain difficulties, due to the only recent introduction of remedial measures. But one estate in particular stands out in terms of the efforts which have been made to redress a rapidly deteriorating physical environment and social climate – Les Minguettes, a massive 'grand ensemble' located on the south-eastern fringe of Lyon (Figure 4.2). In the early 1980s it had come to symbolise the worst of these residential quarters; but since then it has become virtually an experi-

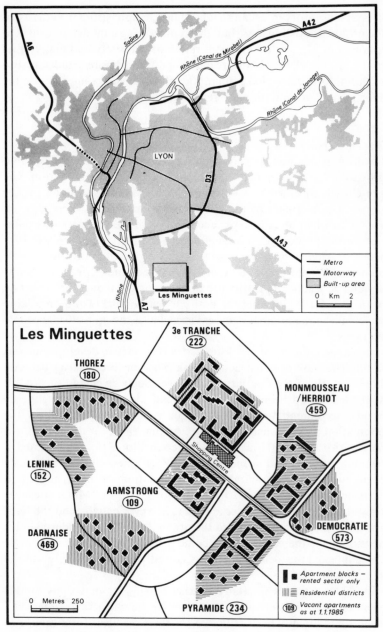

Figure 4.2   The 'Grand Ensemble' of Les Minguettes, Lyon

mental laboratory in urban rehabilitation, emphasising the gravity of the problems existing there but also representing a model for others to follow. Les Minguettes may still retain its notoriety and many of its problems, but change is also readily apparent. A more detailed review of this unfortunate suburb ought, therefore, to shed some light on the effectiveness or limitations of remedial policy.

The early years
Les Minguettes was conceived in the early 1960s at a time of rapid growth of Lyon's population and a shortage of accommodation. The site chosen to house this development lay amidst farmland on the south-eastern fringes of the city in the commune of Vénissieux, an area which had already experienced a period of considerable expansion in the prewar years largely due to the arrival and growth of a series of engineering and chemical industries (notably the vehicle manufacturer Berliet, now Renault Véhicules Industriels). Here was designated a zone of priority urban development (zone à urbaniser en priorité – ZUP) reflecting the desire to build quickly and on a large scale; indeed the original plans envisaged housing up to 40 000 people on this site.

Once the building of Les Minguettes was started, development was rapid. The bulk of construction took place in three phases between 1967 and 1975. By this latter date over 9000 dwellings (nearly all apartments) had been completed, spread amongst nine neighbourhoods, accommodating around 36 000 residents: nearly half of the population of Vénissieux lived here. At that time, for the communist mayor (M. Marcel Houel) and his councillors, this represented a triumph; after all had not many of the ZUP's new citizens previously been unable to find suitable accommodation or been housed in extremely poor conditions? From the town hall Les Minguettes was viewed with pride. Yet a decade later, however enlightened the local authority may have considered the original decision to undertake this development, the estate had become a major nightmare; and while this happened the local council was virtually powerless to prevent the situation arising.

With hindsight it is relatively easy to suggest that signs of this eventual outcome were already evident by the mid-1970s. Other such estates had already been criticised for their repellent form (high rise and high density), for their lack of amenities and services, and for their isolation on the fringe of large urban centres. Les Minguettes was no exception. Out of 132 apartment blocks, 62 are 15 storeys high.[15] The majority were built close together, their spacing largely determined by the working radius of a single crane (to enable it to be used most economically) rather than by any theory of efficient or attractive urban design; thus the towers are grouped together in small clusters of four or five. Certainly there is considerable space between these groups of buildings, but arguably this has not been used effectively, with little of the area originally given over to any form of sports or recreational facilities. Despite a population of the size to be found in many medium-sized towns, Les Minguettes had been conceived essentially as a dormitory settlement, offering dwellings but little else. Even the manner in which the apartments were conceived now appears limited. Comparatively large flats were grouped together with an exactly similar layout throughout every floor of the same block, resulting in up to 60 families with possibly four or five children each (or more) in the one building. Inevitably problems arose through the need to use common facilities such as lifts, as did other undesirable features, not least that of noise, the latter inconvenience being exacerbated by the close spacing of the tower blocks.

By the late 1970s there were already indications that difficulties were emerging at Les Minguettes and that its living environment, for whatever reasons, was perceived increasingly as undesirable. Evidence of this came primarily from the growing number of vacant flats and it was this problem which first prompted action to improve conditions. Many of the apartments, both inside and out, exhibited signs of quite severe deterioration (cracks, leaks, plaster pulling away from ceilings and walls and lifts frequently out of order) caused by various factors, including poor design, cheap materials, insufficient maintenance and vandalism. Added to this were the oppressive and depressing character of the estate's architectural style and the shortcomings in the fields of services, amenities and jobs. However, at this time the solution was seen essentially in refurbishing this environment, particularly through improvements to the flats. It was hoped that this would reduce the number of people leaving, in many cases apparently attracted by the more pleasant surroundings of the low-rise housing estates which had become an increasing feature of the city's urban/rural fringe. Proposals, therefore, were formulated to enable such rehabilitation work to be undertaken, benefiting from a general programme (known as 'habitat et vie sociale' – HVS) already set in motion by the government for this purpose in the late 1970s.

However, in the early 1980s such tentative initiatives were largely overtaken by events: the latent discontent and frustration long felt by many of the residents manifested itself in violence and upheaval. As certain elements of the population, particularly the young, demonstrated in the streets, others left the estate permanently in ever-increasing numbers. Les Minguettes became synonymous with many of the scenes of a breakdown in law and order and destruction which were also a feature of certain of Britain's inner cities at the same period. In the summer of 1981, for example, cars were stolen and burnt by the adolescents of the estate; others were raced around the tower blocks, often involving spectacular chases with the police. Such outbursts continued; relations between the police and the residents of a number of neighbourhoods deteriorated badly, resulting in 'no-go' areas, as the ramming of vehicles and the launching of various missiles from upper windows of the tower blocks became popular anti-police 'sports'. Local folk heroes were born, notably Toumi Djaïda a young North African, who first led, then sought to calm the riots. But just as he developed his role as peace-maker he was arrested and imprisoned for an earlier offence, further inflaming feelings on the estate, only to be subsequently released and pardoned by President Mitterrand following hunger strikes and a march to Paris by his sympathisers. These more sensational events took place against a backcloth of a society becoming increasingly divided and insecure, with a substantial rise in incidents of vandalism and theft, many directed towards the estate's shops, causing a number to close.

A complex problem

Together these various occurrences might be seen as the outward signs of much deeper social malaise affecting certain sections of the population of Les Minguettes. But the explanation for this situation is complex. There is still a tendency to consider the hostile nature of the built environment as a basic cause of the problems. However, by the standards of many areas the accommodation here could be considered highly satisfactory: central heating is provided throughout the area by a collective system and over 80 per cent of households have a telephone installed. Arguably it is not so much basic inadequacies in the quality of the flats or problems of lack of maintenance that have encouraged the population to leave, but the huge scale of the whole residential development and its depressing and suffocating effects. There is little variation in the building style, one horizontal or vertical block after another, producing a virtually mono-functional ensemble of subsidised low-cost, 'public sector' accommodation.

Since the first manifestations of discontent, however, greater significance has been attached to certain of the inherent and problematic social characteristics of the estate. Progressively Les Minguettes has come to house an increasing proportion of foreigners, partly due to the continuing inflow of these people, but also because it has been essentially the French population which has left. Just under 30 per cent of the inhabitants are now officially registered as foreigners, but the presence of a large number of second generation migrants (with French nationality) gives the impression of an even stronger presence. The majority of immigrants originate from North Africa, but in total there are over 40 different foreign nationalities present on the estate. Given the various cultures and living styles of these groups it is of little surprise that tension and mistrust should arise between them. Similar strains exist between certain of the French residents and the immigrant population, particularly the North African contingent. Even within this latter group, however, significant differences exist, with resentment and hostility displayed against the 'harkis' (Algerians who supported the French during the troubles, prior to decolonisation, in the late 1950s and early 1960s).

Thus, Les Minguettes has a large and heterogeneous immigrant population presenting problems of integration and contributing to the unstable base of the estate's society; but the reasons for this concentration are varied and hard to define precisely. Given the modest means of much of the population, such people are naturally attracted to areas of low-cost and subsidised accommodation, the bulk of which (certainly in the quasi-public sector) is located on the periphery of the urban area. The focus upon such areas has also been increased by the squeezing of the private market in many inner areas, as redevelopment and rehabilitation schemes have reduced considerably the availability of cheap, rented flats. It is also suggested that local authorities' housing policies have reinforced these spontaneous tendencies; immigrant families are perceived, rightly or wrongly, as difficult to assimilate in local communities and there would appear to have been attempts to shift them away from certain inner residential areas to some of the more insalubrious peripheral estates, presumably with the idea of isolating and spatially concentrating the 'problem'.

Les Minguettes also features an extremely youthful population, with nearly 45 per cent of its residents aged under 20 (compared with

28 per cent for the city as a whole). This characteristic is also linked to the existence of much larger sized families than are found generally throughout Lyon. The presence of so many young people (over 11 000 on the estate) invariably leads to problems of noise as well as other difficulties such as providing a sufficient range of sporting and recreational activities. There is also a tendency to equate this situation with the existence of the sizeable immigrant population, for amongst these people families tend to be larger; over 35 per cent of the foreign households at Les Minguettes include four or more children and a third of the children aged 5–14 on the estate have a nationality other than French. It is of little surprise, therefore, that in certain schools the majority of the class is made up of such children, a situation which is not always readily or willingly appreciated by French parents. There are a number of other distinctive social characteristics of the population which might be seen as potentially problematic or demanding of more or special resources: it is popularly held, although less easy to substantiate, that Les Minguettes possesses an excessive concentration of 'difficult' families. One illustration of this feature is a greater than average presence of various groups of people who might be considered as less fortunate members of society; for example over 14 per cent of the estate's families have only one parent compared with a much lower proportion (8 per cent) for the city as a whole.

Possibly the worst problem facing the community over recent years, however, has been the substantial increase in the number of people out of work. Between 1975 and 1982 the unemployment rate rose from 4.5 to 13 per cent, the latter figure being considerably above the average for Lyon (8 per cent); the rate is now nearer 16 per cent. Les Minguettes has been badly hit by the adverse effects of the recession on the employment market and the decisions of major employers of local residents (such as RVI) to cut back substantially on their labour-forces. As elsewhere the rise in unemployment has not been felt equally throughout the population. Young people and immigrants appear to be the two groups most affected: in the former case nearly a third of those aged 16–25 who are not continuing their studies are out of work, while in the latter instance approximately a fifth of foreign workers are unemployed. Amongst young immigrants the situation is even worse; over 40 per cent are without a job. But the most depressing feature is that in many cases the prospects of obtaining employment have become extremely remote. With over 1000 young people unemployed, of whom most have neither the inclination or qualifications to pursue any further course of study, it is perhaps understandable that their sense of frustration should become expressed in acts of vandalism.

As on similar estates elsewhere in France, Les Minguettes has experienced the progressive departure of many of the original French families, replaced by a less stable population whose problems have only increased as the recession has intensified. So by the early 1980s the estate represented very much a society 'en crise'. Yet in this situation a number of contradictions existed. Despite the 'label' of a relatively poor and less favoured population, it is of some surprise to learn that over 70 per cent of households at this time owned at least one car! Moreover, not all neighbourhoods exhibit the same social profile, nor have all been affected to the same extent by the estate's various problems. There is some evidence to suggest that it is some of the first and highest tower blocks which have encountered most of the difficulties (such as the districts of Monmousseau and Démocratie). Such anomalies and variations only serve to confirm, therefore, the inappropriateness of offering a single and simple explanation for the troubles of Les Minguettes.

It is also apparent that as conditions deteriorated, the local authority responsible for the estate, Vénissieux, was virtually powerless to intervene, lacking the resources and legal status to do this. The dwellings at Les Minguettes are not under the control of the commune, but are the property of 11 different house-building organisations (HLM companies). Each has been responsible for the allocation and upkeep of its accommodation, and in many cases very different policies have been pursued. It has been argued that certain actions of these companies have contributed to the area's difficulties through, for example, accepting an increasing number of immigrant families and carrying out inadequate maintenance. Yet those charged with managing the apartment blocks have been faced with severe financial problems, for their revenue has declined as tenants have departed and an increased number of those remaining have experienced difficulty in paying their rents. At the same time the outgoings of the HLM companies have risen, for regardless of the number of residents the same overheads have to be paid for and inflation alone has increased this cost. In such circumstances there has been an understandable tendency to fill vacant apartments with non-French families who, because of the shortage of alternative accommodation, readily accept such opportunities. Similarly one means of lowering costs is to reduce repair and maintenance work to a minimum. However, had the HLM organisations shown greater interest in and care of their property in previous years, certain of the present difficulties may not have emerged. So to the serious social and economic problems existing at Les Minguettes, need to be added shortcomings in the administration and management of the estate.

New initiatives

The violence of the summer of 1981, added to the background and build-up of the difficulties outlined above, meant that by the early 1980s substantial remedial action had become essential. Between 1975 and 1982 there had been a net loss of over 10 000 people from Les Minguettes, and by the early 1980s over 3000 residents were leaving the area each year; in 1985 nearly 2500 flats were empty (Figure 4.2). To arrest this decline cosmetic improvements were no longer sufficient: instead major surgery was required. There remained, however, the delicate question of the most appropriate form of intervention to undertake, although it was widely accepted that a plurality of measures was required. Given that the need for rehabilitation of many of the flats had already been agreed, one of the first decisions was to amplify and accelerate this programme, for which additional government funding would be provided. It was also decided, not without some controversy, to demolish a number of the tower blocks in the quarter of Monmousseau where vandalism and physical decay had led to a deterioration of the buildings and where residential densities were amongst the highest with around 110 dwellings per hectare. It is arguable whether this decision was merited, viewed purely in terms of the condition of the buildings, but it also had a symbolic importance, emphasising the commitment which existed to effect substantial changes. With these decisions made and remedial work set in motion, a more detailed and comprehensive plan of improvement was formulated and finalised in 1985 based upon the organisational principles and priorities established by the 'Commission Nationale'.

Prior to this date, however, a sizeable sum had already been invested amounting to approximately 120 million francs for the years 1982–4. Over this period one of the most obvious changes was the demolition in the summer of 1983 of the three towers in the Monmousseau district. It was originally proposed to remove a further six blocks, but the high cost of such a strategy, for property under twenty years old for which the loans negotiated to finance its construction had not yet been fully repaid, encouraged the search for an alternative solution. This produced an ambitious programme of rehabilitation involving a major redesign of the flats which included the addition of balconies, helping to modify and render more attractive the previously austere facades of the blocks. Such work is expensive; the cost of rehabilitating each block is approximately 3 million francs at 1985 prices although part of this total is being met by the government. The policy has been well accepted by the residents who have been encouraged to give their view on the nature of the modifications which they would like to see (within certain limits) in their apartments. However, the fitting of reinforced doors with special security locks to all the entrances to the flats gives some indication of the problems which still exist in the area. Not unnaturally improvement will result in increased rents; but by signing an agreement with the state to modulate the rise in accordance with government norms, the HLM company owning the property gives its tenants the right to apply for a rent subsidy under the APL system, which in many cases ought to cover the greater part of the increase. Logirel, the company responsible for the tower blocks at Monmousseau has adopted such a policy, as have other companies, notably OPAC du Rhône, which is also carrying out extensive rehabilitation of its properties, particularly in the Armstrong district of the estate.

Indeed one of the major features of the strategy to revitalise Les Minguettes has been the changing attitudes of certain of the HLM companies. Traditionally their role has been that of home builders; but, faced with a sharp rise in vacancies, they have been forced to become far more professional and imaginative in the manner in which they manage their property. This change in attitude has manifested itself in various ways. Most of the major companies now have an office 'on site' where tenants are able to discuss their problems, seek advice and report damage or the need for maintenance. Previously contact was often difficult, with the companies' offices based in Lyon. Various initiatives have also been taken to improve the 'mix' of families, with the avoidance of an excessive number of racial groups (or, on the contrary, of a single group), or of families each with a large number of children, in any one block: OPAC has pioneered this approach with some success. For the city as a whole there is also now a special commission (Commission Permanente pour l'Habitat Social) whose aim is to co-ordinate the allocation policies of the different housing organisations, aiming particularly to achieve a more equitable spatial distribution of the various different types of family. Certain companies have sought to promote their properties at Les Minguettes by generating a new image of well-equipped and reasonably priced accommodation, while in limited cases, in some of the more attractive and less densely developed parts of the estate, flats are being offered for sale. In theory there is an attempt to co-ordinate such action, with the different HLM companies having combined to form an association (Association pour la Gestion de l'Ensemble Locatif des Minguettes – AGELM), offering a forum for discussion and the joint formulation of policy. Again, as with rehabilitation work, government subsidies have been made available in an effort to persuade the companies to improve their management, enabling them, for example, to increase their staffs and maintain a presence on the estate.

Considerable efforts are also being made to create a more caring society, providing special help for the least favoured members of the community; and various initiatives aim to effect a general improvement in social and economic conditions. One important step has involved increasing the number of social and educational workers available to advise and guide the residents. The range of help now offered is considerable. Centres exist to assist in the integration of foreign children into a new culture – helping them to improve their language ability or to learn about French cooking. Advice is available to families on how to budget properly, more crèches have been provided and social workers are available to discuss personal or family problems. Not that such initiatives always work as planned, for in many cases if foreign families take advantage of these facilities, they are shunned by the French, or vice versa.

An interesting experiment in the field of education has been to turn a former primary school, closed as the adjacent apartment blocks were bricked up, into a computer laboratory, open to schools or any individual on the estate; it has proved immensely popular. (Similar initiatives have been taken in other problem estates elsewhere in France, all conforming to the wishes of Gilbert Trigano who was asked by President Mitterrand to launch such a scheme). While such a facility might improve the future prospects of obtaining a job for some of the population, the general problem of providing more local employment opportunities remains extremely difficult to resolve. The estate was never designed to accommodate small factories or offices, but it is now hoped to provide a limited number of such premises. However, in the current economic climate and with the estate's unfortunate reputation, it is not obvious that related investment will be forthcoming. Special efforts have been undertaken to provide openings for young people and a number of jobs have now been created amongst the firms carrying out the rehabilitation work. This has had the added advantage of helping to make the younger generations feel part of a community which previously they considered had rejected them. But praiseworthy as such schemes are, employment has only been provided for less than fifty people, still leaving a considerable problem of those without work.

As far as the children on the estate are concerned other measures have been taken to try and improve the opportunities available to them. These include schemes to take a number away each year to holiday centres, in rural areas such as the Ardèche, helping to relieve the boredom and frustration which tend to build up in the summer months. With the same aim of reducing tension in the community, the system of policing has been altered, above all to try to avoid the previous and frequent conflicts which arose between the police and youths on the estate; hence armed patrols have given way to a greater presence of local policemen, each responsible for a small section of the urban area – integration rather than confrontation.

Providing a realistic assessment of the impact of all these various forms of intervention is difficult, not least in view of their recent introduction. Nevertheless, as suggested by one of the stickers given away by Logirel (to promote its properties) 'ça bouge' (things are moving) at Les Minguettes. It is very evident that a concerted effort is being made to improve conditions with strong government backing, for the estate has become a test of the state's ability to reverse the tendency towards marked social and economic deterioration which by the 1980s had become a feature of many of France's postwar suburbs. Certainly there is now evidence of a reduction in the number of vacant apartments in selected areas of the estate where major rehabilitation has taken place, although certain of the newcomers have simply transferred from another area of Les Minguettes, exacerbating the problem of vacancy and abandonment elsewhere.

In contrast to the positive signs, there remains the sad spectacle of one whole district of the estate completely abandoned – la Démocratie. Here nine empty and partially bricked-up tower blocks and nearly 600 empty flats attest to the enormity of the task represented by the rehabilitation of Les Minguettes. Before taking any further action the owners are apparently waiting to see if conditions elsewhere improve significantly. Such an attitude highlights a further problem in effecting improvements. Despite certain common ground amongst the HLM companies, not all appear disposed to pursue the same policy; some still favour demolition and pulling out of the area. But until there is a common will to improve conditions and the estate's image, progress will inevitably be slow.

Finding such common ground is also complicated by the presence

of a large number of interested parties, often each with a different
position to defend or policy to promote. Apart from the eleven
owners of the apartments, the municipalities of both Vénissieux and
Lyon also have strong vested interests in this area. Similarly the
government, through the National Commission, and various of its
ministries are directly involved in the changes which are occurring. All
recognise, however, that the transformation of Les Minguettes is an
essentially long rather than short-term process. It is for this reason
that current thinking is concerned with providing the optimum
conditions in which a new image can be created; hence the interest in
such projects as the further extension of Lyon's modern metro system
to serve this suburb. But even with the help of such ambitious
schemes, a substantial and durable improvement of living conditions,
here and elsewhere on similar estates in France, is unlikely to take
place without more general changes in society related to an upturn in
the economy and a marked shift in attitude over issues such as
immigration.

WIDER DIMENSIONS TO URBAN CHANGE

Improving the quality of urban living in the 1980s has not been
confined to the rehabilitation of run-down or impoverished residential districts, although this has represented a major priority for
investment, particularly from the public sector. Change has been far
wider, embracing the core of the city as well as its suburbs. Faced with
a strong movement of decentralisation and the vigorous challenge
from peripheral retailing complexes, increased emphasis has been
accorded to reviving the image and appeal of the centre and its
commercial activities. Creating a more attractive central area is partly
dependent on persuading private investors to demonstrate a commitment to this zone, but it also requires imaginative policies from local
authorities. While this may involve launching large-scale schemes of
redevelopment, it frequently entails a more modest but none the less
inventive approach. Pedestrian streets (including the special French
version where cars are tolerated and therefore continue to represent a
hazard for people on foot!), the introduction of flowers and shrubs,
the cleaning or repainting of buildings' facades, much improved sign-
posting and the encouragement of various forms of exhibitions or
special events represent but some of the many initiatives pursued over
recent years.

City centres have witnessed other important changes, particularly as they have become the focus for a growing number of new systems designed to improve public transport, a benefit which extends of course to a much wider part of the urban region. Seeking to give priority to public transport is not a new approach in itself, for such a policy has been pursued since the early 1970s. But more recently a growing interest has been displayed in creating new, fixed-track transport systems based on the metro or tramway, and intended to cope specifically with the traffic problems of France's provincial cities. Support for the development of this type of infrastructure was given by the socialist government in the context of the IXth Plan, with nearly 5 billion francs originally allocated to such investment.[16]

Part of this expenditure has been devoted to extending the metro networks already in service at Lyon, Marseille and Lille. Of these the latter scheme is the most recent (the first line was opened in 1983) and technically the most interesting. Use is made of small, totally auto-mated trains, a technique which is reflected in the name of the system – VAL (véhicule automatique léger); it was pioneered by Matra. The ride is less comfortable than at Lyon or Marseille and there is concern that the cost of maintaining the rolling stock may prove high due to its sophisticated nature, but against this are the advantages of low running costs (reflecting the small labour input) and a high level of flexibility: trains can be brought in and out of service very rapidly in response to variations in demand.

However, one of the difficulties of maintaining the development of metro systems during a period of recession is their elevated cost. At Lyon the present extension of the network, a new east-west link stretching for 11 kilometres across the city and involving tunnelling under both the Rhône and Saône, is estimated to cost 4 billion francs (1985 prices): this represents approximately half the total cost in-curred in building the new line (390 kilometres) for the TGV between Paris and Lyon. Attention has, therefore, turned to the idea of developing tramways or light rapid transit systems. These benefit from lower construction costs and greater flexibility of operation, while with reserved tracks and priority at major junctions, speed and efficiency of use are comparable with conditions on rival metro schemes. Yet less than two decades ago trams were seen as incompat-ible with the need to move people about rapidly in city centres, not least because of the delays they provoked for other vehicular traffic. They disappeared from French cities with the exception of a limited number of lines which were retained at Lille, St Etienne and Marseille.

Now in the mid-1980s, in a different set of cities, the tram is making its comeback. In the early part of 1985 the first of the new generation systems opened in Nantes, extending over 11 kilometres and serving the centre and part of the town's western suburbs. The rolling stock is entirely new and each tram has capacity for 168 passengers and a maximum speed of 70 kph – a far cry from the city's former trams, known when they operated in the 1950s as the 'péril jaune', reflecting both their colour and inconvenience to motorists. Over 44 000 passengers now use the system each day.[17] Grenoble has followed this lead, with its own tramway network scheduled to open in the late 1980s. Yet despite the inherent advantages of cost and flexibility that the tram possesses over the metro, not all city councils have been persuaded of such benefits. Where considerations of status and image are deemed important, the metro still has a significant advantage; and after lengthy and at times acrimonious debate, Strasbourg, Toulouse and Bordeaux have opted in favour of the VAL metro system and its advanced technology 'label' in preference to a tram network.

Despite the benefits brought by the schemes discussed above, and widespread efforts to revitalise more traditional bus services, in general the pattern of rapidly increasing usage of public transport evident in the late 1970s has since been less apparent. Partly this may be attributed to changing preferences amongst potential users, but it also reflects the problems faced by large cities in maintaining the number and quality of services during a period of financial restraint. Public transport is run at a considerable loss, with operating revenue rarely exceeding half of the total costs. Part of the shortfall can be recouped by the proceeds from the local transport tax which is paid by all firms employing more than nine workers in urban areas with at least 100 000 inhabitants. But the rest has to be made up by the local authorities, and if the deficit increases this implies higher local taxation. In recent years there has been a marked reluctance to raise the value of this subsidy, not least for reasons of political expediency. The implication, therefore, is that if traffic and receipts should not continue to increase, then if other savings cannot be made, services will have to be restricted. This seems a harsh logic after a number of years of substantial progress, but only confirms that in a period of recession economic rather than social priorities invariably dominate.

Mieux Vivre en Ville?

The 1980s have been marked by an increased emphasis accorded to improving the quality of life in urban areas, particularly in the country's major towns and cities. An essential part of this movement has been inspired or directed by the government, and during their term of office the Socialists might reasonably point to significant progress achieved in this field. One illustration is provided by the impact of measures designed to improve conditions in certain 'problem suburbs'. Over 120 such areas have been identified for special aid and are now benefiting from government assistance, while more than 100 individual projects to enhance the environment in suburban districts have been launched under President Mitterrand's 'Banlieues 89' scheme.

It would be unrealistic, however, to see the government as the only 'actor' in this process. Many other organisations and individuals, ranging from municipal councils and their leaders (the mayor) to quasi-public house-building companies, have played important roles. Indeed in understanding the wider pattern of urban change it is also very necessary to take account of the actions taken by the private sector and institutional investors. Much of the success (or failure) of new retailing and office complexes is dependent upon their decisions. Over the last decade the economic and social climate in which these different partners operate has altered, influencing their attitude to development. Much of the 1960s and early 1970s was a period of large-scale construction, often accompanied by substantial renewal. Now a more modest approach is discernible, partly as the result of changes in demand and the availability of investment funds, but also reflecting a revised philosophy to modifying the urban area with far more emphasis placed on rehabilitation. Greater priority has also been accorded to the effective management of the city and its existing fabric, in part a reaction against the lack of control and co-ordination during the years of rapid growth.

This should not imply that new building no longer plays a significant role in changing the urban environment or has not responded to modified attitudes to development. On the contrary it is in this area that innovation has often been most evident, notably in the five new towns which encircle Paris. They have become a central arena for the expression of a modern generation of French or French-based architects such as Castro, Bofill, Nunez and Gaudin. Although obviously influenced in their designs by the period of early postwar development, they have also sought to reject part of this heritage, especially its worst excesses in the form of seemingly endless rows of similarly designed flats. The result is a more varied, colourful and much richer architectural form, that is more open and less oppressive than its predecessor of the 1960s. Certain designs stand out due to their audacious and spectacular form such as the quarters of the Théâtre and Arènes de Picasso at Marne-la-Vallée; the latter development is centred around two large disc-shaped apartment blocks, popularly likened to two huge Camembert cheeses – such 'progress' has not been without its critics! But the real significance of such evolution in design is its contribution to a wider movement aiming to create a more humane urban environment, suggesting that finally in the 1980s the French are rediscovering that cities are primarily about people.

5 Power to the Provinces

The legislation passed on decentralisation will undoubtedly long be seen as one of the major achievements of President Mitterrand's years in power. From the start of his mandate vigorous efforts were made to push through this programme, strongly supported by the then Prime Minister, Pierre Mauroy, and his minister for the Interior and Decentralisation, Gaston Defferre. The importance and priority attached to this action are indicated by frequent reference to 'la décentralisation' as the 'grande affaire du septennat', and by the inclusion of a specific chapter in the IXth Plan aimed at facilitating the introduction of this legislation and at ensuring, as far as possible, its successful adoption.

While the devolution of power embodied in this process may be seen as revolutionary in character, particularly in a nation such as France long renowned for the excessive centralisation of its economic and administrative systems, the concept of decentralisation is by no means new in relation to the history of the country's recent political and socio-economic development. Throughout much of the postwar period there has been extensive debate over the need to reduce the overwhelming influence exerted by the capital on the lives of French citizens, nurturing numerous initiatives in favour of decentralisation, their variety attesting to the many spheres of activity embraced by this term and to the different interpretations to which its use is given. In the present chapter two themes are highlighted – the redistribution of economic activity away from Paris to the benefit of the provinces and the reallocation of certain decision-making powers of central government in favour of local communities; given the recent and original character of this latter change greater emphasis is placed on the discussion of this issue.

Measures to restrict the continued economic expansion of Paris were first introduced in the 1950s and then reinforced in the two following decades, notably as an ever-wider part of the country became classified as eligible for an increasingly generous array of development aids. Simultaneously regional planning became 'in vogue', reflecting an official acceptance of the need to seek to redress the spatial imbalances in living standards and opportunities existing within the country. Underlying such action was the recognition, by right wing parties as well as the Socialists, that the devolution of political power was also essential to give France a just and representative democratic system capable of reflecting the varied distribution of its population and economic activities. Over time these different currents of decentralisation have not necessarily evolved in the same manner or at a similar rhythm. Indeed it is somewhat paradoxical that as a pronounced slowing became evident in the shift of productive and service industries from Paris to other areas of France, the pressure for the devolution of government responsibilities intensified, culminating in the recent socialist reforms. With this has also come a renewed awareness of the role to be played by the different regions in devising an appropriate planning strategy for their development.

One of the fundamental issues raised by policies of decentralisation concerns the extent to which the process represents merely a delocalisation of activities and institutions, or embodies the transfer of decision-making powers and the necessary financial means to enable the implementation of policy. In this respect a contrast is evident between the general pattern of decentralisation of economic activity and that of government functions. In the former case the movement of plants and offices has frequently not involved the devolution of a corresponding responsibility for policy formulation, whereas in the second instance the transfer of decision-making authority has represented a key element of the process. Herein lies the principal innovative character and interest of the Socialists' measures, while the objective behind such reform of enabling local citizens to participate more fully in decisions affecting their communities explains the widespread demand for such action. But as with any new process and in this instance one representing a radical departure from previous practices, its introduction has not been without controversy, even within the socialist party itself. Nevertheless, the programme of decentralisation set in motion in the early 1980s represented a significant shift in the balance of power away from central government in favour of local authorities, and was seen by the Socialists as vital to the efficient modernisation of French society in the 1980s.

DECENTRALISING ECONOMIC ACTIVITY: THE BALANCE SHEET

The present outflow of economic activity from the capital represents but a mere trickle compared with the surge of outward movement which was characteristic of the 1960s and early 1970s. During that period decentralisation, as now, was very much 'la grande affaire', although in this case involving essentially the redistribution of industry throughout the country. The basic aim was simple – to slow down the growth of Paris and promote expansion in the provinces. As such the policy formed a key element of a much wider strategy of regional planning aimed at reducing the many inequalities (in wages, job opportunities, access to services and living standards) which existed between different parts of France. The first tentative steps towards this goal were taken in the early 1950s with the introduction of restrictions on the creation of further industrial floorspace in Paris and of financial aids in a limited number of zones (principally those housing heavy industry) to encourage new industrial development. Progressively these measures were reinforced and as early as 1958 extended to cover the tertiary sector.

Prior to the recession the results of this policy were considered as largely positive. Between 400 and 500 thousand jobs are estimated to have been diverted away from the capital; not all were accounted for by direct transfers, for many of the new employment opportunities created in the provinces were linked to expansion projects of major firms such as Renault and Thomson which retained an important part of their activities in the Paris region. However, it was argued that without restrictions on development in and around the capital, these new factories would invariably have been built in this area. Furthermore, decentralisation policy was seen as having played a major part in the industrial 'take-off' of a series of predominantly rural regions situated mainly in the Paris Basin and western France. Thus throughout the 1960s and early 1970s regions such as Centre and Bretagne benefited from the arrival of a diverse range of industries, leading to rates of employment growth in this sector often exceeding 4 per cent per annum. Invariably there was also an important spin-off for other businesses (ranging from sub-contractors to retailers) in the areas to which these plants were transferred.

Despite some protest from industrialists and local politicians, little opposition was evident concerning the restrictions on expansion at Paris. Certainly the number of jobs offered by the industrial sector in the capital stabilised and then started to decline, causing the proportion of the country's work-force in industry located in the Paris region to fall from around 25 per cent to only 20 per cent; but this aroused little protest. The continued and strong expansion of service activities largely served to mask this negative effect and overall unemployment remained low. Generally decentralisation was not seen as a damaging process. On the contrary it was viewed much more as a spontaneous and logical response by firms during a period of rapid economic growth. The implication, therefore, is that a dispersion of industry would have occurred anyway (although perhaps not on the same scale), irrespective of restrictive legislation.

Ten years on, in a very different economic and political climate, the policy of decentralisation is not necessarily viewed in such a favourable light. At a time of low economic growth and a declining employment market, the task of redistributing activities becomes far more arduous and contentious. Faced with such conditions there are few regions prepared to sacrifice jobs in favour of a competitor. At the same time, following a longer period of reflection, a growing number of shortcomings have been identified in the process of decentralisation. Again it is during a period of recession that such negative features tend to become emphasised and seen as exercising a more influential role, particularly when decentralisation has significantly altered the basic structural characteristics of a region's employment base.

Decentralisation – the limitations

Almost from the first years in which decentralisation developed on a large scale, two underlying weaknesses of the process were detected: first it was argued that new plants were located or relocated too close to the capital and second that in many cases these creations represented merely manufacturing units, with the management activities of the firm remaining in Paris. Over time these trends have been accentuated. Thus the majority of new factories decentralised beyond the boundary of the Paris region (i.e. Ile-de-France) have been established within a radius of 60–200 kilometres from the capital. Undoubtedly this brought a number of advantages for the towns and often the semi-rural areas of this belt which had previously been accustomed to an outflow of population and a low level of economic activity (both caused by the proximity and dominance of Paris). But it did little to satisfy the demands of more distant regions (in for example the central and south-western parts of France), equally wishing to participate in and benefit from this growth mechanism. Such results question not just the efficacy of decentralisation strategy but equally the efficiency of the policy of seeking to induce a more equitable spatial distribution of industry through the provision of various financial and fiscal incentives to stimulate development in the country's 'less favoured' regions.

The choice of a location within relatively close proximity to Paris might be seen as the result of the interplay of two sets of forces. On the one hand, in a generally tight labour market, firms were attracted by the presence of a relatively cheap work-force, (readily available in areas where the modernisation of agriculture had resulted in the release of a large number of potential workers); to this was allied the search for a similarly inexpensive (by Parisian standards) site that was adequately equipped and reasonably accessible. The question of labour supply might be seen as influenced not just by the need to augment a firm's productive capacity but also by various changes in manufacturing processes, notably the use of an ever-increasing range of standardised products capable of being manufactured on a very large scale. Such mass production techniques were seen as ideally adapted to the comparatively unskilled labour-force widely available throughout the capital's hinterland. On the other hand, given that it was generally only the production side of a company's activities that was involved in such a move, ease of contact was essential with the firm's central services (and in some instances with established suppliers and sub-contractors) still concentrated in Paris. Frequently this factor may be seen as having favoured sites adjacent or relatively close to the main motorways radiating from the city, especially to the west and south; towns such as Evreux, Chartres and Dreux all benefited from this process.

The essence of the above comments, therefore, is that the policy of encouraging industrial decentralisation has not served to breathe new economic life into some of the country's more remote or depressed areas, as might originally have been anticipated. Indeed it has been argued that despite the redistribution of a large number of jobs, in itself the transfer of industry away from Paris has done relatively little to modify the basic economic geography of France. With few exceptions the underlying cleavage, dividing a more advanced and economically rich eastern region from a much poorer, less developed western counterpart, remains valid after more than thirty years of efforts directed at its eradication.[1]

Even where decentralisation has led to the creation of a substantial number of new jobs in previously under-industrialised regions, the wisdom of official policy in this field and the resulting benefits have been contested. In the northern part of Brittany, for example, strong emphasis was given (in the 1960s and early 1970s) to encouraging the location of electronics industries specialising in the manufacture of telephone systems. At the time, given the urgent need to modernise and expand the capacity of France's antiquated and inadequate telephone network, the demand for such equipment was high, ensuring that factories operated to their limit; but it also meant that certain districts such as the Trégor (Côtes-du-Nord) and particular towns such as Lannion and Guingamp became highly (even excessively) dependent on a single industry. Now the position is very different.[2] The above shortcomings of the telephone system no longer exist and consequently the demand for the related basic equipment has diminished considerably, posing an acute problem for the related manufacturers and their employees. The former are looking to reduce their work-forces, a situation complicated by the merging of the telecommunications interests of the two French giants, Thomson and CGE, and the resulting quest to rationalise their operations. At a local level, and notably in the above area of Brittany, redundancies resulted, provoking protests in the form of sit-ins and marches amongst a disillusioned work-force. In this region finding alternative employment and effecting a longer term diversification of the economy are daunting tasks in the current economic climate, and emphasise the doubts long-expressed by local unions over the possible adverse consequences of a policy of decentralisation too reliant on one activity.

Of perhaps greater concern, however, is the somewhat paradoxical notion that decentralisation has reinforced rather than diminished the influence of Paris on the rest of France. Through the progressive concentration of firms' control functions in the capital, an ever-increasing proportion of the productive activities of the country's provincial regions has become dependent upon these Paris-based headquarters. The previous example of Brittany highlights some of the problems which may result from this situation; here most of the jobs in the telephone industry are in large Paris-based firms (which are also now nationalised) giving local authorities and union representatives little opportunity to influence significantly the companies' policy making. Other imbalances have been induced by this segregation of functions, noticeably concerning the qualitative character of related employment: highly skilled and management jobs have been retained within the Paris region to a far greater extent than more routine blue-collar occupations. The benefits accruing from higher wages and other spin-off effects have been, therefore, generally to the much greater benefit of Paris than provincial France.

Many of the same criticisms apply to the more recent pattern of decentralisation of office and research-based activities. The volume of movement has never been very high (averaging at most 3–4000 jobs a year in both the public and private sectors since the late 1970s), although there is evidence of a significant number of long-distant moves, contrasting markedly with the industrial sector; for example over an extended period insurance companies and pension funds have decentralised part of their services to towns of western France such as Poitiers and Niort, government research centres in telecommunications have been established in Brittany (e.g. Lannion) and Grenoble, while in advanced sectors of production such as aerospace Toulouse has grown not only as an important centre of production but also of research and development work. For those critical of achievements in this field it is once again in the qualitative nature of decentralisation that the most significant shortcomings are considered to exist. As with the industrial sector, those activities which have 'moved' most readily have been linked to the routine administrative or data-handling activities of firms, again relying on a modestly qualified work-force and generating relatively few multiplier effects. Headquarters, functions of firms have been rare candidates for decentralisation, demonstrating the continued importance of accessibility to a series of specialist services and labour skills, and proximity to clients and other potentially influencial decision-takers, in determining their location; few centres outside Paris are sufficiently large to have been able to offer this range of advantages.

Current policy

Such criticism of the manner in which decentralisation has operated should not imply that overall the policy has not produced various positive results; the fact that jobs might have been created at a greater distance from Paris and that they have frequently only offered employment for people with relatively few qualifications should not mask the considerable achievement of directing, over a thirty year period, in excess of half a million workers away from the capital. Certain factors, however, do suggest that decentralisation may no longer be an easy or even appropriate spatial strategy to pursue, particularly during a period of recession. The persistence of a depressed economy has acted as a major constraint on the availability of mobile capital, with firms reducing their investment in new factories.

Frequently their chief concern has become an excess rather than a shortage of capacity, leading to a new emphasis on policies of rationalisation (sometimes involving the closure of plants) and of adapting existing productive units. Furthermore, at the height of the decentralisation movement, a significant lead was given by the country's major industrial groups; yet now these companies are seeking to reduce their work-forces rather than augment their manpower. A strategy heavily reliant upon their investment decisions is obviously, therefore, no longer appropriate; similarly against a background of high unemployment, the shortage of labour, which frequently represented a strong motivating force affecting a firm's decision to move in the 1970s, has lost much of its significance and influence. Also it is of little surprise that after an extended period of decentralisation, the number of 'candidates' susceptible to transfer should become limited.

In these circumstances even the government's own regional planning agency (DATAR) has recognised the need for a modified and more selective approach to decentralisation. This revised attitude has been evident in various ways. First, in terms of overall regional policy, government priorities have altered: the simple idea of decongesting Paris has long been superseded. Emphasis has switched to the urgent need to compensate the loss of jobs in those areas hit most severely by the recession, notably the Nord and Lorraine, and a series of smaller centres such as St Etienne, St Nazaire and Toulon. Thus, one of the first measures introduced by the socialist government in relation to regional planning was a revised system of financial aids to firms willing to move to such areas, which had the effect of generally increasing the amount of assistance available (see also the discussion in Chapter 3). To this end a new form of grant was created (prime d'aménagement du territoire – PAT) relating to development projects in both the secondary and tertiary sectors. Not only was this subvention more generous than its predecessors (up to 50 000FF per job created in the zones of maximum assistance such as parts of the north, north-east, west and Massif Central), but it also had the potential advantage of being authorised in many cases by the regional councils of the regions in which the investment was to take place (although it is still paid by central government) – a practical example, therefore, of the government's wider policy of administrative decentralisation and an attempt to reduce the bureaucracy associated with such decision-making.

This desire to transfer responsibility to the regions was also seen in the creation of a second form of grant (prime régionale à l'emploi – PRE) which in this case was funded by the regions themselves. The PRE cannot be added to the PAT but along with other forms of assistance now offered by the regions, such as covering part of the interest charges of loans, offering low-cost premises and providing or guaranteeing loans, it does provide a much more comprehensive and flexible local system of aids than was previously available – to the extent that one criticism has been that complexity and confusion now exist for those firms contemplating seeking assistance. None the less, some success might reasonably be claimed for this revised policy. In 1984 over 800 development schemes involving more than 40 000 jobs qualified for a grant under the PAT scheme; this compared favourably with the situation in the early 1970s when similar annual totals were being recorded. However, the current minor role played by decentralisation in this process is indicated by the fact that only around 750 of the 40 000 jobs previously cited were the result of transfers from Paris.[3]

As far as decentralisation itself is concerned, the greater selectivity associated with present policy is indicated by the increased emphasis placed on influencing the location of tertiary activities; not only would this appear logical due to the continued expansion of employment in this field, but also because of the ever-increasing concentration of the country's labour-force in service activities. Moreover, certain businesses subsumed within this sector, notably those associated with various forms of consultancy, have proved particularly dynamic. Hence the considerable interest in encouraging such decentralisation shown by those responsible for regional planning strategy in government ministries or agencies, as well as amongst local authorities and development organisations.

However, as with the expansion of the industrial economy twenty years ago, where such movement occurs it might be seen as an essentially spontaneous rather than government-induced process. Banks and insurance companies were amongst the first to decentralise, establishing a series of major regional offices as the volume of their business activities increased. Now the same tendency is evident amongst a series of other 'service' organisations as they too have reached a stage in their development where the expansion of their activity justifies a regional network of offices. Not surprisingly, the feature is evident currently in the location strategies of firms concerned with data processing and electronics, especially the manufacturers of computer products; and a number of the leading foreign-based companies such as Hewlett-Packard, Control Data and Canon, having established their headquarters at Paris, have since expanded in this manner.

Naturally organisations such as DATAR aim to encourage these trends, although their ability to influence decisions in the private sector is often limited. Conversely, they have probably played a greater role in engineering transfers in the public sector. Again the emphasis has switched towards advanced technology and research activities, compared with the banking and financial sectors which were seen as the main targets in the 1970s. One theme to remain constant, however, has been the policy of promoting the transfer of sizeable sections of large or prestigious organisations away from the capital – the idea of mounting a series of 'coups' destined in part as a means to influence others. Lyon is one city which has benefited particularly from this strategy over recent years, with the arrival of EdF's nuclear engineering and design company (SEPTEN), the decentralisation of a sizeable part of SNCF's commercial and computing services and the transfer to the city of the science faculties of the Ecole Normale Supérieure. Indeed Lyon also seems to have been notably successful in attracting firm's regional headquarters, and in 1985 the city was selected as the site for Interpol's new World headquarters, to be decentralised from its former Parisian location at St Cloud.

The appeal of Lyon might be linked to a number of potentially attractive features of the city's business environment; these include the services and office accommodation offered by the new and now expanded central commercial district of la Part-Dieu, a favourable image as a progressive and expanding centre, benefiting from a location at the head of a dynamic region (Rhône-Alpes) housing over 5 million people, and the city's high level of accessibility from other business capitals (notably Paris due to the substantial reduction in journey-times between the two cities brought by the TGV).[4] For Lyon the ability to persuade a large or prestigious organisation to locate in the city offers a series of benefits, aptly illustrated by the case of Interpol. It is not just the jobs that will be directly created by Interpol that are important, but also the various indirect effects resulting from the organisation's presence – a demand for hotel accommodation and conference facilities, the improvement of telecommunication and data transmitting services and in the longer term, with the growth of the city's international community, the provision of facilities such as an international lycée to meet the needs of these residents.

The above features have not been unique to Lyon: similar changes, related to the same set of processes, have been evident in a number of the country's other regional capitals such as Marseille, Bordeaux, Lille, Strasbourg, Nice and Toulouse; in the latter case, for example, decentralised sections of the aerospace industry have acted as the dynamic force behind the city's recent economic development. More generally the growing strength of these cities as business centres has been demonstrated by the manner in which the market for office floorspace in the private speculative sector has evolved over recent years. Outside Paris, it is here where the demand for space has been greatest leading to the emergence of a growing shortage of supply. This has occurred despite a continuing programme of new building, although its scale is well below that which existed during the speculative boom of the early 1970s prior to the recession.

Such trends have led to the growing acceptance of the idea of a restricted set of provincial cities that have acquired the necessary dynamism to sustain their growth as business centres independently of Paris. This in turn has lent support to the notion of a certain renaissance of the 'métropoles d'équilibres'. Although first designated in the mid-1960s to act as major provincial counterweights to Paris, and initially seen to benefit from a policy of preferential government investment, a decade later this particular development strategy was largely considered to have lapsed. Yet arguably it is only now that the wider multiplier effects resulting from such action have become fully apparent. Furthermore, the idea of a spatial concentration of firms in a limited number of major provincial centres would seem to have a particular applicability to the current expansion of office-based activities. However, in assessing the role of these cities as growth points and as potential challengers to the dominance of Paris, a certain caution needs to be exercised. All the regional centres are now experiencing a decline in the number of jobs they offer (albeit essentially as a result of a reduction in industrial employment), and even Lyon still possesses only a very small office market compared with the capital.

Paris – a new dilemma

Viewed from many provincial cities and regions, it might seem highly desirable to continue to divert firms and jobs away from Paris; but it is far less evident that a similar opinion is now held by those responsible for planning and development in the capital. Just as elsewhere in France, the economy of the Paris region has suffered from the depressant effects of the recession on investment and jobs. Decentralisation was tolerated, even welcomed during the rapid growth years of the 1960s and 1970s; at that time it frequently implied not so much the substantial shift of employment from Paris, but the creation of a large number of totally new jobs in the provinces. But in the very different economic climate of the late 1970s and 1980s, decentralisation has been seen to represent an important loss for the capital which is not easily compensated.

To suggest that the capital's economy faces increasingly severe difficulties might at first view appear surprising. Numerous statistics are available (and are frequently published by those responsible for promoting the region) to demonstrate the continuing economic strength and vitality of Paris. In a region (Ile-de-France) covering little more than 2 per cent of the country's land surface is concentrated over 18 per cent of the total population, nearly 25 per cent of urban residents and slightly more than a fifth of the national workforce. In the latter case this represents around 4.5 million jobs, of which the majority (70 per cent) are in the tertiary sector. Paris houses a quarter of all such employment in France, and remains the primary focus for jobs requiring a high level of qualification or attracting a substantial remuneration – 60 per cent of the country's research workers and 40 per cent of the top executives are concentrated in the region. Nearly two-thirds of the country's largest companies (those employing more than 500 workers) have their head office in the Paris region, and in the influential branch of banking and insurance over 70 per cent of all offices and agencies are located in the capital. The list could be extended, doubtless reinforcing the image of a region which would appear to have lost little of its traditional power and dominance.

Yet other indicators portray a very different picture of the capital, suggesting a substantial decrease in its former vitality. Twenty years ago the region's population was increasing at around 1.5 per cent per annum, well in excess of the national average; currently the yearly growth rate is approximately 0.3 per cent, slightly below the national mean. Further confirmation of the altered demographic situation is given by the pronounced reversal which has occurred in migrational patterns. In the mid-1960s immigration into the Paris region exceeded emigration annually by over 60 000 people; now there is a strongly negative balance, with a net migrational loss of around 41 000 residents each year. Employment growth has also been severely curtailed: there is a now substantial overall loss of jobs in industry (averaging around 30 000 each year), while the rate of increase of tertiary employment has eased considerably to around 1.0 per cent each year, almost half the level recorded in the late 1960s and early 1970s. Manufacturing still employs around 1 million people in the city, and in certain branches such as the car and electronics industries between a quarter and a third of the total national labour-force is found in the capital; but little more than two decades ago over 60 per cent of employment in these industries was concentrated in Paris. As jobs have disappeared, unemployment has risen. Since 1975 the number of people out of work has doubled to a total of over 400 000 a decade later, representing nearly 8 per cent of the labour-force. This is still lower than the national average, although in certain inner suburbs such as St Denis and Aubervilliers, where industrial decline has been pronounced, considerably higher rates are recorded. There is, therefore, ample evidence of Paris having lost part of its former substantial drawing power for population and economic activity.

For many people it is not hard to find a 'culprit' responsible for this situation. While it is accepted that the recession and improvements in productivity have combined to reduce manpower requirements, particularly in industry, the government's policy of decentralisation is considered to have been of fundamental importance in undermining the region's economic base. From the mid-1950s two restrictive measures were introduced progressively on development in the capital – the need to obtain official sanction for any new constructions above a fixed floorspace limit (agrément) and the requirement to pay a special tax (redevance) on such projects: this latter tax was set at a variable rate throughout the region in order to give preference to certain locations (particularly the new towns), despite the general policy of constraint. By the early 1970s these measures applied to industrial premises exceeding 1500 square metres of floorspace, and to office developments involving over 1000 square metres of floorspace, with an 'agrément' required by both the developer and the user.

Much has been written and debated about the efficacy of these controls. Some have argued that the agrément became essentially a device to induce a dialogue between expanding Paris-based firms and the government, frequently resulting in the negotiation of investment plans, with limited expansion being allowed in and around the capital in return for a commitment to expand elsewhere in one of the country's priority development regions; for others the procedure was seen as exercising a major constraining influence on investment and resulting in the loss of a substantial number of jobs. Whatever the exact role played by these measures, as the labour market deteriorated in the late 1970s, with increasing redundancies and higher unemployment, there were growing demands, especially from certain local politicians and trade union leaders, to remove such constraints; the expectation was that this would act as an important means by which to stimulate new economic development.

Relaxing development controls
Initially such pressure was resisted, but under the Socialists a rethinking of strategy occurred, resulting in a substantial relaxation of previous constraints. This was first carried out in 1982 with the abolition of the redevance for new factories and the relaxation of the conditions for granting an agrément in the case of industrial firms employing less than 100 workers. The changes represented a useful complement to measures already being taken by the local councils of various departments of Ile-de-France, and by the regional council itself, to favour industrial regeneration; these included limited grants and loans to assist businessmen in setting up firms, extensive advice on running a business and the provision of new premises especially adapted for small firms. The latter initiative was considered particularly important although in practice it has produced mixed results.[5] Despite the attraction offered by new factory floorspace, even with subsidies it has remained relatively expensive, an almost inevitable consequence of a location close to the heart of the capital; in certain instances, therefore, the take-up of space has been below expectation.

Even where successful, such schemes represent only a minor brake on the underlying tendency for industrial activity and employment to disappear; for the department of Paris it has been estimated that while nearly 50 000 square metres of new or refurbished industrial and workshop floorspace are being added each year, at least three times as much is being lost.[6] The continuing reduction of manufacturing activity has been even more dramatic in some of the traditionally industrial inner suburbs such as Nanterre, where a number of large companies such as Citroën have abandoned their premises or severely pruned their work-forces. Protests at this process have continued, with the communist party being vociferous in expressing its hostility to the continuing 'casse de l'industrie dans la région parisienne';[7] in their case it is seen to be caused as much by the long-standing desire of multinational enterprises to diversify their activities to areas where labour is little unionised, as by purely economic forces.

Despite the concern over industry, increasing efforts were also being undertaken to persuade the government to ease controls on office development. In part this recognised the importance of office-based activities to the regional economy, as well as this sector's continued ability to create jobs, in contrast to the majority of manufacturing industries. But it was also a response to the growing shortage of new floorspace which became progressively more apparent in the early 1980s, especially in prestige locations with the virtual completion of 'la Défense'. A positive reaction to these demands was forthcoming at the beginning of 1985 when further significant revisions were made by the government to decentralisation policy, affecting both the industrial and office sectors. The need for an agrément was abolished for all forms of new commercial development (i.e. factories, warehouses and offices) in the five new towns of the Paris region and for speculative office building irrespective of its location (although such approval still has to be obtained by the users of such space). Similarly, for firms who wish to construct or extend their own factories and offices built for specific clients, the floorspace thresholds at which an agrément becomes necessary were doubled to 3000 and 2000 square metres respectively.

Most of the previous controls, therefore, have been removed. Certain remain, such as the need for users of new office floorspace to obtain an agrément where they take up over 2000 square metres (although there is nothing to stop them acquiring up to this limit each year), which may limit the effectiveness of the new measures in stimulating construction. The redevance is also still retained for office development, but since the rates at which it is levied were fixed in the early 1970s, it can hardly be considered a punitive tax. What is clear is that a much less restrictive and more flexible official attitude has now been adopted to development in the Paris region; and this may be seen as partly attributable (together with factors such as a renewed confidence in the economy) for the upsurge in new office projects which had become evident by the end of 1985.[8]

The revised thinking of the government was also demonstrated by its decision to give greater encouragement to foreign companies to invest in the capital, particularly where it concerns the creation of a European or French headquarters; the granting of an agrément is likely to be automatic in these cases. The appeal of such firms (particularly American and Japanese companies) is that they are amongst the few to continue to invest on a relatively large scale. As such there is intense competition from cities as diverse as Brussels, London and Geneva, where no development controls exist, equally eager to benefit from this investment; hence the need for Páris to increase its competitiveness by removing unnecessary obstacles to development. Indeed greater competition is also emerging within France as individual regions, anxious to strengthen their economies and to exercise their newly gained freedom and powers in matters of economic development, are also increasing their promotional activities abroad; this should be seen as of little surprise, for foreign companies create around 13 000 new jobs in France each year (Table 5.1).

The result of these various changes is a very different policy and attitude towards decentralisation. For much of the postwar period the basis of the government's regional planning strategy was to favour 'province' at the expense of Paris. To achieve this a firm policy of constraint was adopted in the capital, coupled to a range of incentives available in less-advantaged parts of France. The 'carrot' remains largely intact, indeed in some cases reinforced, but the 'stick' has been virtually abolished. However, given that the scale of decentralisation towards the provinces is already extremely modest, it could be argued that the government's liberalisation policy is unlikely to induce a radical change in this situation. Conversely the impact on the geography of location within the Paris region is potentially much greater. It is already clear, for example, that speculative office development is being attracted above all to certain prime sites in inner western

Table 5.1   Jobs created by foreign firms in France, 1985

Area of origin	Total jobs
USA and Canada	2 448
United Kingdom	2 033
West Germany	1 805
Benelux	1 670
Switzerland	1 390
Japan	1 092
Scandinavia	507
Other countries	2 453
Total	13 398

Source: DATAR.

suburbs, in direct opposition to the long-established planning aim of trying to target such expansion towards more deprived northern and eastern suburbs.

Nevertheless at a time when the capital's economy still appears remarkably healthy when viewed through many 'provincial' eyes, the decision to accord a further advantage to Paris by facilitating office development has not been greeted favourably by all interested parties. The government's response to such criticism has been that it is strongly in the country's interest as a whole to maintain a buoyant economy in the capital, and when this appears threatened appropriate remedial action needs to be taken. While the economic logic may be sound, it still might be seen, however, as a bitter pill to swallow in regions such as the Nord and Lorraine already faced with high unemployment, vacant industrial sites and empty office blocks.

DECENTRALISATION UNDER MITTERRAND

Despite the success associated with the policy of directing economic activity away from the capital, this form of decentralisation has always been characterised by strong control from central government and has rarely involved a corresponding transfer of decision-making authority. For much of the postwar period such features might also be seen as representative of the wider pattern of organisation of French society. By the 1960s there had been a reluctant acceptance by central government of the general lack of independence existing amongst local communities in policy-making; relatively few major decisions could be made without reference to government ministries in Paris (or their departmental off shoots) or to the government's representative in the form of the Prefect. Subsequent reforms sought to modify this position but only modest progress was achieved in altering the balance of power between central and local government.

So when the Socialists were elected in 1981, France still represented a highly centralised state particularly by the standards of other West European countries. Yet within less than a year the first legislation had been enacted to radically change this position, as the country was firmly placed on the path towards decentralisation. The desire for change and the forces motivating it were not new. It had been widely accepted that the powers of the basic administrative units of local government (the commune and department) were too limited to respond effectively to many of the needs of their citizens, but previously the political will to transform this system had been largely absent. The fundamental aim, therefore, of the government's programme was to accord far greater freedom of action to local authorities in deciding upon and carrying out their policies.

This principle applied to the municipal and general councils of the country's communes and departments which were to be freed from the control previously exercised by the Prefect over their activities; it was also to become applicable to the regional councils as the 22 regions were accorded an equivalent legal status to the communes and departments, and adopted as a third tier of local government. Reform, however, was not only directed at granting these authorities more autonomy, but equally at considerably widening their areas of responsibility so that, in theory, a substantially greater number of matters concerning local communities could be resolved at this level. It was strongly argued that such a system was much more efficient than its predecessor where constant approval from Paris was required; equally it was seen as representing a major increase in democracy as many aspects of people's lives would now be determined by the policies of locally-elected officials. Decentralisation was also to be a feature of services remaining under the control of central government, involving a transfer of certain officials from various central government departments to local areas; again the aims were to expedite their work and ensure that wherever possible decisions were taken close to the people they affect.

The socialist policy-makers also turned their attention to France's major urban centres and to the possibility of decentralising part of the administrative functions of their centrally-based councils, applying the same principle that had been used at a national level. Paris, Lyon and Marseille were initially concerned by the government's proposals. Although these cities would already experience a strengthening of their administrative powers as a result of the legislation on decentralisation applying to the country's communes and departments, the issue involved here was to make the exercising of these responsibilities more efficient and democratic. It was argued that residents felt themselves increasingly isolated from those responsible for decision-making in fields such as housing allocation, education and sports and recreational amenities. This was a consequence not only of the large and extensive size of the urban areas but also of the centralised character of services within them. Equally it was considered important that local inhabitants themselves should be given greater opportunities to participate in the management of the areas in which they live.

Thus it was proposed to divide the three cities into a series of smaller administrative districts (arrondissements), each with its own elected council and mayor, and specific set of responsibilities.

Once in power the Socialists moved swiftly to present their plans for decentralisation, with François Mitterrand immediately pledging himself to this programme. The first bill, introducing an initial package of devolutionary measures and setting out the framework for future action, was placed before Parliament in July 1981 and became law in March 1982; then in the following four years a further series of Acts was passed, giving substance to these earlier proposals. Despite the socialist government's original haste in introducing its legislation, it should not be thought that its ideas on decentralisation were formulated only during the short period which it had been in power. Already in the late 1970s, as an opposition party, the Socialists were arguing strongly against the excessive centralisation of power and advocating the measures they deemed essential to transform this situation: nor was such thinking absent from the parties of the then governing majority. Valéry Giscard d'Estaing had long expressed his support for increasing the powers of local authorities, and indeed spent over three years preparing such a programme. Moreover, a tentative step towards decentralisation was taken in 1979 when the government's funding of communal and departmental operating budgets took the form, for the first time, of a single 'envelope', leaving the final decisions on how the money was to be spent to the local authorities concerned. In addition, more ambitious changes relating to a significant relaxation or removal of government controls and increased responsibilities for local councils were to be considered by the National Assembly when Giscard and his supporters were ousted from power. It was left, therefore, to the socialists to seize the initiative. This they did fully, putting forward an even more radical programme of reform.

The new legislation

The process of implementing decentralisation has passed through three stages.[9] Of these, the first might be considered an essentially institutional step concerned primarily with the devolution of power, the details of which are set out in the Decentralisation Act of 2 March 1982. A key aim was to remove various controls which the government previously exercised over the affairs of local authorities, notably concerning their expenditure: previously communal and departmental budgets had to be approved by the Prefect. This requirement has been removed, although local authorities' accounts are still vetted (although only after they have been adopted) by a series of newly created 'Chambres Régionales des Comptes'. Indeed the functions and powers of the Prefect himself have been modified considerably. In the past this state official acted as the executive officer for the departmental (general) and regional councils; thus substantial authority and influence were vested in the Prefect. Now executive power has been transferred to the respective presidents of the above councils. Other changes (discussed later) have affected the Prefect not least the granting of a new title; they became Commissaires de la République (Commissioners of the Republic). At the same time as this important shift of power was instituted, it was also decided to give local authorities far greater freedom of intervention in economic affairs. Finally, it was intended that no tier of local government should be subject to any form of administrative control exercised by another.

A second stage of decentralisation, initiated in 1983, occurred with the transfer of various new functions to the communes, departments and regions.[10] In undertaking this task the government sought to select an appropriate areal scale for each of the administrative responsibilities to be decentralised and to favour those levels of the hierarchy of local authorities which previously possessed relatively little autonomy; the government also had to take account of a pre-existing distribution of functions, for its aim was certainly not to undertake a complete reorganisation and reallocation of activities between the echelons of local government. Based on these principles it thus chose, for example, to make the regions the principal bodies charged with planning and economic development, and to transfer a greater number of new powers to the departments and regions than to the communes, as the municipal councils of these latter areas had long been entrusted with a much wider range of administrative tasks than their departmental or regional counterparts.

Transferring functions from central to local government also implied the need for a corresponding redistribution of resources, particularly financial. This was effected through a further set of governmental measures set out in 1983 which sought not just to increase the income of local authorities but to give them as well far greater freedom in determining how their money was spent.[11] To augment local finances, the government chose first to transfer to the departments and regions the right to levy certain taxes; for example, the receipts from car taxation became an additional source of departmental income. A second and more important form of new funding was to come directly from the government itself. Even before decentralisation central government contributed to the current and investment budgets of local authorities; these grants have now been revised and increased, based on the principle first adopted in the late 1970s of providing a global sum, leaving the decision on how it is spent up to individual councils. Consequently, since 1983 local authorities have been provided annually with three financial 'envelopes' – one to cover the cost of providing services (dotation globale de fonctionnement – DGF), a second to assist with investment as in new building or infrastructural projects (dotation globale d'équipement – DGE), and a third and entirely new grant to compensate for the additional costs associated with the transfer of new administrative functions (dotation globale de décentralisation – DGD).

Together central government subventions to local authorities now represent a sizeable sum – over 111 billion francs in 1985[12] – although this still only amounts to around 30 per cent of their total income, of which the principal source remains various traditional forms of local taxation such as the tax on businesses (taxe professionelle). These transfers have benefited essentially the councils of the country's departments and regions (largely because it is these bodies which have received the majority of new functions). However, the use to which such resources are put varies between these two local authorities, illustrating the different influences they exert on the lives of their communities. The bulk of the region's expenditure is devoted to capital investment, whereas in the case of the department most of its spending is taken up by the running of the various services for which it is responsible (Table 5.2). Furthermore, the size of the departmental budget is considerably greater than its regional equivalent.

Providing the appropriate funding for local authorities to undertake their new responsibilities has represented a vital part of implementing decentralisation. But other 'resources' have also been essential to this process, not least the recruitment of new personnel. The third and most recent stage of decentralisation, therefore, has been concerned with this specific issue and has resulted in a series of changes embodied in legislation passed between July 1983 and January 1985. Two major problems confronted the government. The first was the need to produce a unified set of conditions of employment and a clearly defined career structure for the large body (approximately 800 000) of civil servants employed by local authorities.[13] Such a

Table 5.2   Local authority expenditure, 1984

Local authority	Expenditure (billion francs)		
	Current expenditure	Capital expenditure	Total
Commune	181.1	100.4	281.5
Department	86.3	28.2	114.5
Region	5.5	9.7	15.2
Total	272.9	138.3	411.2

Source: Adapted from *Le Monde*, La France des Régions (1986).

measure would not only harmonise the extremely diverse system of employment contracts which existed previously, but also hopefully assist in the recruitment of the necessary highly-qualified administrators required particularly to run the new services provided by the departments and regions. These conditions have now been created. The second problem, which has yet to be resolved finally, concerns the status that should be accorded to the considerable body of local councillors. All are now elected directly to the various municipal, general and regional councils, and in many cases have substantially increased responsibilities. The current issues relate to matters such as the amount of absence employers should accord to employees who are councillors and, above all, the nature and size of the remuneration that they should receive. It is this latter question which poses a particular difficulty, for while it is accepted that the present system of paying expenses is unsatisfactory, replacing it by a considerably more expensive system of salary payments has unwelcome implications in a period of strict budgetary constraint on local finances.

Special cases
All the above measures apply to the various local authorities located on mainland France. In slightly modified form they are also applicable to Corsica, while in the case of the country's overseas territories (e.g. the islands of Guadeloupe, Martinique and Réunion) the legislation on decentralisation has also been introduced, but with special provisions to take account of these areas' particular conditions. The only other exceptional case is represented by the cities of Paris, Lyon and Marseille for which specific legislation was eventually passed after lengthy and at times bitter debate in December 1982.

Corsica's position is particularly interesting, with the government moving swiftly to give the island greater autonomy and being prepared to go further in this direction than in other areas of France. This was seen as a partial response to the region's numerous difficulties, which owe much to its turbulent history and largely inhospitable natural environment. Despite considerable investment and various initiatives to modernise Corsica's economy, the results have been seen by many as disappointing, with the benefits from development affecting only a limited area of the country, situated essentially around the periphery, and a restricted sector of the population; in many cases those who have shown most initiative and obtained the greatest advantage from government-led improvement projects have been members of the large immigrant community (repatriates from North Africa and foreign workers) rather than the indigenous Corsican population, provoking resentment amongst this latter group. There is also an important political element to the island's problems. To a long history of internal feuding have been added more recently the unrest and violence associated with growing demands for some form of independent status: such action has been pursued forcibly by an extremely determined, although disparate, separatist movement.

Decentralisation has given Corsica a new statute (Decentralisation Act 2 March 1982) and led to the creation of a directly elected regional assembly (upon which the regional councils on mainland France have been modelled) with wide powers to intervene and influence the island's affairs.[14] This is revealed in the functions which have been devolved to the assembly, which include responsibility for matters such as education and cultural services, and are more extensive than those accorded to regional councils elsewhere in France. In addition three specialist bodies, jointly run by the island's council and central government, have been set up to help tackle key issues relating to Corsica's future development in the fields of agriculture, irrigation and transport links with the mainland. These and other measures obviously imply the need to transfer the necessary financial means to enable the effective operation of new responsibilites. Again this was agreed by the government in accordance with its general programme of decentralisation, and indeed in the case of Corsica extra resources, particularly of personnel, have been made available to assist with new management tasks. Thus the government was prepared to accept a substantial devolution of power to the new regional assembly, although for certain autonomist groups this was still seen as inadequate. But given the clamour for independence in other parts of

France, reasons of political expediency suggest that the government could not have gone further along this path without considerable risks. Part of the present disenchantment also reflects that greater autonomy alone will not radically transform the island's economy and prospects for development; this is a much longer-term and more complex process, and a subject over which it is likely to prove difficult to convince a population that has long felt unfairly treated.

Who does what?

The transfer of new functions to the various levels of local government began in the early part of 1983 and continued over the following three years. Some commentators from the then opposition parties suggested, somewhat mischievously, that the length of this process reflected uncertainty and even disenchantment over decentralisation amongst the ministerial ranks of the government; but the Socialists resolutely maintained that it was essential that devolution should be progressive, allowing local authorities to become accustomed gradually to functions for which they generally possessed little experience or prior competence. The form of decentralisation varied between functions. In some instances the transfer of responsibility was not total, with the state and local authorities sharing the administration of certain services; in other cases responsibility was divided between the various levels of local government, as occurred with education and economic policy.

La commune

The most significant change at the base of the hierarchy for the mayor and his municipal council has been the considerable increase of powers relating to urban planning. Previously, this task was often largely undertaken by the departmental agency of the Ministry of Urbanism, Housing and Transport (Direction Départementale de l'Equipement – DDE), with decisions over the licensing of new building work taken by the Prefect. Now it is up to each commune to produce its own detailed land-use plan (plan d'occupation des sols – POS) and the mayor decides whether or not to issue a building permit. Similarly, for wider-scale structure planning involving a number of communes, it is now the responsibility of the relevant municipal councils to initiate this process. Not that the state has relinquished all its rights; structure plans still have to be submitted to central

233

4. *The mysteries of decentralisation.* Decentralisation represented a major reform for the Socialists, yet at the local level it was not without its complexities and ambiguities.

government for approval and the state has reserved the power to authorise itself building projects which are considered of 'national interest' (such as a major factory or research laboratory of a foreign company).

Le département

The departmental general councils have gained a considerable number of new administrative functions. By far the most important, not least in terms of the value of the accompanying transfer of financial resources, is responsibility for a series of social and public health services (and particularly the payment of benefits), a field in which the department previously shared administration with central government. Even now the state retains control of certain activities. Thus while it would seem logical that such 'community' services should be provided by local rather than central government, the division of responsibility has led to the suggestion that the result is greater confusion rather than heightened efficiency; one illustration that has been cited is that abortion services remain the province of the state, while those concerned with contraception have been transferred to the department.[15]

In the field of education the department now has certain responsibilities, having taken charge of the country's 'collèges' (for pupils aged between 11 and 14). The administration of the rest of the school system, however, has been split between the communes (primary education) and the regions (lycées and special schools). As for the state, it retains control of higher education although regional councils have the power to submit recommendations based on their priorities for development and investment. In a related area, the provision and organisation of school transport (outside the main urban areas) is now also to be undertaken by the department. Finally a number of other diverse and generally minor management tasks have become departmental responsibilities such as the administration of main public libraries and (where appropriate) certain of the country's smaller ports.

New functions obviously mean an extension of the influence exercised by general councils within their respective departments, but their power is also very substantially increased by the transfer of executive power from the Prefect to the president of the council. This change is of fundamental importance (as it is in the regions), giving the president authority to sanction the numerous financial commitments made by the council. Generally the department is now much freer to devise policies, a feature illustrated further by the powers the general council possesses to assist firms in funding expansion programmes or to help them overcome short-term financial difficulties. The importance of the departments as administrative bodies may be gauged by the size of the budgets which their councils manage: in the case of Rhône (a small department but containing the city of Lyon) the annual budget in 1985 amounted to 2.7 billion francs. Together these new responsibilities have greatly increased the demands upon the administrative services which work for the general council, particularly in such departments as finance, management and economic development. Inevitably this has necessitated a considerable increase in staff including the recruitment of personnel of a high calibre to command newly-created senior posts. Frequently many of the people recruited into these services were previously employed in similar capacities by the Prefecture; indeed it has not been uncommon for high-ranking officials to 'change sides', attracted by a better career structure and higher salaries now being offered by the departments. A similar movement has also been taking place amongst civil servants previously working in the departmental services of various government ministries. So, as responsibility has been transferred to the general council a corresponding reallocation of personnel has occurred. One illustration is given by the Ministry of Urbanism, Housing and Transport (DDE) which will lose over 6000 of its staff from its departmental offices.[16]

The enhanced role of the general council could also be seen as giving increased political significance to the election of its members – councillors have a mandate for six years, with elections in half the country's constituencies taking place every three years. Whereas once these elections might have been seen as concerned essentially with local matters, now they are viewed much more as a judgement of central government policy and a measure of the popularity of the major political parties. This was certainly the case of the 'cantonales' held in March 1985, particularly as they represented the last major test of the socialist government's standing before the general election in 1986. Inevitably, therefore, the main issues for many of the electorate would seem to have been those related to the government's austerity measures, falling living standards and high unemployment rather than which party might be most efficient at running school bus services. There was, therefore, a certain predictability about the results, with the then opposition parties taking over 53 per cent of the vote, which led to right wing parties having control of 69 departments compared with the Left's total of 26.[17] For the party that gave the general councils their substantial increase in power, it must have seemed ironic that this should be exercised in the majority of cases by their political opponents.

La région

From its original role as an appropriate geographical area within which to formulate the spatial priorities of the country's economic development, the region, following the reforms of 1982 and the modification of its legal status, has now become fully established as a third level of local government, with its own specific set of functions. These betray its origins, for they remain strongly linked to the fields of economic planning. The regional council plays an essential role in the elaboration of regional development plans, which under the Socialists became an integral part of the process of formulating the country's National Plan. It also has an important remit to encourage economic growth, with much wider scope for intervention than other local authorities. Not only is the region able to offer various forms of grant to assist firms, but additionally it can finance or guarantee loans, provide industrial sites for companies, or arrange for the necessary expertise to advise on or assist with any aspect of an investment. Funds may also be made available to firms in short-term difficulty, with the object of helping to preserve jobs. Regional authorities are not allowed to own a financial stake in private companies, but they are now able to become shareholders in semi-public, 'mixed-economy' companies which frequently play a vital role in urban and regional development.

Further confirmation of the region's importance in promoting economic growth is seen in its new responsibility for the organisation of a diverse range of programmes and courses in vocational training and adult education, and for administering apprentice schemes. Here the type of project for which assistance is provided varies greatly between regions; it may be to compensate inadequate technical education in schools, to help retrain displaced workers in the major heavy industrial regions or simply to provide a means for people to develop a new career, whether this be long-distance lorry-driving or hairdressing – courses in both these professions have been run by the regional council of Haute-Normandie. Helping to adapt a region's labour-force to the requirements of its businesses is obviously seen as vital to its longer-term economic future. But in seeking to fulfil this need, a certain sense of frustration has emerged at a regional level, for most of the funds allocated for this purpose are still distributed by the government itself. A number of administrative functions in fields such as education, the environment and urban development have also been devolved to the regions, but compared with the principal concern for planning and economic development, they are of only minor significance. The region has thus been endowed with an essentially strategic role.

The other advantage for the region is that executive power has been vested with the president of the regional council, giving this latter body the same autonomy as its departmental counterpart. Once again the controls formerly exercised by the Prefect have been removed. Not only has this produced a similar increase in responsibility, but it has also led to the same process of transfer of administrative services from the regional Prefecture to the council. However, it was not until March 1986 that the regional council became a directly elected body, giving it an equivalent status to the corresponding bodies in the communes and departments. The delay in instituting this measure was seen by the Socialists as a natural consequence of its evolutionary approach to decentralisation, whereas the opinion of the Right was that it simply represented a means of postponing further 'self-inflicted' electoral damage. Certainly this might appear to have been the case, for as a result of these elections twenty of the country's twenty-two regions are now controlled by the Right; only Nord – Pas-de-Calais and Limousin remain in the hands of the Left. Whatever the truth about this delay, it undoubtedly hindered the regions in establishing their own identity and authority. Moreover, many of the former regional councillors tended to orginate from the ranks of the 'notables' rather than from within the younger and generally more dynamic members of the community; this suggested that if the regions were to be innovative and progressive in their approach, change was highly desirable.

PLM

Compared with the changes that decentralisation has brought about in the communes, and particularly the departments and regions, those introduced in the three cities of Paris, Lyon and Marseille contitute a much more modest affair. In each case it is still the municipal council of the commune which retains most power, but it has ceded certain limited powers to newly created councils which now exist for each of a series of small electoral districts (arrondissements) – Paris has 20, Marseille 16 and Lyon 9. The main role of such bodies is to act as a means of expression for local residents; the arrondissement council has to be consulted by the mayor of the commune over most matters which concern its area, particularly in relation to new building projects. Responsibility for a number of social and recreational facilities such as crèches, playing fields and small parks has also been transferred to these local councils, while they are also involved in the allocation of part of the stock of 'social housing' lying within their boundaries. But their budgetary means are extremely limited (to cover only their running costs) and any form of 'technical' assistance is provided by personnel seconded from the administrative ranks of the municipal council.

THE REALITY OF DECENTRALISATION: CONTROVERSIAL ISSUES

Few people would dispute the logic behind the Socialists' legislation on decentralisation. France's highly centralised state machinery had become outmoded and inefficient, and too remote from the daily lives of the majority of its citizens, leading to widespread agreement on the need for this reform. However, while the principle of decentralisation has never really been at issue, the manner in which the processes of devolution and deconcentration have been carried out has been criticised. This in turn has given rise to debate over the effectiveness of the new measures and the extent to which they have produced the desired changes.

The haste with which the first legislative measures were prepared led to claims of confusion and imprecision over many of the proposals; but following extensive parliamentary discussion, the initial stage of setting out the government's programme and removing state administrative controls over local authorities was finally accepted without major opposition. More controversy surrounded the choice of exactly which functions should be transferred and to which level of local government they should be assigned. In this context it seems reasonable to question why certain areas of responsibility have not been seen as suitable candidates for decentralisation. Housing is such a case, with control for its funding resting firmly in central government hands. Yet this is a matter in which there is considerable community interest and, judging by the present shortcomings in the system of housing provision, one which would benefit greatly from a revised approach. The process of decentralisation has also been characterised by considerable delay between the announcement of a particular measure and the publication of the appropriate texts indicating the means by which it was to be achieved. Even once decided upon, the implementation of certain reforms has often been extremely slow, although given the complexity of the legislation and upheaval involved in the changes this might be seen as inevitable. In addition, certain transfers of staff and other resources have necessitated detailed negotiation between government ministries and local authorities, again tending to complicate and retard the process, and causing irritation amongst councils anxious to exercise and exploit their new powers.

War over Paris

Despite such general, albeit at times begrudging, acceptance of the government's measures, this should not imply that major battles have not been waged over decentralisation. One of the most acrimonious conflicts, leading to an undignified confrontation between Jacques Chirac (mayor of Paris) and the late Gaston Defferre (then Minister for Decentralisation), occurred over the proposals to dilute the local power base in the country's major cities. The measure was partly politically inspired, as a means of limiting the personal authority (which was seen as excessive) of Jacques Chirac in his administration of the capital. But to 'sell' the idea effectively it was presented as a natural extension of the wider process of decentralisation, while to avoid the criticism of a direct attack on the mayor of Paris it was proposed to treat Lyon and Marseille in similar fashion. Monsieur Chirac and his supporters were highly critical of the government's proposals. They argued that rather than being more efficient and contributing to greater participation of the local population in decisions related to their respective parts of the city, the effects would be to complicate decision-making, to increase costs and, therefore, local taxation and to produce conflict between new district councils and the municipal council: in sum more bureaucracy, more waste and more dissatisfaction for those people affected by the changes. Worse still, in the eyes of Jacques Chirac, there had been no prior consultation with him over these proposals!

The 'battle for Paris' raged throughout the latter part of 1982, with the government unwilling to shift its ground, and the opposition, mobilised by the capital's mayor, continually denouncing its proposed action, calling at one stage for a referendum on the subject. In the end (December 1982) the goverment succeeded in passing its legislation, having agreed to limit the powers of the new district councils (conseil d'arrondissement) – not quite a draw but some honour was preserved on each side, although Jacques Chirac vowed to repeal the legislation once the opposition regained power.

Given that the changes resulting from this reform could hardly be described as revolutionary, it is tempting to question whether the controversy was justified. In all three cities power remains firmly vested in the municipal councils and their mayors, with the district councils having little say in the major decisions affecting the running and development of their cities. Nonetheless, their presence and role appear to be appreciated by the local population, and in dealing with many routine affairs they have considerably reduced part of the administrative load of the municipal council; now residents at least have a body with which they can identify and which they can contact easily. Conversely certain matters considered by the municipal council inevitably take longer to resolve due to the need to consult the district councils. This is the case with the modification of local land use plans (POS); while it might be desirable that residents should now possess an official channel through which to express their views, as a result of increased consultation the process of revision has become a far more protracted operation, causing the delay or sometimes even abandonment of building projects. Yet such change in procedures is still relatively modest, and Jacques Chirac would seem to have been misguided when he argued in July 1982 that 'I doubt if it is possible to impose such an obviousuly pernicious reform on a population which, according to all the evidence, will reject it and express clearly this rejection'.[18]

Monsieur le Préfet

When in the late 1970s the administration of Valéry Giscard d'Estaing proposed a programme of decentralisation which maintained the role of the Prefect and his traditional powers, there was a scornful reaction from the then left wing opposition; how was it possible to talk of effective decentralisation while retaining one of the principal symbols of the state's very considerable influence on local affairs? Not unnaturally, therefore, when the Socialists were in a position to implement their own proposals, a key element was the removal of the Prefect's power to influence the decisions of local authorities and the institution of a revised role for this agent of the state. At the time the intuitive reaction of most commentators was that the newly created Commissaire de la République had been considerably downgraded compared with his much more illustrious predecessor. Previously the authority of the Prefect had been absolute and the privileged contacts he frequently enjoyed with government ministers and their departments were seen as vital in obtaining the necessary resources to finance local development schemes. It was also not uncommon for much of the expenditure of the Prefecture to be borne by the budget of the general council, not least because the department's finances were controlled by the Prefect.

Now it was the turn of the heads of the general and regional councils to demonstrate their authority, a task that some seemed to perform with considerable relish, now they were released from their formerly subordinate role. To emphasise the point, certain Prefects found themselves transferred to less prestigious accommodation, while generally their expenditure became strictly controlled. Since these first reactions, however, there has been a reappraisal of the role and power of the Commissaire de la République, leading to the conclusion that the loss of authority and influence is less than was first imagined. Indeed, the term Prefect is increasingly coming back into common usage and in fact has never ceased to be used to describe the career grade of this state civil servant.

The 'new Prefects' are still required to perform a wide range of important tasks on behalf of the state. Although they no longer have control of departmental and regional budgets, they are still required to verify the legality of the various financial and other transactions undertaken by the different local authorities. This may be illustrated by reference again to town planning, for while the Commissaire now has no direct influence over the contents of local land use plans, these still have to be submitted for his approval (*a posteriori*) to ensure that they have been correctly drawn up and respect all relevant legislation. As the direct representative of the Prime Minister and his various ministers, the Commissaire retains the further important role of supervising the application of government policy. He is thus responsible at a local level for ensuring that measures such as those designed to help create jobs, limit inflation, or assist with industrial conversion projects are being implemented. Similarly it is his function to oversee the introduction of the regional plan and to ensure that the various contracts linked to it are carried out in accordance with their provisions.

In certain spheres the Commissaire has even seen an increase in his powers, notably through the control he now exercises over the different departmental services of government ministries (e.g. agriculture, industry, equipment, health and social affairs). Previously there was a direct line of command and communication between the heads of these departmental offices and their respective ministers in Paris: now they report to the Prefect, who in turn communicates with Paris. Not surprisingly this change has not been greeted over-enthusiastically by government officials, but given the loss of a considerable number of their former responsibilities, departmental heads have had little capacity to resist. Up to half the former functions of the once all-important DDE in matters such as transport, roads and rural development have been transferred to the general council: not that this has prevented certain heads from trying to by-pass the Prefect! Control of these services (and, therefore, by implication of their expenditure, even if it is now reduced) gives the Commissaire a further vital role in local affairs and suggests that it is important for the president of the general council to co-operate with him to ensure the efficient running of the department. In many cases this has occurred, despite a certain initial antagonism between the two officials.

However, the new presidents of departmental and regional councils are often themselves highly influential figures, not least because of their ability to have accumulated a number of important responsibilities. This is the case, for example, of the veteran politician Jean Lecanuet. Among the many offices which he held in the early part of 1986 were those of deputy at the National Assembly, mayor of Rouen, president of the general council, regional councillor and president of the association of mayors of the department of Seine-Maritime: he is also a member of the European Parliament. Yet there is little that is exceptional in this situation, and concern has long been expressed at the opportunities which exist for politicians to effect such a 'cumul des mandats', not least because of the considerable power with which they become invested, a situation which is obviously open to abuse. There is also a financial side to this issue, for as the number of public offices held increases, so too does the level of remuneration through the associated salaries and retainers; together these may represent a substantial amount which is either tax-free or taxed at only a low rate. The Socialists have naturally been opposed to such a privileged system and duly sought to introduce change. This came in

December 1985, although not without controversy, when legislation was enacted which will progressively restrict politicians to holding only two major offices. But, notwithstanding this reform, where council leaders have acquired a powerful position, there is often a desire in conducting their affairs to avoid any intervention by the Prefect and to 'short-circuit' the system by dealing directly with government ministers; after all political reputations are at stake!

There is still, therefore, a degree of ambiguity surrounding the present position of the 'Préfet'. Certainly these officials have lost part of their former power and the overriding infuence they were able to exert over local affairs. But as the state's representative they retain a series of important and demanding functions; and they are still responsible for the regulation of numerous and diverse matters (ranging from the maintenance of public order to the authorisation of extended opening hours for cafés). The prestige of the office remains and in the eyes of many citizens the Prefect, even in his new guise, continues to be the 'homme fort' in the region.

Accepting responsibility

Devolution of power also implies the transfer of accountability and it is by no means clear that all local authorities have readily welcomed this new responsibility. Undoubtedly there are advantages but drawbacks exist as well, including certain potential dangers. It has been generally accepted as desirable that councils should have greater powers to intervene in the economic affairs of their respective regions, not least through the provision of financial assistance to firms. Jobs are obviously of vital importance to local communities. However, such intervention requires that the relevant council possesses the necessary competence to assess realistically a company's commercial prospects, but many small authorities simply do not have this type of expertise. Again few councils have the experience of prospecting for new investors: ideally a specialist marketing service is required but only the larger authorities have the financial capacity to afford such an organisation. In the search for investment, there are also dangers from competition between councils, not just between different regions of the country, but even within the same department, each authority trying to out-bid the other with more generous or a greater range of aids. Without careful control, therefore, providing assistance to firms contains a number of risks, seen in the reluctance of many councils to make a major commitment to such a strategy.

Problems posed by additional responsibilities would seem most likely to arise for the municipal councils of relatively small communes in carrying out their requirements relating to urban planning and development. Preparing or modifying a local land-use plan necessitates the use of specialist technical services, but rarely are these available (or affordable) locally in small communities. Hence the continued need to make use of the resources of the DDE (as has traditionally been the case) or, where available, to enlist the help of the department's own planning section working for the general council; there is even some competition since the DDE has agreed to make such services available freely. In one sense this solves the commune's problem, but in another it means that the notion of the commune being independent is illusory. Despite decentralisation there are still controls operated (in this field and others) by one local authority over another, and by government departments over certain activities of local councils.

Many mayors see it as only natural that they should have the authority to issue building permits in the area over which they have jurisdiction; but again in smaller communes where the mayor does not benefit from any technical services or specialist advisors this is not always seen as a desirable responsibility. Making the 'correct' decision requires a sound understanding of the relevant legislation and considerable powers of judgement; and should the decision be contested it also requires that the commune has the necessary resources to defend its position. The government has been prepared to authorise certain guarantees to cover this eventuality, but there are still a number of mayors who regret they are no longer able to hide behind the Prefect, whose responsibility it was formerly to grant building permits. His role was particularly useful for he was seen as an essentially neutral power in these matters; if he said no to a proposal, then it was not seen to be the direct fault of the mayor (even if he was in full agreement with the decision and had recommended it himself), and thus did not put into question his standing with the local electorate.

Questions of finance

One of the most vexed issues of decentralisation has concerned the financial implications of the reform, and the extent to which the state has been prepared to compensate in its entirety the extra expenditure incurred by local authorities as a result of their new responsibilities. For the Socialists the question was straightforward: they adopted the principle that the resource allocations to local authorities to help cover running and capital costs (DGF and DGE) should rise in line with inflation – (thus in 1984 with the inflation rate at 6.9 per cent the increase in the DGF and DGE was 7.0 per cent;[19] respective figures for 1985 were 5.2 per cent and 5.6 per cent). Similarly, for the compensation paid to cover new functions (DGD), this was to equal the cost of the particular service to the state at the time of its transfer. Therefore, as far as the socialist government was concerned it had fully honoured its commitments.

Opposition parties and a large number of council leaders saw matters rather differently. They argued that the transfer of resources was inadequate; moreover, in their view the state had rid itself of the responsibility for a number of services (in fields such as health and social security, vocational training and education) which were costly and for which it was difficult to limit expenditure, placing the unwelcome onus for raising extra taxation to pay for them firmly on local authorities. The government had, as one commentator remarked, 'transféré les emmerdements et les déficits'[20] – and why should it worry, for (at that time) the majority of general councils were in opposition hands. Therefore, even if the state raised its grant to local authorities in line with the level of inflation, expenditure would be likely to rise more rapidly. It was also evident that it would cost councils more (at least initially) to run the equivalent services provided in the past by central government, given the need to acquire and equip offices and recruit personnel; thus the principle of compensation on the basis of previous cost was unrealistic. Finally, the sources of taxation which have been transferred to assist local authorities meet their increased expenditure were seen as inappropriate; for example, with the relatively depressed state of the car market taxes from the registration and licensing of vehicles (allocated respectively to the region and department), were seen as unlikely to rise substantially in value.

To this type of argument socialist ministers responded that during a period of financial restraint it was inevitable that, just as with central government expenditure, limits have to be placed on local authority spending. Equally, it was emphasised that the basic philosophy of decentralisation is that it gives local government the freedom to decide on its policies and priorities. But many councils have seen this as unconvincing, particularly concerning such services as education, health and social assistance where cost-cutting is difficult as strict government controls apply concerning their nature and quality.

Dissatisfaction over such matters has helped provoke wider criticism of the overall cost and cost-effectiveness of decentralisation. The process itself has been expensive, and estimated in 1985 to have involved already an outlay of at least 1 billion francs, covering items such as new buildings and the additional staff which have had to be provided.[21] In the longer term the existence of two parallel systems of local administration is also likely to prove more costly; under decentralisation not only are there still in place the departmental offices of the different ministries (although with reduced status) but also a series of 'duplicate' services, answering to the general council, to look after new responsibilities. Further, it is seen as inevitable that decentralisation will lead to a progressive increase in local taxation, although arguably this is but part of the price to pay for a more autonomous system of local government. Finally, it is worth recalling that centralisation also implies additional costs in terms of the loss of time, energy and money in having to make constant reference to Paris.

THE REGION AND REGIONAL PLANNING

One of the significant changes brought by decentralisation has been to establish the region as a third level of local government. The new status and importance accorded to this area are readily apparent from the recent increase in regional expenditure; this rose by nearly 84 per cent between 1982 and 1984, as the majority of the regions' new functions were transferred, rising by a further 12 per cent in 1985, double the rate of increase applying to the two other tiers of local administration.[22] Overall in 1985 the regions spent around 17 billion francs. Although this total was still much lower than the expenditure of the communes and departments, which together amounted to approximately 420 billion francs, it represented a growing and nonetheless substantial injection of capital into the regions, aimed specifically at promoting economic development and improving infrastructure.

A key function assigned to the region is responsibility for determining the main planning priorities for economic and social development within its area, re-affirming and enhancing its traditional role. Since the regions were first established in 1955 this role has varied. Thus during the 1960s, and with the launching of the IVth and Vth National Plans, attempts were made to include a regional dimension to certain parts of the government's investment programmes, but the decisions on how money was to be spent were still taken by central government. By the following decade attitudes had been modified. Less emphasis was now given to the idea of regionalising the national plan, but more importance was placed on the need for the regions to be able to express their opinions on the priorities for investment and development.

The growing authority of the regions was confirmed by legislation passed in 1972 which gave these areas their own statute and established the regional council, although at this stage the latter body was constituted by nominated representatives rather than directly elected members. Their enhanced status, increased powers and independent resources enabled the regions to take a much more active role in promoting economic expansion often by assisting in the financing of new infrastructure, and in devising development plans: indeed the Prefect was obliged to consult the regional council over matters of government policy related to regional development. From this grew a first attempt, in the context of the VIIth Plan, to reconcile the priorities formulated by each region with those set by the government at a national level. The result was the launching of a series of regional priority programmes (programmes d'actions prioritaires d'intérêt régional – PAPIR). Unfortunately the experience was not followed through; the country's worsening economic position in the late 1970s meant that government investment priorities became increasingly sectoral rather than spatial in orientation, and regional ambitions were forced into a lowly second place behind the overriding objective of modernising the country's productive base. Advance planning for what became the defunct VIIIth Plan (due to the change of government) only confirmed this thinking.

Once in power the Socialists adopted a different view. They attached far more importance to the formulation of regional development plans and to a general decentralisation of the planning process. Regional councils took responsibility for drawing up social and economic development strategies. To assist with this task they were able to call on their own technical services, while before finalising their proposals, they were required to seek approval from the region's economic and social committee, a consultative body comprising representatives drawn mostly from local businesses, professional organisations and trade unions. In implementing these modifications the government was seeking to link more closely regional aspirations with national priorities; the aim was to integrate planning at these two levels far more closely.

Contractual planning

Under this revised system of 'planification décentralisée', embodied in legislation enacted in July 1982, the new national plan (IXth Plan, covering the period 1984–88) was organised around 12 priority plans (programmes prioritaries d'exécution – PPE), inspired by the experience of the earlier 'priority programmes' set up under the VIIth Plan. These plans covered such themes as research and innovation, energy, education and training, communication industries, and health and social conditions. Simultaneously each region was asked to produce its own regional plan, setting out its priorities for investment. This document was then to be used to help finalise the contents of the national plan. Consultation between the regional councils and central government aimed to ensure that wherever possible regional plans took account of the state's investment priorities, set out in the PPE, and that similar consideration was accorded by the government to the propositions of the regions. The final state of the process was reached with the signing of a contract (contrat de plan) between the government and region (Fig. 5.1).[23] This sets out those aspects of the national and regional plans which are compatible and for which each partner is prepared to guarantee a given level of investment; these guarantees are made not just for the plan as a whole, but for each of its subsections. In addition supplementary contracts may be drawn up to cover specific items of development. This contractual aspect of planning policy was seen by the Socialists as an important innovation, and has been applied in other circumstances. Frequently the government has negotiated contracts with local authorities independently of the 'contrat de plan', while regional councils have also adopted this procedure.

One illustration of the negotiation of specific contracts is provided by current attempts to improve road access to certain of the skiing resorts in the Alps. Along many of the road arteries which penetrate this region there is a recurrent problem of congestion, associated particularly with the period of school holidays in February and 'la grande transhumance des skieurs'. Travelling is most difficult on

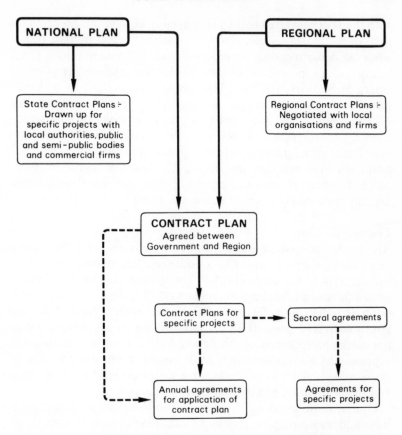

Figure 5.1   The contractual planning system

successive weekends during this month, as one wave of holidaymakers is replaced by another; conditions are rendered especially irksome and hazardous by the huge volume of traffic (estimated to exceed 500 000 vehicles during this period) and by the constraints of the weather (fog, snow and ice). Access is most difficult to the major resorts of the 'Tarentaise' area (e.g. Val d'Isère, les Arcs, Courchevel, Tignes), all of which are served by a single and still relatively narrow main road (N90).

Now, following extensive discussion, a joint agreement has been concluded between the government and the general council of the department of Savoie, designed to provide much needed relief. A motorway extension is to be built between Chambéry and Albertville, with the N90 converted to dual carriageway beyond this point. In the first stage the state's contribution amounts to 250 million francs, while the department has agreed to provide 350 million francs. Other changes are proposed, and include the electrification of the rail link to Bourg-St Maurice, enabling TGV services from Paris to penetrate into the heart of this area and thus hopefully help alleviate congestion on the roads. (It is also hoped to encourage hoteliers and letting agencies to stagger bookings to a far greater extent.) However, essential as such improvements to regional communications might be (although their necessity has been questioned due to the relatively short duration of severe congestion), past indecision means that benefits are unlikely to occur before the 1990s.

Contrats de Plan

All the regions have now concluded contract-plans with the government, committing each side to a considerable scale of investment; over the duration of the plans (1984–8) the state has agreed to invest 35 billion francs and the regions 27 billion (1984 prices).[24] Moreover, it is estimated that over 50 per cent of the money pledged by the government is for projects which conform with the priorities set out in the twelve programmes of the national plan. Some satisfaction was expressed by socialist ministers at this result, particularly in view of the considerable haste with which the formulation of regional plans and the negotiation of subsequent contracts took place.

Overall most spending is to go on improvements to communications and transportation, followed by the development of agriculture and linked industries, the rehabilitation of run-down urban districts, the promotion of research and the improvement of education. The nature of planned activity, however, varies between the regions, although a number of general trends may be detected. Many areas of central and western France are seeking to improve the efficiency of agriculture (e.g. Aquitaine, Midi-Pyrénées, Bretagne) or to stabilise and diversify employment opportunities in rural areas (e.g. Auvergne and Limousin). In those regions with an existing base of technologically advanced industries further development of this sector is a major priority (e.g. Rhône-Alpes, Alsace, Provence-Alpes-Côte d'Azur), whereas in those less fortunate parts of the country still dependent on a heritage of now outmoded heavy industries, particular emphasis is given to facilitating the process of conversion through programmes designed to promote retraining, rehabilitate urban areas, and improve educational and research actitivities (e.g. Nord – Pas-de-Calais and Lorraine).

The region of the capital (Ile-de-France) stands out due to the large proportion (66 per cent) of the five-year budget which is allocated to improving transport infrastructure (Figure 5.2); most is to be spent on completing the link between the A1 and A6 via the A86 ring motorway which has long been designed (but only very slowly built) to relieve pressure on the oversaturated boulevard périphérique. Whether this ambitious scheme will ever be completed is questionable for the idea of pushing an eight-lane motorway with its attendant problems of noise and pollution through the salubrious 'gin and tonic' belt of the outer suburbs of south-west and western Paris has met with ferocious opposition from local residents and councillors. So, what is desirable for one part of the community, (in this case seeking to reduce the nuisance-effect of the périphérique to inner-city residents by shifting traffic further out), is often unacceptable to another. This principle has applied elsewhere. The regional plan often represents a difficult compromise between competing interests, particularly in regions where there are major contrasts in the patterns of activity, as between a major urban area and a remote upland periphery.

Other problems have emerged. In the selection of their priorities, not all regional councils were prepared to follow the government lead, particularly where control was in the hands of opposition parties. In Rhône-Alpes, for example, despite the large-scale and serious character of the social and environmental difficulties found in suburban housing estates such as Les Minguettes at Lyon, no provision for remedial action has been made in the regional plan negotiated with the state, necessitating protracted attempts by the government to negotiate a separate contract. But such disagreements might be seen as insignificant compared with the polemic generated by the government's decision not to honour a clause in the plan drawn up and agreed with the region of Alsace. The contract stipulated that Strasbourg should be the French choice of location for the building of the synchrotron (used to accelerate electrons) proposed by the European Science Foundation. For the region this represented a major 'coup', corresponding exactly with the desire to enhance the status of Strasbourg as a European and scientific city.

Belatedly, however, Grenoble also appreciated the sizeable potential benefits in terms of employment opportunites and research spin-

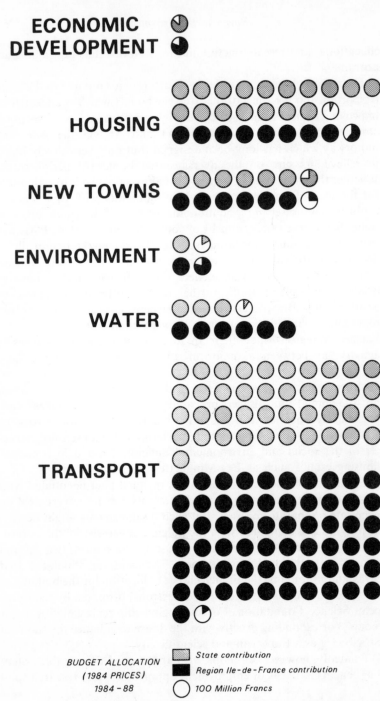

ECONOMIC
DEVELOPMENT

HOUSING

NEW TOWNS

ENVIRONMENT

WATER

TRANSPORT

BUDGET ALLOCATION
(1984 PRICES)
1984 – 88

State contribution
Region Ile - de - France contribution
100 Million Francs

Figure 5.2   The budget for the contract-plan of Ile-de-France

off that would result from such an investment. Moreover, it had a strong case to argue, given the importance of its existing research laboratories in nuclear physics and electronics. Aided by the strong support of local politicians (including Louis Mermaz, the then president of the National Assembly and the leader of the general council of Isère), extensive lobbying by the city's scientific community and pressure from the Atomic Energy Commission (CEA), on the 17 October 1984 the government decided to back the site of Grenoble in preference to Strasbourg.[25] Reaction in Alsace was understandably bitter and hostile, resulting in an almost total boycott by local political leaders (right wing parties are strongly in control in the region) of President Mitterrand's visit to the region in the following month. Subsequently the regional council challenged the decision in the courts, with the result that the government's action was declared illegal, although this is unlikely to alter the eventual location of the synchrotron. Not unnaturally such an episode was a setback to the creation of a new relationship between the regions and central government. Failure to respect its commitment in Alsace obviously invited unfavourable conjecture about the government's attitude concerning other regional contracts. Confidence in the efficacy of 'decentralised planning' would have been much stronger without this 'faux-pas'.

Further problems arose in 1985 with the decision of the administrative court in Montpellier to annul the contract between the state and Languedoc-Roussillon, basing its judgement on the illegality of the plan as the necessary consultation on its contents with the local communes and departments had not occurred.[26] Criticism of the plans has also arisen over the general vagueness with which they were written and the lack of rigour behind their costing; and in most cases, partly for these reasons, it it unlikely that they will be fully implemented. Yet despite difficulties and false manoeuvres the new system of regional planning might be seen as a substantial advance, and a useful example of decentralisation in practice. In this latter context it illustrates the still considerable influence of the Prefect and his continued role as a privileged intermediary between central government and local authorities, for it was through the Commissaire de la République that negotiations over the contract plans occurred. But for a socialist government seeking greater local democracy, one of the main achievements was to establish a planning process that is two-way, contrasting with the system's previously uni-directional character.

DECENTRALISATION – FOUR YEARS ON

Decentralisation was an issue of fundamental importance for the Socialists. Before his election as President, François Mitterrand wrote that the welding together of the French nation had been dependent on the existence of strong central government; now to prevent the breakup of the country the devolution of this power was necessary.[27] By March 1986, following the direct election for the first time of.the regional councils, this latter process was largely complete (at least from a legislative point of view), just four years after the publication of the original charter for decentralisation. It is, therefore, ironic that as this stage was reached the Socialists should be forced out of government.

Implementing decentralisation has been a major task, in terms of both the scale and scope of the related legislation, which by the beginning of 1986 amounted to 48 Acts of Parliament and 269 related decrees.[28] The aims were to increase local democracy and create a more efficient system of administration, whereby a far greater number of decisions could be taken by authorities no longer remote from or inaccessible to the population they serve; but determining the extent to which these objectives have been realised is still probably premature. It is generally accepted, however, that the socialist legislation has provided an appropriate framework for such reform to occur, although certain doubts remain. The ability of local authorities to freely determine their policies must be questioned when the bulk of their financial resources still originates from (and is, therefore, controlled by) central government. Claims of greater efficiency might also be challenged. Decentralisation could be argued to have created more bureaucracy, with an increase in the number of local government officials and a duplication of personnel, as similar services coexist in the administrative systems of the department and Prefecture. A vertical overlap of responsibility is also apparent, as France now has four tiers of government administration. There have been protests of 'too much' local government, with often each level of the hierarchy exercising some responsibility in the same area of policy (economic development is one example); arguably this leads to confusion and is potentially wasteful of resources.

The essence of decentralisation, however, has been the transfer of power away from central government and its administrative services; but where have the benefits gone? Each of the mayors of France's 36 433 communes has seen some increase in his authority, but such officials have long enjoyed considerable independence in their actions and can hardly be judged to have been the major beneficiaries of devolution. The battle for honours is between the new executives of the departments and the regions. At the moment the former authorities undoubtedly have most power, controlling sizeable budgets. One result is that many smaller communes within the departments have simply seen their dependency upon the Prefect and his services replaced by a similar reliance on the president of the general council and his administration. Obviously the exercise of such control is contrary to the spirit of decentralisation, but in the quest for power and influence this would appear to be of little consequence. Against a departmental council seeking to extend and strengthen its authority, the corresponding regional body might seem poorly placed. Yet certain of the region's responsibilities suggest that the role it plays in local affairs is likely to increase substantially in future years; in particular its function in encouraging economic development and devising accompanying policies is highly significant. Furthermore the region is essentially a body concerned with investment strategy, vital in assuring future development, while the department has traditionally been primarily concerned with the provision and management of a varied range of services. In its role as an investor, and through its responsibility for strategic planning, the regional council also has the advantage of a close relationship with central government through the contractual arrangements linking national and regional plans. For some, however, this represents a constraint, limiting the regional council's freedom of action. Nonetheless, generally the region benefits from a dynamic image (partly reflecting its youthfulness as an institution) and might be seen as a body anxious to increase its influence. Yet the departmental council, with its new freedom of action and the desire to extend its powers might now be expected to offer a greater challenge to the region's authority in certain areas of its activities, especially in matters of economic policy.

As decentralisation moves into a more mature phase, the outcome of such power struggles will doubtless become clearer. There are certain issues, however, which remain unresolved by the original legislation and to which a solution, at least in the short term, appears unlikely. It has long been argued that France's numerous small communes are ineffective and inefficient units of local administration, and that many ought to be amalgamated; decentralisation was seen as a means of effecting such change, but ultimately the Socialists avoided taking action on what is still a highly sensitive matter. Conversely, they originally demonstrated a much stronger commitment to reforming local taxation, giving local authorities greater control over the origin of their income; hopefully this would have avoided much of the controversy over the adequacy of the state's transfer of financial resources to local authorities. But again the socialist policy-makers were defeated, largely by the complexity of the problem. Some further dissatisfaction has been expressed over the failure to modify any of the regional boundaries, delimited over 30 years ago, largely for administrative convenience rather than functional coherence. In certain cases separatist movements have added their weight to demands for at least a partial redrawing of the map. Decentralisation thus appears likely to remain a major policy-issue for a succession of future governments.

One intriguing and vital question also requiring clarification is the extent to which the devolution of government power will assist in a corresponding relocation of economic activities. If this effect is to be positive, it would seem to depend as well on the willingness of government departments and other public organisations, which play a significant part in a company's decision-making process, to decentralise certain of their responsibilities. But here progress has been slow, with government ministries showing a notable reluctance to move part of their services away from the capital as intended under recent legislation: cynics might suggest that they appreciate where effective power still lies! However, a change in attitudes now seems inevitable and has already been evident amongst various of the more enlightened major banking and credit organisations.

With decentralisation now seen as 'irreversible' the Socialists merit recognition for having had the political courage to launch and carry through their ambitious programme, although many of the ideas were not new. Despite the very substantial character of the changes which have occurred, they have not produced the anticipated dramatic upheaval. Instead France has experienced 'une révolution tranquille'.

The State of the

...he present decade France remained under the
...ugh by 1986 the performance of the economy
...dence than it had five years previously. A new,
...ned optimism had emerged over the prospects for
a r... ...tes of growth: certainly this was the view taken by
the OECD ... the early part of 1986. Thus, during the period of
socialist reign, contrary to the predictions of many right wing critics,
the country did not experience an economic collapse and society was
not split apart: the anticipated disaster resulting from a left wing
administration did not occur.

Equally, however, the years of socialist government did not produce the revolution of which many of its supporters dreamed. A new
France, rid of inequality and injustice, characterised by a more caring
society and based on a prosperous and expanding economy had not
been born. Instead economic growth proved sluggish and many of the
basic divisive features of society showed themselves highly resilient to
change. This led to the questioning of the soundness of the Socialists'
economic management and of their judgement, with criticism in the
latter case generated by the hesitancy and prevarication evident in
resolving matters such as the 'Greenpeace affair' and the constitu-
tional crisis in New Caledonia. In the eyes of some critics the fault had
its roots in the presidency, for whatever the talents of François
Mitterrand as a politician and philosopher, his qualities as a 'bon
gestionnaire' were seen as far less apparent, certainly during the first
five years of his reign.

Yet against this negative backcloth might be balanced the considerable progress achieved in both the social and economic spheres during
the period the Socialists were in power. Whatever the government's,
shortcomings it demonstrated a strong commitment to reform, particularly during the early 1980s, representing a significant break with
the past. Progress in the social field included a series of measures to
improve the working environment and general conditions of the
working-class, a new freedom for the media and a revised attitude to
law enforcement. Not all of the government's attempts at reform
encountered success, notably in relation to education, the 35-hour

week and a reorganised private rented sector in the housing market; but certain measures, such as lowering the retirement age to 60, represented important landmarks in the social progress of a country.

Over the years 1982–4 some justification did appear to exist for the view that the Socialists' handling of the economy had been inept: the country was heavily indebted, unemployment was rising rapidly, growth was virtually non-existent and a remarkable volte-face had occurred in government policy. Little more than two years later, however, the coalition government led by Jacques Chirac inherited a transformed and healthier economy. Change had led not just to a much reduced level of inflation and a substantial fall in the foreign trading deficit, but also to revised thinking over investment strategies with increased funding for research and a major restructuring of key sectors of industry: in the latter case it is questionable whether a right wing administration would have achieved comparable results, for despite the severity of reductions in manpower which accompanied this process, trade union opposition remained largely muted. Moreover, the return to profitability of the majority of nationalised industries by 1986 could be interpreted as evidence of the success of the government's policies.

Socialist intervention was not confined to the social and economic arenas: it also featured an important political component, with the government accepting the challenge to carry through a major programme of devolution. Given that the Socialists had long argued for such reform, this action and its generally favourable response might be seen as predictable; the same applies to certain aspects of social policy which were also widely acclaimed. Even the government's economic strategy might ultimately be viewed as successful, at least in terms of creating a sounder and more efficient base from which to generate growth. Yet the cost of this particular victory was high, for it was achieved only at the expense of a substantial rise in unemployment, leading to the split with the Communists and the alienation of much of the traditional support for the socialist party. As this occurred there were others, notably Jean-Marie Le Pen and his National Front party, only too willing to exploit such disenchantment. The government's failure was not so much that the jobless total had risen, but that it had failed to honour a key electoral promise.

Despite the early reforming zeal and undoubted achievements of the Socialists, their legacy for the Chirac administration included a series of unresolved problems. In the social sphere the increase in criminality remained a highly contentious issue, not least due to the continuing increase in violence and terrorist attacks, and the Right's insistence on the need for a more vigorous campaign against crime. Immigration was an equally controversial subject, with the Chirac government again adopting a more repressive stance on the issue than their predecessors. Misunderstanding and resentment persist amongst both French and foreign communities. In the latter case the feeling prevails that inadequate efforts are being made to integrate immigrant populations into French society and to provide an equality of opportunity. For the French there is still a popularly held view that foreigners (particularly of North African origin) are largely responsible for many of the country's ills and a major source of abuse of welfare and health benefits; and hence the desirability of reducing their number.

The need to eradicate misuse of the social security system points to a wider problem of the increasing difficulty faced by governments in controlling related expenditure. At issue is not so much the question of abuse, but that the French have become far greater consumers of various forms of benefit and health and social services. This has resulted from people living longer, from their expectations rising in terms of the quality of service, and from the fact that particularly during the recession greater numbers have retired or joined the ranks of the unemployed. The result is a considerable strain on resources, provoking a delicate political problem of on whom additional payments should fall.

Relative calm may have returned to the classroom, but uncertainty still prevails over the future of the educational system. Change at the secondary level is one priority, particularly to tackle the problem of too many teenagers being ill-equipped to enter a highly competitive labour market. But it is in higher education that reform is essential; otherwise there is the danger that the current malaise in the university system will become an endemic feature. There is also a more general need, as part of the process of reviving the French economy, to promote the achievement of a higher level of educational attainment amongst young people and to develop a more flexible system capable of adapting more readily to society's changing requirements; the decentralisation of control which took place under the Socialists may assist in achieving this goal.

Although the economy now appears stronger than for several years, this should not imply that weaknesses no longer exist. Jacques Chirac may have inherited fewer urgent and controversial 'problem cases' than Pierre Mauroy had five years previously, but difficult issues requiring careful arbitration remained. Further rationalisation in the steel industry appeared inevitable as the problems of over-capacity and a residue of out-dated plants were still apparent. Similarly, and in the short term, more urgent problems faced the beleaguered French ship building industry, as chronic world over-capacity and lack of orders have induced even the Japanese to rationalise their activities. Amongst the nationalised industries, Renault and CdF-Chimie stood out as heavy loss-makers and a significant and unwelcome drain on the public purse, while the reconstruction of the country's vital telecommunication industries remained incomplete. From a geographical perspective continued efforts were essential to help regenerate activity in the depressed local economies of a growing number of industrial 'black-spots'. These included traditional areas of decline represented by the northern coal and steel towns, and many of the country's small and medium-sized ports, notably those hit by the crisis in the shipbuilding industry such as Dunkerque, La Ciotat and La Seyne; but they have also come to encompass a series of centres such as Lannion, dependent on a more modern industrial base (in this case telecommunications), where the rapid pace of technical progress has induced the premature obsolescence of manufacturing plant.

Decentralisation has been an essential reform, and one of the few over which there has been no question of its reversibility (contrary to certain other aspects of socialist policy such as nationalisation). Yet even in this case a certain disillusionment has emerged as the extent to which a significant increase in local democracy has occurred seems questionable. In many spheres Paris still remains the effective focus of decision-making. This raises the wider issue of the extent to which the state should intervene in determining how society and the economy are managed and in organising people's lives. In France there is a strong tradition of a powerful state, operating in a highly interventionist manner; not just as a purveyor of services, but also as a major employer and an influential guiding force in the determination and implementation of economic and social policy. As a result the all-pervading role of the state has been held increasingly to act as an excessive infringement of personal liberty, and should be curtailed allowing greater individual freedom (and responsibility).

Having been elected with a firm commitment to devolution, the position of the Socialists might have been interpreted as one which would lead to a lessening of the influence of central government. Yet such a view would appear to contradict the basic philosophy of a socialist party which favours the existence of a supportive and interventionist state. Indeed such an approach seemed to prevail during the early years of socialist rule with the programme of nationalisations, the revival of national planning, government inspired plans for the major branches of industry, a consistent rise in public expenditure and the advocacy of a single and unified system of public education. However, in this latter case, the strength of public feeling against this idea and in favour of the 'école libre' suggested that in enhancing the role played by government, socialism had lost touch with reality and the aspirations of many people. Moreover, there appeared to be a basic flaw in the argument that extolled the benefits of a caring state, for as public spending had risen so too had the ranks of the unemployed and impoverished.

Realisation of this change of mood might be held partly responsible for the modified character of socialist policies during the government's last two years of office. Laurent Fabius together with a number of other like-minded ministers such as Edith Cresson, at that time responsible for industrial policy, promoted a rather different approach to the state's role in society, away from direct intervention and in favour of greater liberalism; the Socialists appeared to have come to terms with the market place, a conversion which led to the suggestion that, in effect, after 1984 France no longer had a left wing government. The notion that the state should withdraw from certain of its traditional responsibilities and offer increased opportunities for individual expression was advocated with far greater force by the Right when they assumed office; not only might this be seen as indicative of the considerable scope which exists for such change, but also of the fundamental importance of the movement of decentralisation which is already under way.

Advocating a lessening of the state's influence, leads to the further question of whether government policy, in a western capitalist economy, is indeed capable of exerting a significant impact on the pattern of economic development. While government action undoubtedly affects the nature of the precise path along which the economy is steered, external forces play a key part in determining its overall direction. Continuing changes in the nature of capitalism itself might be seen to have underpinned the restructuring of the economy in France and other western countries, irrespective of the government in power and its specific set of policies. Increased investment in capital and technology, the further internationalisation of capital and the growing spatial division of labour on a world basis have all produced basic changes in the structure of employment, the size of the labour-force and the location of economic activity. The recession itself was set in motion largely by forces operating beyond the boundaries of France rather than by any specific change of direction in the economic policy of the French government. Similarly, in 1986 as the country appeared to emerge from the shadow of recession, this change corresponded with a much wider movement of slow recovery amongst western industrialised nations. Thus some caution is required in assigning too readily to one particular administration blame for the depressive effects of the recession or credit for reversing this tendency.

Arguably within any nation there is also a collective responsibility which influences the manner in which society and the economy develop. The attitudes and reactions of people to accepting the challenge of change might be seen to play an important role in determining the form and degree of success of a country's development. Consequently, while an upturn in international trading and a government economic strategy pursued in sympathy with this trend might offer the appropriate framework within which renewed growth and prosperity could occur, for this to be effective a fundamental change is required in people's approach to work. In this respect one factor capable of constraining progress in France is the persistence of marked inequalities in society; even the Socialists were only able to effect minor modifications to this position. The contrast is not only between the affluent and the poor, although the spread of incomes in France remains far wider than in many other European countries, but also between those whom society in some way protects and those who remain potentially vulnerable, outside the system. Various accounts point to the existence of a significant set of privileged classes in France,[1] not least many of the country's 2.6 million civil servants and certain workers in public service sector activities. Members of these groups have been largely sheltered from the recession, their jobs and incomes guaranteed. Such conditions might be held to foster attitudes of indifference towards the commitment to work and related responsibility.

It has been argued that under recession French society appears to have maintained an excessive rigidity, with the protection of existing standards of remuneration and security of employment becoming prime but unacceptable concerns amongst a significant section of the population.[2] As a result certain categories of people, unable to benefit from such advantages, have found themselves exposed and at risk, inducing feelings of rejection and alienation; the young have become particularly vulnerable, seen in their current difficulties in entering the labour market. Furthermore, the notions of creating a more efficient economy and of adopting a highly protective attitude to both jobs and wages appear incompatible. The rigid defence of acquired benefits is no longer a realistic attitude in a much changed and highly competitive international economic environment, where the intensity of competition is only likely to increase as more of the world's industrialising nations attain maturity. Greater flexibility and adaptability, and above all the adoption of an enhanced notion of efficiency, would seem essential in the organisation of work if a sustained increase in national wealth and individual living standards are to be achieved. Just as society's restrictive approach to change might be seen to have contributed to the past pattern of economic decline and loss of jobs, so the acceptance of a more enlightened and less rigid attitude could be conceived as a vital key to future prosperity, and to its accessibility to a greater number of French people.

Notes and References

1 France in the 1980s

1. *Tableaux de l'Economie française* (Paris: INSEE, 1985).
2. *Economie et Statistique*, no. 171–2, 1984.
3. *Le Monde*, 9 May 1984.
4. *Le Monde*, 11 April 1986.
5. *Le Monde*, 19/20 January 1986.
6. M. Cézard and D. Rault, 'La Crise a freiné la mobilité sectorielle', *Economie et Statistique*, no. 184 (1986), 41–62.

2 Society in Disarray

1. *Le Monde*, 30 May 1984.
2. *Le Monde*, 21 December 1982; *Le Monde*, 29 February 1984.
3. *Le Figaro*, 19 April 1984.
4. J-Y. Potel (ed.), *L'état de la France* (1985), 509.
5. *Le Monde*, 8 February 1985.
6. *Le Monde*, 19 February 1985.
7. CESDIP, *Les Coûts du crime en France* (Paris, 1985).
8. G. Bonnemaison, *Face à la délinquance: Prévention, Répression, Solidarité* (1983).
9. P. Mauroy, *A Gauche* (1985).
10. *L'Expansion*, Les Sept Crises (1984), 153.
11. O. Marchand and E. Martin-Le Goff, '200 000 emplois à nouveau perdus en 1984', *Economie et Statistique*, no. 176 (1985), 3–12.
12. J-L. Heller, 'Emploi et Chômage en Mars 1986', *Economie et Statistique*, no. 183 (1985), 21–35.
13. P. Rongère, 'Droit et Pratique du licenciement en France', *Regards sur l'Actualité*, no. 110 (1985), 27–39.
14. INSEE, *Données Sociales* (Paris, 1984).
15. *Le Monde*, 17 July 1984.
16. *Le Monde*, 9 January 1985.
17. *Le Monde*, 17 January 1985.
18. P. Mauroy, *A Gauche* (1985).
19. O. Marchand *et al.*, 'Des 40 heures aux 39 heures: processus et réactions des Enterprises', *Economie et Statistique*, no. 154 (1983), 3–15.
20. B. Schwartz, *L'Insertion Professionnelle et Sociale des Jeunes* (1981).
21. Délégation à l'Insertion Professionnelle et Sociale des Jeunes en difficulté, Missions locales: Point 84 (1985).
22. *Le Monde*, 27 January 1984.
23. *Le Monde*, 5/6 May 1985.

24. Conseil Economique et Social, *Le Travail clandestin* (1983).
25. *Le Monde*, 16 March 1984.
26. INSEE, *Les Etrangers* (Paris: INSEE, 1984).
27. *L'Express*, 3/9 May 1985.
28. A. Griotteray, *Les Immigrés: le Choc* (1984), 85–98.
29. F. Gaspard and C. Servan-Schreiber, *La Fin des Immigrés* (1985), 122–7.
30. *Le Monde*, 26/27 January 1986.
31. 'Les Jeunes dans la Société', *Le Monde, Dossiers et Documents*, no. 114 (1984).
32. J. Malézieux, 'Emploi et Résidence des populations d'origine étrangère: le cas d'Aulnay-sous-Bois', *Annales de Géographie* 94 (1985), 546–60.
33. *Le Monde*, 30 March 1983.
34. *Le Point*, 1 April 1985.
35. R. Pesce, *Développement social des Quartiers* (1984).
36. L. Stoléru, *La France à deux vitesses* (1982).

3. Restructuring the Economy

1. J. Fourastié, *Les Trente Glorieuses* (1979).
2. *L'Expansion*, Les Sept Crises (1984), 15.
3. M. Delattre, '1979–1984: une nouvelle donne pour les branches de l'Industrie', *Economie et Statistique*, no. 186 (1986), 3–30.
4. Conseil Economique et Social, Informatique et Emploi (1984), 36–8.
5. O. Marchand and E. Martin-Le Goff, '200 000 emplois à nouveau perdus en 1984', *Economie et Statistique*, no. 176 (1985), 3–12.
6. J. Wahl, *Le Pétrole Vert français* (1983), 8.
7. G. Gouzes, *Tradition et Modernité de l'Agriculture française* (1985), 116.
8. M. Delattre, op. cit.
9. *Le Monde*, 25 August 1984.
10. 'La Politique Industrielle', *Les Cahiers Français* (1983).
11. 'Nationalisations industrielles et bancaires', *Les Cahiers Français* (1984).
12. *Les Echos*, 6 February 1984; *Le Figaro*, 30 March 1984.
13. *Le Quotidien de Paris*, 14/15 April 1984; *Le Monde*, 14 April 1984.
14. 'Groupes Publics et Politique Industrielle', *Regards sur l'Actualité*, no. 112 (1985), 3–27.
15. 'Bilan Economique et Social 1983' (Paris: *Le Monde*, 1984).
16. *Le Monde*, 28 February 1986.
17. 'Bilan Economique et Social 1984' (Paris: *Le Monde*, 1985).
18. P. Aydalot, 'The Location of New Firm Creation: The French Case' in D. Keeble and E. Wever (eds), *New Firms and Regional Development in Europe* (Beckenham: Croom Helm, 1986).
19. *Le Monde*, 10 October 1984.
20. *Le Monde*, 24 July 1985.
21. *Le Monde*, 17 January 1986.

22. *Le Monde*, 14 December 1984.
23. *Les Echos*, 26 April 1984.
24. *Le Figaro*, 25 April 1984.
25. *Le Monde*, 14 December 1984.
26. Delattre, op. cit., 18.
27. *Le Monde*, 13 March 1985.
28. *L'Expansion*, 8–21 February 1985.
29. Conseil Economique et Social, 'Le Devenir de l'Industrie française de l'Automobile', *Journal Officiel de la République Française'* (1984).
30. *Le Monde*, 17 April 1985.
31. *Problèmes Economiques*, no. 1915, 13 March 1985.
32. 'Le Commerce en 1985: une bonne année pour les hypermarchés', *Economie et Statistique*, no. 186 (1986), 55–65.
33. G. Mermet, *Francoscopie* (1985), 383.
34. *Le Nouvel Economiste*, 7 June 1985.
35. *Le Nouvel Economiste*, 12 April 1985: *Le Monde*, 31 May 1985.
36. Syndicat National des Fabricants d'Ensembles d'Informatique, de Bureautique et de leurs Applications Télématiques, Parc français des Ordinateurs – Enquête 1985 (1985).
37. *Le Monde*, 7 January 1986.
38. *Le Figaro*, 10 January 1985.
39. *01 Informatique*, no. 901, 14 April 1986.
40. *Ville de Paris*, no. 62, February 1985.
41. J. Joly (ed.), 'Grenoble et son Agglomération', *Notes et Etudes Documentaires*, no. 4769 (1984).

4 Revitalising the City

1. P. Merlin, 'Pour une véritable priorité au logement social à Paris' (Paris: *La Documentation Française*, 1983).
2. F. Chabiron, 'Le Financement du Logement: l'Intervention de l'Etat', *Regards sur l'Actualité*, no. 102 (1984), 45–55.
3. *Le Monde*, 19 January 1985; *Le Monde*, 25 January 1985.
4. *Le Figaro*, 29 April 1985; *Le Monde*, 24 October 1984.
5. *Le Monde*, 27/28 May 1984.
6. *Le Monde*, 28 February 1984.
7. F. Seigneur, 'Projets d'Urbanisme de la Ville de Paris', *Regards sur l'Actualité*, no. 109 (1985), 3–21.
8. *Le Moniteur des Travaux Publics et du Bâtiment*, 23 March 1984.
9. J. Tuppen and P. Mingret, 'Suburban Malaise in French Cities: The Quest for a Solution', *Town Planning Review*, 57 (1986), 187–201.
10. *Le Monde*, 17 May 1985.
11. Conseil Economique et Social, 'La qualité de la vie dans les banlieues des grandes villes', *Journal Officiel de la République Française* (1983).
12. H. Dubedout, *Ensemble refaire la Ville* (1983).
13. R. Pesce, *Développement social des Quartiers* (1984).
14. *Le Monde*, 12 August 1983.
15. M-P. Ambrogelly and M-H. Farrouch, 'Vénissieux: les Minguettes, qui

habite la ZUP?', *Points d'Appui pour l'Economie Rhône-Alpes*, no. 25 (1983), 7–16.
16. J. Le Garrec, *Demain la France* (1984).
17. *Le Monde*, 27/28 April 1986.

5 Power to the Provinces

1. 'Les Disparités Régionales', *Economie et Statistique*, no. 153 (1983).
2. *Le Monde*, 16 December 1984; *Le Monde*, 7 May 1985.
3. *La Lettre de la Datar*, no. 85, March 1985.
4. J. Tuppen, 'Core Periphery in Metropolitan Development and Planning: Socio-Economic Change in Lyon since 1960', *Geoforum*, 17 (1986), 1–37.
5. *Le Monde*, 17/18 February 1985.
6. *Le Monde*, 17/18 February 1985.
7. *Le Monde*, 29 November 1983.
8. *Le Marché immobilier en France – 1986* (Paris: Bourdais, 1986).
9. 'La Décentralisation en marche', *Les Cahiers Français*, (1985), 3.
10. 'Décentralisation: les Textes et la Pratique', *Regards sur l'Actualité*, no. 102 (1984), 7.
11. *'La Décentralisation en marche'*, op. cit.
12. *'La Décentralisation en marche'*, op. cit., 61.
13. B. Jean-Antoine, 'Etat et Collectivités Locales: les 'nouveaux' fonctionnaires', *Regards sur l'Actualité*, no. 105 (1984), 20–33.
14. F. Bertrand, 'Le nouveau statut de la Corse', *Regards sur l'Actualité*, no. 88 (1983), 47–56.
15. *L'Express*, 8/14 March 1985.
16. *Le Monde*, 4/5 August 1985.
17. *Le Monde*, 19 March 1985.
18. *Le Monde*, 27 February 1985.
19. *Le Monde*, 13 November 1984.
20. *L'Express*, 8/14 March 1985.
21. *L'Express*, 8/14 March 1985.
22. *Le Monde*, Le Monde des Régions, (1986).
23. 'Décentralisation et Planification', *Regards sur l'Actualité'*, no. 103 (1984).
24. *Le Monde*, 5 June 1984.
25. *Le Monde*, 21 and 24 November 1984.
26. *Le Monde*, 14 August 1985.
27. F. Mitterrand, *Ici et Maintenant* (1980).
28. *Le Monde*, 7 February 1986.

6 1986—The state of the Nation

1. F. de Closets, *Toujours Plus*, (1982); A. Wickham and S. Coignard, *La Nomenklatura française* (1986).
2. M. Albert, *Le Pari français* (1985).

Select Bibliography

General

ADA, *Bilan de la France 1986* (Paris: La Table Ronde, 1986).
M. ALBERT, *Le Pari français* (Paris: Seuil, 1985).
J. ARDAGH, *France in the 1980s* (Harmondsworth: Penguin, 1982).
R. BARRE, *Réflexions pour Demain* (Paris: Pluriel, 1984).
F. DE CLOSETS, *Toujours Plus*, (Paris: Grasset, 1982).
F. DE CLOSETS, *Tous Ensemble* (Paris: Seuil, 1985).
J.-M. COLOMBANI, *Portrait du Président* (Paris: Gallimard, 1985).
'Demain la France', *L'Expansion* no. 269, October/November, (1985).
L'Expansion, Les Sept Crises 1973–83 (Paris: Pluriel, 1984).
L. FABIUS, *Le Coeur du Futur* (Paris: Calmann-Lévy, 1985).
'La France en 1984', *Annales de Géographie* 93 (1984), no. 517.
J. LE GARREC, *Demain la France*, (Paris: Editions la Découverte, 1984).
V. GISCARD D'ESTAING, *Deux Français sur trois* (Paris: Flammarion, 1984).
D. HANEY et al., *Contemporary France*, 2nd ed (London: Routledge & Kegan Paul, 1984).
P. MAUROY, *C'est ici le Chemin* (Paris: Flammarion, 1982).
P. MAUROY, *A Gauche* (Paris: Albin Michel, 1985).
G. MERMET, *Francoscopie* (Paris: Larousse, 1985).
A. MINC, *L'Avenir en Face* (Paris: Seuil, 1984).
F. MITTERRAND, *Ici et Maintenant* (Paris: Fayard, 1980).
Le Monde, L'Année Economique et Sociale 1985 (Paris: Le Monde, 1986).
'La Population française de A à Z' *Les Cahiers Français*, no. 219 (1985).
J.-Y. POTEL (ed.), *L'état de la France et de ses habitants* (Paris: Editions la Découverte, 1985).
L. STOLERU, *La France à deux vitesses* (Paris: Flammarion, 1982).
A. WICKHAM and S. COIGNARD, *La Nomenklatura française* (Paris: Pierre Belfond, 1986).
T. ZELDIN, *The French* (London: Collins, 1983).

Social issues

J. BERQUE, *L'Immigration à l'Ecole de la République* (Paris: La Documentation Française, 1985).
G. BONNEMAISON, *Face à la délinquance: Prévention, Répression, Solidarité* (Paris: La Documentation Française, 1983).
Conseil Economique et Social, 'Le Travail clandestin', *Journal Officiel de la République Française* 25, February 1983.
A. CORDEIRO, *L'Immigration* (Paris: Editions la Découverte, 1984).

268

Délégation à l'Insertion Professionnelle et Sociale des Jeunes en difficulté, Missions locales: Point 84 (Paris: La Documentation Française, 1985).

'1975–1985: Dix ans de Chômage en France', *Regards sur l'Actualité* no. 115 (1985).

F. GASPARD and C. SERVAN-SCHREIBER, *La Fin des Immigrés* (Paris: Seuil, 1985).

A. GRIOTTERAY, *Les Immigrés: le Choc* (Paris: Plon, 1984).

INSEE, *Contours et Caractères – Les Etrangers en France* (Paris: INSEE, 1986).

J. MARANGÉ and A. LEBON, *L'Insertion des Jeunes d'origine étrangère dans la société française* (Paris: La Documentation Française, 1982).

OECD, *Youth Employment in France* (Paris: OECD, 1984).

A. SAUVY, *Le Travail noir et l'Economie de demain* (Paris: Calmann-Lévy, 1984).

A. SAVARY, *En toute liberté* (Paris: Hachette, 1985).

B. SCHWARTZ, *L'Insertion Professionnelle et Sociale des Jeunes* (Paris: La Documentation Française, 1981).

The economy

B. BELLON and J.-M. CHEVALIER (eds), *L'Industrie en France* (Paris: Flammarion, 1983).

J. BLANC and C. BRULE, 'Les Nationalisations françaises en 1982', *Notes et Etudes Documentaires* nos. 4721–2 (1983).

G. BREMOND, *La Révolution Informatique* 2nd edn (Paris: Hatier, 1983).

Conseil Economique et Social, 'Informatique et Emploi', *Journal Officiel de la République Française*, 30 March 1984.

Conseil Economique et Social, 'Productivité, Croissance et Emploi', *Journal Officiel de la République Française* 14 August 1984.

Conseil Economique et Social, 'Le Devenir de l'Industrie française de l'Automobile. Situation et Perspectives de l'Industrie française des Poids lourds', *Journal Officiel de la République Française* 17 August 1984.

G. GOUZES, *Tradition et Modernité de l'Agriculture française* (Paris: Ministère de l'Agriculture, 1985).

H. MACHIN and V. WRIGHT (eds), *Economic Policy and Policy Making under the Mitterrand Presidency, 1981–1984* (London: Frances Pinter, 1985).

'Mutations technologiques et Formations', *Les Cahiers Français* no. 223 (1985).

'Nationalisations industrielles et bancaires', *Les Cahiers Français* no. 214 (1984).

'La Politique industrielle', *Les Cahiers Français*, no. 212 (1983).

'Le Tissu industriel', *Les Cahiers Français* no. 211 (1983).

J. TUPPEN, *France* (Folkestone: Dawson, 1980).

J. TUPPEN, *The Economic Geography of France* (Beckenham: Croom Helm, 1983).

J. WAHL, *Le Pétrole Vert français* (Paris: Flammarion, 1983).

Urban change

R. BUTLER and P. NOISETTE, *Le Logement social en France 1815–1981* (Paris: Maspéro, 1983).

Conseil Economique et Social, 'La qualité de la vie dans les banlieues des grandes villes', *Journal Officiel de la République Française*, 17 December 1983.

D. CORNUEL and B. DURIEZ, *Le Mirage urbain* (Lille: Editions Anthropos, 1983).

H. DUBEDOUT, *Ensemble refaire la Ville* (Paris: La Documentation Française, 1983).

H. HEUGRAS-DARRASPEN, 'Le Logement en France et son financement', *Notes et Etudes Documentaires* no. 4794 (1985).

P. MERLIN, 'Les Politiques de transport urbain', *Notes et Etudes Documentaires* no. 4797 (1985).

R. PESCE, *Développement social des Quartiers* (Paris: La Documentation Française, 1984).

I. SCARGILL, *Urban France* (Beckenham: Croom Helm, 1983).

Decentralisation and regional planning

J. BAGUENARD, *La Décentralisation*, 2nd edn (Paris: Presses Universitaires de France, 1985).

P. BERNARD, 'L'Etat et la Décentralisation', *Notes et Etudes Documentaires*, nos. 4711–12 (1983).

'La Décentralisation: les Textes et la Pratique', *Regards sur l'Actualité*, no. 102 (1984).

'Décentralisation et Planification', *Regards sur l'Actualité*, no. 103 (1984).

'La Décentralisation en marche', *Les Cahiers Français*, no. 220 (1985).

J-P. LABORIE *et al.*, *La Politique française de l'Aménagement du Territoire, 1950–85* (Paris: La Documentation Française, 1985).

LE MONDE, *La France des Régions* (Paris: Le Monde, 1986).

D. SCHMITT (ed.), 'La Région à l'heure de la Décentralisation', *Notes et Etudes Documentaires*, no. 4772 (1985).

'Trente ans de décentralisation industrielle en France', *Cahiers du CREPIF*, no. 7 (1984).

Index